foundlings

Edited by

Michèle Aina Barale,

Jonathan Goldberg,

Michael Moon, and

Eve Kosofsky Sedgwick

foundlings

LESBIAN AND GAY

HISTORICAL EMOTION

BEFORE STONEWALL

Christopher Nealon

DUKE UNIVERSITY PRESS

Durham & London   2001

© 2001 Duke University Press

All rights reserved

Printed in the United States of

America on acid-free paper ∞

Designed by Amy Ruth Buchanan

Typeset in Carter & Cone Galliard

by Tseng Information Systems, Inc.

Library of Congress Cataloging-in-

Publication Data appear on the last

printed page of this book.

FOR MY GRANDMOTHER,

MARY DiBENEDETTO

acknowledgments

Writing this book was fun. Not continuously, I admit, but ultimately—and lots of people made it that way. Before I ever thought of writing it, first of all, my teachers at Williams College set me on its path, and I am still grateful for the example of their critical intelligence and watchful pedagogy: Wendy Brown, Wahneema Lubiano, Christopher Pye, Anita Sokolsky, and Karen Swann.

At Cornell, Shirley Samuels and Mark Seltzer were always supportive; I owe a particular debt to Timothy Murray, who (with great foresight, and faith in me) got me a job at the Human Sexuality Collection in Cornell's Kroch Library, where I was first able to read the materials for chapters 3 and 4. Brenda Marston, Phil McCray, Mark Dimunation, and the staff at Kroch welcomed me to into the community forming around the archives there. Throughout the long winters and subtle summers in Ithaca, my fellow graduate students—most of all Trevor Hope, Dana Luciano, Sally Jacob, and Chris Sturr—offered open minds and unmatched intellectual friendship. I am grateful to Lauren Berlant for taking me out to lunch in Chicago one morning in 1994 and giving me permission to think of this project in something like its current form. And I am especially indebted to Judith Butler, whose fantastic, phantasmatic readings of Willa Cather in a 1991 seminar gave me my first sense of what her novels could communicate.

In Seattle, dear friends made what might have been two lonely years of writing a delight: Patrick Baroch, Russ Craig, Lee James, Steven Manson, Laura Pierce, Mike Ranta, and Kent Whitehead. I am especially thankful for the chance to have worked at the youth center at Lambert House, where the kids, the volunteers, and the staff (Zan Loosier and Lynn Hyerle) gave me a living example of how a queer childhood and youth, however embattled, might be viable, joyful, and defiant all at once.

My colleagues at Berkeley have been extremely generous with their conversation, encouragement, and feedback. Sharon Marcus read the entire book twice, with great care and acuity; and Kevis Goodman offered crucial readings of the introduction and the first chapter just in time for my fourth-year review. Stephen Best has kept me on my toes, always urging me to keep "the scandalous formulation" in sight; and Colleen Lye has opened my eyes to all the places this book might lead me next. Jeffrey Knapp watched out for me while serving as chair of the department; and Catherine Gallagher was kind enough to let several of us read a draft of "Counter-History and the Anecdote" before its publication. I am also thankful for two sources of financial support from Berkeley—a Humanities Research Fellowship and a Regents' Junior Faculty Summer Research Grant—and for the help of Paul Hurh, whose efficient editing will make the book clearer and more accurate.

At Duke, Michael Moon and Jonathan Goldberg gave me hope for a book whose four chapters seemed sometimes too far-flung actually to *make* a book; their work, and their care with new work, is an inspiration. I am also very lucky to have worked with Ken Wissoker, Richard Morrison, and Leigh Anne Couch at Duke Press.

I would also like to thank the editors of *American Literature* and *New Literary History,* who published earlier versions of chapter 2 (*American Literature* 69.1) and chapter 4 (*NLH* 31.4).

I should not write a book on foundlings without mentioning the love and support my family has provided me: I hope I do it justice in these pages. My love to my grandmother, Mary DiBenedetto; to my parents, Jerome and Claudia Nealon; and to my sister and brother-in-law, Jennifer and Chris Smith.

In San Francisco, for always making me laugh, Chris Groves, Dennis Palmieri, and Eric Schulz. Upstairs, thanks to Aglika Angelova for playing the piano in the afternoons (and for not playing it in the morning). Other lucky encounters in the Bay Area have enriched this book—among them the chance to talk with Fabio Cleto and Ann Weinstone, whose work (respectively) on camp and queer childhood lit up connections for me as I was finishing it.

To Pam Thurschwell, with whom I grew up at Cornell, my love and gratitude for years of friendship and critical regard. Finally, I would like to thank Rob Hardies: he is everything a Decembrist could ask for, and more precious to me than I can say.

April 2000

It takes time to make queer people. —Gertrude Stein

This book gathers together some texts produced by gay men and lesbians in the United States in the first half of the twentieth century—poems by Hart Crane, novels by Willa Cather, gay male physique magazines, and lesbian pulp fiction—to argue that, during this period, queer writers and artists were groping their way toward a notion of homosexuality defined by a particular relationship to the idea of history. This relationship, which I call "foundling," entails imagining, on one hand, an exile from sanctioned experience, most often rendered as the experience of participation in family life and the life of communities and, on the other, a reunion with some "people" or sodality who redeem this exile and surpass the painful limitations of the original "home." The figures for what unites these new sodalities vary, of course, among the texts I have chosen: Crane imagines a secret, surpassing vitality that links American men in a Whitmanian brotherhood of hope for the future, while Cather dreams of a diaspora of lonely, artisanal sensitives; the editors of the physique magazines trumpet a "movement" of physical culture that will make America the latter-day fulfillment of Greek bodily and political ideals, while pulp authors such as Ann Bannon write about a network of Greenwich Village lesbians whose erotic entanglements and struggles against prejudice mark the beginnings of recognizably contemporary urban queer culture. Across differences of sex, genre, and two generations, however, the manifestations of this foundling imaginary share two characteristics: a determined struggle to escape the medical-psychological "inversion" model of homosexuality that was dominant in the United States in the first half of the century and a drive toward "peoplehood" that previews the contemporary "ethnic" notion of U.S. gay and lesbian collectivity. Before describing how I read these foundling texts, I offer a brief historical sketch of the other two models of American homosexuality between which they move.

We may think of the inversion model of homosexuality—the idea that homosexuals are people whose souls are trapped in the body of the "other" sex—and of the ethnic model—the idea that gay men and lesbians, either separately or jointly, constitute a people with a distinct culture—as two poles between which the history of U.S. lesbian and gay sexuality was shaped in the twentieth century. Roughly speaking, the inversion model enjoyed dominance in the first half of the century, while the ethnic model rose to prominence in the second. The two notions have always been deeply bound up with each other, however, and each of my four chapters takes up the ways that paying attention to their shared articulation can illuminate lesbian and gay texts for us; in the following paragraphs I offer a formal separation between them for the sake of preliminary clarity.

The understanding of gay men and lesbians as "inverts" emerges in nineteenth-century German sexology, with the writings of Karl Ulrichs, whose Urnings (male homosexuals) and Urningin (female homosexuals) owe their names to a passage in Plato's *Symposium* that describes two Aphrodites, a "heavenly" and a "common": the tributary pull of the two versions of the goddess of love inspires, respectively, love of men and of women (Mondimore 29). Ulrichs's choice of mythological nomenclature already suggests a tension between advocacy on behalf of homosexuals as a kind of "people" (since they are ancient) and clinical categorization of them as a "type" (since they seem to fit a psychological pattern). In fact, Ulrichs's writing on inversion is taken in each of these two directions in the 1880s and 1890s, as Richard von Krafft-Ebing damningly encapsulates it as an example of degenerate *per*-version in his influential *Psychopathia Sexualis* (1886), while John Addington Symonds, in "A Problem in Modern Ethics" (1896), makes a plea for the unpunishing dignity of Greek attitudes toward it—attitudes promisingly revived, he finds, in the fraternal poetry of Walt Whitman (Cory 86). Later, just after the turn of the century, Edward Carpenter tries with great invention to work the inversion model into a notion of "the intermediate sex" who have a historical status that exceeds the merely clinical. Suggesting their special sensitivity in matters of the heart, Carpenter argues for a historical mandate to value homosexuals of both sexes, since members of "the intermediate sex" will serve as mediators in the twentieth-century war of the heterosexual sexes (Cory 142).

As it turns out, the Victorian inversion model did not disappear in the twentieth century, despite competition from psychoanalysis and social-psychological sexology. Indeed, as both Thomas Laqueur and Judith Butler have shown, the idea of inversion lingers on in the psychoanalytic understanding of homosexuality, which depends not only on a notion of the two sexes as "opposites" (as opposed to, say, neighbors) but also on a notion of "primary bisexuality" or the coexistence of masculine and feminine impulses in all persons, so that homosexuality becomes a kind of psychical inversion: it is the man "within" a lesbian that motivates her to love a woman, and the woman in the man that presses him to love a man (Laqueur 149–53, 233–34; Butler, *Gender Trouble* 60–61). Outside the psychoanalytic idiom, meanwhile, both lesbian and gay vocabularies of self-definition, and, later, the "expert" medical-psychological writing on homosexuality, also continued to depend on Victorian notions of the homosexual as invert. Two examples are Radclyffe Hall's portrayal of lesbian subjectivity in *The Well of Loneliness* (1929)—in which, for clarification, the hero, Stephen Gordon, reads Krafft-Ebing, not Freud—and the work of the psychologist George Henry, whose 1948 *Sex Variants* encodes homosexuality as a secondary sign of a root disorder in gender identity, essentially an inversion (Terry). Even Alfred Kinsey's dispassionate study of homosexuality in the 1948 and 1953 *Sexual Behavior* volumes, based as it was on statistics about frequency of sexual contact, and not on the subjective experiences of its interviewees, was consumed by lesbians and gay men alongside, and not instead of, earlier models (partly, no doubt, because Kinsey offered no descriptive vocabulary for the lived experience of homosexuality). Kinsey's research decisively shifted the focus of sexology from pathology to statistical analysis and from Europe to America; even so, American lesbians and gay men were still consuming both old and new sexology. The Victorians and the social scientists appeared side by side, for instance, in the well-known 1956 volume edited by gay activist Daniel Webster Cory, *Homosexuality: A Cross-Cultural Approach*.

One reason for the collocation of such different sexological methods in a single volume is that, whatever their differences concerning the degree or kind of pathology at work in the homosexual, the languages of psychoanalysis, Victorian sexology, and social-scientific sex research are all primarily focused on describing the genesis of homosexual individuals (or, in Kinsey's case, the prevalence of certain types of individual experience within a population). By World War II, however, these languages would begin to prove inadequate to historical change rung by the emergence of large, urban lesbian and gay communities.[1] Another vocabulary, generated by lesbians and gay men themselves, and more attuned to collective experience than to individual identity, begins to be visible around World War I and picks up momentum after World War II: a vocabulary for what I call the "ethnicity" model of American homosexuality.

The anthropologist Gayle Rubin succinctly describes the historical and cultural changes that encouraged the development of the ethnicity model in the United States and Western Europe. In this passage from her 1984 essay "Thinking Sex," Rubin distinguishes modern, "ethnic" homosexuality from the homosexual behavior of other cultures and epochs.

> The New Guinea bachelor and the sodomite nobleman are only tangentially related to a modern gay man, who may migrate from rural Colorado to San Francisco in order to live in a gay neighborhood, work in a gay business, and participate in an elaborate experience

that includes a self-conscious identity, group solidarity, a literature, a press, and a high level of political activity. In modern, Western industrial societies, homosexuality has acquired much of the institutional structure of an ethnic group.

The relocation of homoeroticism into these small, quasi-ethnic, nucleated, sexually constituted communities is to some extent a consequence of the transfers of population brought about by industrialization. As laborers migrated to work in cities, there were increased opportunities for voluntary communities to form. Homosexually inclined women and men, who would have been vulnerable and isolated in most pre-industrial villages, began to congregate in small corners of big cities. [17]

Although Rubin's rendition of the historical background of this "quasi-ethnic" homosexuality is extremely general, more detailed work in lesbian and gay history locates the wave of urbanization she mentions at the turn of the twentieth century. And all of this scholarship overwhelmingly supports Rubin's basic claim to the link between industrial modernity and contemporary homosexual community, further specifying World War II as a turning point in its consolidation, since the war segregated men and women from each other in the armed forces, made possible a brief experiment in integrating women into the work force while men were fighting, and also led, at peacetime, to a massive settlement of GIs in coastal urban centers like San Francisco and New York. Each of these demographic shifts has been shown to have facilitated the development of lesbian and gay communities.[2]

Rubin's description of the emergence of an "ethnic" lesbian and gay community implies a wide variety of cultural practices that grew up alongside it. The bare bones of the ethnicity model, for instance, are to be found in the simple but enduring lesbian and gay practice of listing famous homosexuals from history—a gesture of genealogical claiming for which literary historian Rictor Norton finds evidence as far back as the sixteenth century but which he suggests picks up a great deal of momentum in Anglophone settings after the 1897 publication of an English translation of Havelock Ellis's *Sexual Inversion* with its list of famous "inverts." Norton points to the use of such lists as a gesture of political defiance—most famously by Oscar Wilde in his rehearsal, at his 1895 trial, of all the illustrious historical adher-

ents to "the love that dare not speak its name"—and to their recurrence in
U.S. queer novels of the 1930s such as Blair Niles's *Strange Brother* (1931) and
Richard Meeker's *Better Angel* (1933), as well as in late-century work such
as Larry Kramer's 1985 AIDS-activist play *The Normal Heart* (Norton 218–
24). Indeed, the practice of producing queer lists survives and flourishes in
contemporary mass culture, in the form of books such as Leigh Rutledge's
1987 *The Gay Book of Lists* and Dell Richards's 1990 *Lesbian Lists,* as well as
in a wide variety of literary anthologies such as Steve Hogan and Lee Hud-
son's 1998 *Completely Queer: The Gay and Lesbian Encyclopedia.* Such com-
pendia, designed to combat a homophobic belief in the lonely singularity
of gay men and lesbians, expend their self-justifying energy in the assem-
bly of illustrious literary and artistic queer names—Sappho, Shakespeare,
Michelangelo, Dickinson, Whitman—and in the collation of evidence for
the social dignity of homosexual roles from cultures both geographically
and historically far-flung—most frequently, in U.S. contexts, evidence of
the normal status of male-male pederasty among the classical Greeks, and
of the high value, in many Native American tribes, placed on the spiritual
services of *berdache* or "two-spirit" figures.[3]

These modest, defiant lists of homosexuals, once gay men and lesbians' prime and lonely strategy for describing queer historical presence, now
form part of a much wider array of lesbian and gay projects of historical
and cultural reclamation that aim to uncover a sense of what Norton calls
the "cultural unity" of homosexual experience in history. To be sure, feminist lesbian writers and queer writers of color in the United States have
tried to make clear to their reading publics that contemporary gay men
and lesbians are as much divided by differences in sex, race, and class as
they are "united." Audre Lorde's *Zami,* Joan Nestle's *A Restricted Country,* and Samuel Delany's *The Motion of Light on Water* are among the best
examples. Following on the critical assessments of queer cultural unity in
these texts, lesbian and gay scholars in the U.S. academic left have pointed
out the political problems with the primarily white, middle-class practice
of claiming non-white or otherwise historically distant "ancestors." Scott
Bravmann's *Queer Fictions of the Past* is the first full-length academic study
of the problems queer historians face as they try to weigh the tension between middle-class desires for a unified queer "heritage" and the actual vicissitudes of political difference in forming their narratives. But the debate

about whether "we" can ever really claim "ancestors" across multiple historical divides is a grass-roots one as well, conducted in queer newspapers and in conversations among friends (98).

Even in light of these strong political cautions, however, the lure of the ethnicity model remained strong at the end of the century, not least because it continued to be widely encouraged in queer consumer culture, especially its national print culture—which for half a century has been one of the most powerful links among lesbians and gay men in the United States. There are no lesbian and gay radio stations or television stations and, until the advent of the Internet—now a major avenue for socializing and for circulating information among queer people—city and regional newspapers, and the books available in liberal or queer bookstores, have been the very glue of the "imagined community" of U.S. lesbian and gay culture. Indeed, the conceptual force of Benedict Anderson's phrase is plainly evident in the myriad ways contemporary U.S. gay men and lesbians signal their sense of collective agency to each other across abstracting distances by consuming certain images and metaphors—not least the rainbow flag attached to cars and homes and clothing and countless product logos (for cruises, for magazines, for CDs); and the figure of "the tribe," represented by books with titles like *Joining the Tribe* (Linnea Due's collection of interviews with and stories about young men and women "growing up gay and lesbian in the '90's"), *Reviving the Tribe* (Eric Rofes's guide to gay male mental and sexual health in the second decade of the AIDS epidemic), and *Members of the Tribe* (a collection of cartoon caricatures by Michael Willhoite, modeled on the format of the "gay list," in which the uniform style of the cartoonist encourages the reader to experience Anne Frank, Sergei Eisenstein, Gore Vidal, and Senator Joe McCarthy as ethnically similar). The ethnic model of American homosexuality, whose first armature was the simple list of worthy forerunners, has been elaborated in contemporary mass culture into an ambient notion of the "peoplehood" of lesbians and gay men.[4]

Such are the large historical changes—the dissemination of sexological theories, the mass migration of military and labor forces, the formation of urban queer subcultures, and their integration into a mass market—that Jonathan Dollimore summarizes as a movement "from pathology to politics" (169–230). The questions that animate this book, however, are meant to challenge that formulation. What did such changes feel like? Was there really a movement from inversion to ethnicity, from isolation to people-hood, that women and men living through it could experience as such? What is the subjective experience of the birth of a new social movement, or even a new ethnicity?

The texts I have gathered in the four chapters that follow suggest that before Stonewall, literary and mass-cultural writing in the United States re-flects neither an immersion in "pathology" nor an inevitable movement in the direction of what we now call "lesbian and gay culture": neither inver-sion nor ethnicity, that is, in any pure form. What such texts do illuminate is the tension between them, which manifests itself in an overwhelming desire to *feel historical,* to convert the harrowing privacy of the inversion model into some more encompassing narrative of collective life. This is why I think of my materials as "foundling": the word allegorizes a movement be-tween solitary exile and collective experience—one that is surely still a part of contemporary queer culture but that is foregrounded in the two genera-tions that connect Hart Crane and Willa Cather to muscle magazines such as *Physique Pictorial* and lesbian pulp novels such as *Odd Girl Out.*

I should pause here to emphasize that while I want to be respectful of the differences among early-, middle-, and late-twentieth-century lesbian and gay cultures, I am nonetheless tracking a dilemma or tension between indi-vidual and communal identities that animates texts across those differences. We find this dilemma—which foundling texts suffer as the untenability of the inversion model, on one hand, and the inaccessibility of an ethnic model, on the other—rephrased in contemporary queer culture, where it operates in political debates about how important sex is to lesbian and gay identity or how innate it is; and in academic arguments about whether homosexu-ality is an "identity" in the first place. Before I return to the last of these questions, I want merely to suggest that their persistence across the century prevents us from looking to the present for greater or more reflexive knowl-edge about the historical significance of homosexuality than what the past holds.

If I reject a purely progressive or liberationist narrative of the develop-ment of U.S. queer politics and culture in the twentieth century, though, it is not because I think the past one hundred years reflect no change at all. I am simply persuaded by a different narrative, one that traces a movement from isolated, urban queer subcultures to a subculture networked across urban centers, then to a "national" queer culture linked by lesbian and gay print media and by shared habits of commodity consumption, and then—most recently—to a globalized queer culture facilitated by tourism, migration, and Internet communication. This other narrative does not imply progress toward liberation in the sense that a "pathology to politics" story does; a wide variety of commentators have been careful to point out that with each new stage of queer integration into urban, national, or international systems new problems of representation, cultural integrity, and political danger emerge to replace or reshape old ones.[5] What our retrospect from the vantage of a global queer culture does allow is a way of reading early- and mid-century identity struggles, like those in foundling texts, as signals of the deeply unfinished business between desire and history whose terminus, if it has one, may not lie within the realm of "queer culture" at all. As I hope to make clear, then, I am most attracted to the exemplarity rather than the uniqueness of my source materials.[6]

So foundling texts do not tell stories of inversion. In this regard they are to be distinguished from the major texts of the emerging canon of lesbian and gay literature in the twentieth and twenty-first centuries, which thus far has been drawn primarily from cosmopolitan literatures of England and Europe, most of them in a modernist vein: the work of Oscar Wilde, Thomas Mann, Marcel Proust, André Gide, Virginia Woolf, or Djuna Barnes. Next to *The Picture of Dorian Gray, Death in Venice, Remembrance of Things Past, The Immoralist, Orlando,* and *Nightwood,* foundling texts look adolescent, hapless, literal-minded. We can see this in choices of genre: Crane, Cather, the muscle editors, and the pulp novelists all make use of coming-of-age narratives to link their solitary heroes to a larger community, whereas Gide's Michel and Barnes's Nora Flood and Robin Vote are wandering cosmopolites, expatriates who traffic, like Wilde's Lord Henry, in the language (and the narrative arc) of degeneracy. None of these decadent texts reaches toward anything like a "community" that outpaces the hostile language of inversion. Indeed, the texts of the Anglo-European canon seem allergic to anything like the contemporary model of community: even Proust's famous "freemasonry" of inverts is constituted by a deep ambivalence among its members about each other's perversion (Bersani 129). It is as though the inversion model, first formulated in the centers of European culture, is diffused in its transmission to America shores, where it becomes a background against which writers struggle but never a narrative destination.

On the other hand, foundling literature is not what we could call an "ethnic" literature, either: we must reserve that designation for the vast (and exuberantly multi-ethnic) body of U.S. queer literature that has been published since Stonewall, by which time a national lesbian and gay culture provides a pool of character types (the queen, the ingenue, the bartender) and narrative tropes (coming out, first love, breaking up, homophobic violence) to draw on. The post-Stonewall literature of queer ethnicity—whether in the short stories of Achy Obejas or Norman Wong, the performance art of Holly Hughes, the later novels of Edmund White, or the plays of Tony Kushner—depends on a complicity with queer audiences that foundling texts never assume. When Hughes recalls in one monologue that her WASP parents used to worry that the expressive flamboyance of her childhood made her seem "ethnic," the joke the audience shares is the pun between her failure to be "straight" and her failure to be "white" (3). And when Obejas titles her first short story collection *We Came All the Way from Cuba So You Could Dress Like This?* the joke with her lesbian readers is that her characters' first ethnicity, their Cuban-ness, will be complicated by another "ethnicity" of butch lesbianism whose sign—masculine dress—is both absorbed and misunderstood in the parental address of the title. Both texts are secure in the assumption that readers have split identifications between their "family of origin" and their "chosen family," to use the current parlance. But foundling texts make no such leap. Their ideas of sodality (if not readerly complicity) are based on hopeful analogies to other historical forms: Whitmanian brotherhood, Native American extended family, Greek pederasty. Only the lesbian pulps do not make this analogical move; but even among Ann Bannon's Greenwich Village lesbians, whose relative freedom from the closet brings them closest to a contemporary queer literature, the social and erotic network that links them in a flush of self-discovery is always in danger of disruption by avenging husbands and over-eager male suitors.[7]

The historical analogies that populate foundling texts, I should point out, make my choice of the word *foundling* a metaphorical one: the texts I have gathered are not orphan narratives after the fashion of *Great Expectations* or *Anne of Green Gables*. It is true that most of the women in Bannon's fiction, for instance, are very conveniently orphaned and Cather's protagonists are most often separated from their families by ambition or a deep sense of difference from them, but the orphandom in the texts is never at the center of a plot's arc. Similarly, in Crane's poems, the lyric value placed on brotherhood far exceeds that placed on parental figures, much as the gestures toward family in the muscle magazines (captions noting the family situations of physique models, for instance) always feel secondary, an afterthought. But I have not written a narrative history of the figure of the foundling in lesbian and gay culture. Recent literary-critical work on the figure of the orphan or the foundling, focused on English Romantic poets and early American texts, has examined the orphan as a trope for experiences of artistic alienation and economic disenfranchisement, or for forms of scapegoating and cultural marginalization during tumultuous historical change, reinvesting the figure of the orphan with broad historical and cultural meaning.[8] I share that last gesture, although my notion of what counts as orphandom is more metaphorical at the outset, and it is also the starting point for a notion of potentially shared identity, based on queer writers' historical analogies rather than on figures of orphans.

The analogies that animate foundling texts, especially those analogies that equate an inarticulate homosexuality with a distant racial, ethnic, tribal, or national form, have led me in all the chapters that follow to turn my attention to the racial politics of foundling imagination. All of the primary texts in this book are by white writers and artists; most of them trade in primitivist or at least anachronistic fantasies that earlier cultural modes are less punishing of secret desires than their own. It is not true, however, that foundling writing must be produced by white people: James Baldwin's *Go Tell It on the Mountain* and John Rechy's *City of Night* are both good examples of texts that easily fit the coming-of-age and neither-invert-nor-queer-ethnic model of foundling writing I have laid out here. It is true that foundling texts by white people tend to participate in an unpolitical and sometimes racist set of beliefs about the simplicity of racial analogies; I have tried to balance the obvious political limitations of such analogies with the benefits of historicizing them. These benefits may be considerable, if we begin to see the twining of race with sexual fantasy as a story about different but simultaneous modes of writing history. I have, of course, learned a great deal about this relationship of modes by reading the work of U.S. queer writers of color (among them contemporary writers such as Delany, Lorde, Wong, and Obejas, but also early-century writers we now claim as illuminating queer desire, such as Nella Larsen and Jean Toomer). I have also been provoked in this regard by Gilles Deleuze and Félix Guattari, who write in *Anti-Oedipus* about the historical promiscuity of sexual fantasy:

> In delirium the libido is continually re-creating History, continents, kingdoms, races, and cultures. Not that it is advisable to put historical representations in the place of the familial representations of the Freudian unconscious, or even the archetypes of a collective unconscious. It is merely a question of ascertaining that our choices in matters of love are at the crossroads of "vibrations," which is to say that they express connections, disjunctions, and conjunctions of flows that cross through a society, entering and leaving it, linking it up with other societies, ancient or contemporary, remote or vanished, dead or yet to be born. Africas and Orients, always following the underground thread of the libido. . . . A love is not reactionary or revolutionary, but it is the index of the reactionary or revolutionary character of the social investments of the libido. (352)

Deleuze and Guattari are not suggesting, in this passage, that racial identities are "merely" fantasy material; on the contrary, they are proposing that fantasy is never merely private. They are also helpful in pointing the way to an antiracist reading practice that historicizes rather than punishes the racialized sexual fantasies of modern subjects, white and non-white alike. And, further, they are helpful in suggesting that "the libido" and race may be names for different historical temporalities—one of them, sexuality, cycling and recycling pieces of the other, race—whose large movements (migrations, displacements) individual lives cannot themselves encompass. Sexuality in this reading is an "individual" phenomenon only insofar as it is historical; and it is "fantasy" only insofar as the material for fantasy depends on the "investments" of the social body. It is always strung between different speeds of time and different registers of experience, between the private and the public. Or, as Deleuze and Guattari put it, desire itself is foundling: "the unconscious is an orphan" (49).

If the texts I have chosen here suffer a political naïveté about race that demands historicizing, they are also in danger of being assimilated into a queer reading practice that assumes the movement "from pathology to politics," so that they come to represent, for better or for worse, what "we" presume ourselves to have transcended: the closet, isolation, dubious and literal-minded analogies to other cultures. And it is true that all the materials I have gathered here do traffic in something like queer mythology, if by "mythology" we mean Fredric Jameson's notion that myths are what writers who dream of describing history collapse into when they cannot gain access to objective historical knowledge ("Figural Relativism" 164). In each of the chapters in this book, however, I try to suggest that it is exactly the "mythological" features of the texts—their hopefulness, their naïveté—that historically illuminate them for us. Through the lens of a foundling imagination, in other words, we can see homosexuality in twentieth-century U.S. literature and culture, not as an early stage in the formation of an autonomous sexual-political "identity" that has "liberated" itself over the past seventy years, but as a historiographical struggle: specifically, a struggle to find terms for historical narration that strike a balance between the unspeakability of desire, especially punishable desire, and group life. "History is what hurts," Jameson writes, meaning by "history" the name we give to the impossibility of reconciling personal life with the movements of a total system (*Political Unconscious* 102). If that is true—and I believe it is—then the pain and the painful delight in these foundling texts are among the most richly "historical" of any a lesbian and gay movement might choose to claim, since they extend our idea of "the historical" to include the desire for its conditions.

I begin to specify what such a desire can look like in chapter 1. Surveying seventy years of Crane criticism, I point out that both his detractors and his champions resolve their difficulty with Crane's notoriously "ecstatic," dense lyrics by subliming him out of literary history: he seems to his critics not a modernist or a metaphysical or a romantic poet but somehow all of these, ransacking "the history of styles" and floating lost beyond it. This subliming of Crane out of literary history is always linked, I suggest, to a notion that he fails to write history; this notion is linked, in turn, to his homosexuality. Hostile critics, that is, have suggested that Crane failed to digest the stern imperative of Anglophone literary modernism to write history as a story of decline and argue that the basis of this failure is a promiscuous male homosexual dispersal of energy, which appears in the poems as an adolescent overexcitement about new technologies such as airplanes and radios. Crane's defenders, meanwhile, have tended to write him as an Icarian overreacher, whose sheer commitment to the means of poetry is traceable to the ahistorical *jouissance* of gay desire. Against these claims, I argue that Crane is in fact an acute theorist of history and that his poems, so often read as the product of uninterpretably private fantasies, actually offer a supple and legible vocabulary for the unnoticed sensory experiences out of which historical narration emerges. In readings of short lyrics from Crane's first book, *White Buildings,* as well as sections from Crane's long poem *The Bridge* and a posthumously published fragment addressed to his critics, I show that Crane's homosexuality prompts him to shape a poetic language of shared but occluded historical experience. Gay critics such as Thomas Yingling have shown Crane's inventiveness in reworking the tropes of the inversion model of homosexuality in his love poems; but this tropological "queering" is only half the story. Crane's desire to communicate historical experience in a lyric address to what Allen Grossman calls his "hermeneutic friends" and to imagine them as the basis of an American fraternity marks his poems as foundling texts.

In chapter 2 I show what a search for "hermeneutic friends" looks like in sustained narrative form. Reading four of Willa Cather's novels—*The Song of the Lark, One of Ours, The Professor's House,* and *Sapphira and the Slave Girl*—I show that Cather's entire career can be understood as a sustained and creative effort to imagine kinship relations among characters without making recourse to the heterosexual marriage plot of the realist novel. I argue that Cather achieves this aim by creating "affect-genealogies," coming-of-age stories that establish for her young heroes a lineage of invisible kin, who always share three things: their unfitness for family life, their identifications with European high culture and against American mass culture, and their faintly inverted gender identities. Cather liked her male protagonists to be ever so slightly feminine, and her female heroes to be boyish. And she is fiercely proud of these inversions: she believes they make her men less brutish and her women less frivolous. They also are the bodily ground for what Cather will argue throughout her career really connects people: not relations of family or nation but the quiet dignity, sometimes terribly lonely, of people who live the life of the imagination. That Cather insists on the bodily visibility of this seemingly intangible difference is both a confirmation of its allegorical relation to homosexuality, I argue, and the source of its interest as a theory of history. In short, Cather's characters, strung between their gender inversions and some ineffable peoplehood of dreamers, give evidence on their bodies of what one character calls "the open secret" of "passion": a struggle to give form to desire that is invisible only to people who believe that material progress is what gives meaning to life. I conclude the chapter with a survey of how this matrix of concerns about feeling and affiliation still silently controls the terms by which contemporary readers of Cather are trying to understand the relationship of her sexuality to her art.

The musclebound images in physique magazines of the 1950s and early 1960s might seem a long way from Cather's early-century struggle with the marriage plot. But in chapter 3 I show that, at mid-century, the magazines are hashing out answers to many of the same questions about homosexuality and history that Cather faced. Like Cather, the muscle magazine editors believed that adolescence encodes an "open secret" in the social body, the secret of beauty—and, like Cather, they believed this secret could operate as a social bond, and a source of historical narration. In a brief introduction, I show how Bob Mizer, the editor of *Physique Pictorial,* insisted on linking images of the taut, muscular bodies of their adolescent male models to written text that poses homosexuality, not as a problem of individual desire, but as an appealing condition in the social body, a kind of contagious "courtesy" that should be the basis for a worldwide fitness movement. The rest of the chapter traces the role of the physique magazines in a mid-century struggle over how to read the relationship between individual gay male bodies, on one hand, and an invisible gay public that might or might not turn out to be the source of some historical change, on the other. Alongside readings of the relationship between word and image in the muscle publications themselves, then, I look at how physique culture was interpreted from outside—by *Sports Illustrated* (which abhorred it as evidence of homosexuality in American sport), the U.S. Supreme Court (which judged it, in 1962, not to be obscene), and by social-psychiatric sexologists (who equated excessive bodily athleticism with a gender identity disorder). In a conclusion devoted to contemporary gay male celebrations of 1950s muscle culture, I show how the way that culture is represented as a "simpler, more innocent" male homosexuality actually masks the unfinished struggle of the magazines to de-individualize homosexuality by placing it in history—to escape the loneliness of the model of individual gender pathology and to confirm the wholesome masculinity of a vast "secret public" of musclemen.

This unfinished struggle between the explanatory powers of isolation and collectivity, between ideas of inversion and a dream of peoplehood, is nowhere more sharply etched than in the production and consumption of the lesbian pulp novels of the 1950s and 1960s. In chapter 4 I focus on how the ambivalent heroines of lesbian pulp novels have shaped the criticism of the genre. The protagonists of the most famous novels of the era, Ann Bannon's Beebo Brinker series, are torn between hating themselves for being inverts and celebrating the erotic networks their sexuality forms. The pressure Bannon places on her characters to come to terms with themselves as "trapped in the wrong body" is so intense, I show, that the plots of Bannon's novels are essentially determined by the tension between butch and femme bodily styles: femme lesbians, who can "pass" as straight, flee their butch lovers, who cannot disguise their masculinity, only to return when the affections of men prove hollow; or, in another arrangement of this plot, a woman who has married a man finally abandons him in order to hunt down her femme lover from college, only to end up playing femme herself to the same butch—Beebo Brinker—from whom the first femme had fled. I argue that subsequent criticism of Bannon's novels, which has focused primarily on their highly mobile femmes, cannot choose between labeling them realist and labeling them melodramatic: are the novels to be remembered primarily as "self-hating," because of the violent instability of the relationships they depict, or are they to be canonized as camp melodrama, whose erotic rondelé reflects the proud sexual autonomy of women? My own answer to this question is that focusing on Bannon's butch, Beebo, allows us to read the novels so as to accommodate the histories of both celebration and shame they describe: in Beebo's "masculine" physique, which over the course of five novels ages from adolescence to menopause, Bannon finds a way to make the inversion model feel historical. Beebo accrues the experience of being unable to pass, that is; and this experience becomes a source of sexual dignity. Age, however, more than a particular butch or femme identity, affords this historicization—or, age in combination with a romance involving both terms of the butch-femme pair. I close this chapter with a reading of a 1992 Canadian film about lesbian pulp, *Forbidden Love,* whose delightful toggling between interviews with older lesbians and a fictional, pulp-style butch-femme romance suggests ways of reading both inversion and an "ethnic" peoplehood into the queer past.

Before turning to my four chapters, I would like to offer a brief description of how I think this book fits into the ongoing work of queer studies. One of my primary aims in writing *Foundlings* was to try to resolve a tension in the United States between lesbian and gay studies, on one hand, and queer theory, on the other. The difference between these two designations has been succinctly phrased by Michael Warner in terms of method, as a difference between historical and psychoanalytic models of interpretation ("Introduction" xi); and by Lisa Duggan, in terms of the institutional placement of queer scholars, as a difference between historians and literary critics ("The Discipline Problem"). In both understandings of this tension, what is at stake is the problem of how to relate the uncovering of a lost or submerged U.S. lesbian and gay history to the project of formulating a nonpunishing but specific account of the origins of homosexuality.

The debate that has most often emerged from the collision of these two projects goes something like this: queer theorists, determined to write a story of the origins of homosexuality, assign themselves to understanding the (logically, if not temporally) "presocial" intersection of matter and language in the figure of sexuality and therefore tend to produce "radical" understandings of homosexuality—that is, theories that locate homosexuality at the very margins or origins of culture itself. This approach is true of all the major American theorizations of the last decade: Leo Bersani's *Homos,* Judith Butler's *Gender Trouble* and *Bodies That Matter,* Teresa DeLauretis's *The Practice of Love,* Lee Edelman's *Homographesis,* and Eve Kosofsky Sedgwick's *Epistemology of the Closet.* Historians of U.S. lesbian and gay sexuality, meanwhile, engaged in the project of capturing lost information about past queer lives, place the objects of their study firmly within the realm of the cultural, as articulate—if contingent—historical forms. This means that the understanding of homosexuality in the historical work is less "radical" and more "political"—less about the untapped possibilities at the root of culture and more about the accumulated example of past attempts at survival. This political emphasis can be found in broad, summary histories of the twentieth century, such as Lillian Faderman's *Odd Girls and Twilight Lovers,* as well as histories of particular places and shorter periods, such as George Chauncey's *Gay New York,* which covers the turn of the century, or Elizabeth Lapovsky Kennedy and Madeline D. Davis's *Boots of Leather, Slippers of Gold,* which is focused on lesbians in Buffalo, New York, from the 1930s to the 1950s. What emerges from the differences between queer theory and lesbian and gay history, then, is something like a debate about ideology and historical self-consciousness: is homosexuality most potent as a force for social change when it is inarticulate, unconscious, and acting as a threat to representation? or when it clothes itself in specific historical and political forms, which pose challenges to particular arrangements of power and authority? Does homosexuality have to be the conscious possession of a person or a group of people—an identity—for it to shape history? [9]

My own solution to this problem partakes of something that James Chandler recently called "the return to history" in literary criticism, under whose rubric we can include the new historicism. Chandler's *England in 1819* offers a genealogy of new historicism, with its interest in particular locales and specific scenes, that links it back to debates about "uneven development" in Marxist historiography—debates about why some dates, 1789 or 1939 or 1819, say, seem supersaturated with "history" (108–9, 131). This genealogy moves Chandler to ruminate on what exactly the "history" is that saturates certain dates (and, since he is a Romanticist, certain poetic figures), and he concludes that it is something like a Lukácsian historical "consciousness," a historical "phantasm" irreducible to mind or body, the material world, or the world of the imagination. What gives this historical phantasm a Marxist genealogy for Chandler is its illumination, for the historical (or protohistorical) subject, of her membership in a collectivity imagined as "revolutionary" (554).

I am especially sympathetic to such formulations, which arrive at a sympathetic, unpunishing description of the relationship between historical fantasy and historical "experience." What attracted me to Hart Crane, Willa Cather, physique magazines, and lesbian pulp novels, and what made me want to collect them and give them a common name, was my sense of the vulnerability of all of the texts to history. In the very articulation of their desire to "feel historical," that is, each of my foundling texts resorted to means so delicate, so unapproved, that in retrospect they seem utterly in danger of being swept aside on the grounds of their naïveté. Crane's enthusiasm for the fraternal possibilities implied in the construction of the Brooklyn Bridge or Cather's belief that a return to some "Native American" artisanal culture was a way to resist modernization and the pressures of heterosexual marriage: these seem too counterfactual to hold up as "lesbian and gay history." The same could be said of the muscle magazines' insistence on the moral purity of their Greek ideals of beauty or on the lesbian pulps' constant recourse to melodramatic, transporting sex as a solution to homophobia. These strategies, in other words, are all mythological rather than historical. But the very subjectivity, the very "mythology," of all of these strategies told me a story that seemed historical: the story of discarded attempt—of unfulfilled desire and the incomplete historical project of connecting personhood and peoplehood it cathects.

In one sense, then, I am participating in a new historicist project that Catherine Gallagher and Steven Greenblatt summarize as an insistence on the historical worth of the fragmentary, islanded, or anecdotal utterance. In an essay called "Counterhistory and the Anecdote," which was written as a kind of retrospective on the past thirty years of literary historicism, Gallagher and Greenblatt offer a clarifying linkage between a resistance to the traditional, narrative history of "great men" and the lure of the anecdote. Surveying the heady intellectual changes of the 1960s and 1970s, they write:

> Along this counter-historical continuum—from poststructuralist negativity, through the recovery of the *longue durée* and the history of the losers, to the envisioning of counterfactuals and provisional historical worlds—our sense of delayed and alternative chronologies, of resistances to change, its unevenness, and the unexpectedness of its sources, grew more complete and assured. . . . At certain points along this range of counter-historical endeavors, anecdotes became prime carriers and expressions of various counter-historical desires: to foster scepticism about the depth or thoroughness of historical explanation; to counteract narratives of development or progress; and to imagine a more complete array of the options at a given moment in the past, instead of selecting only those realized as "historically significant." (53–54)

In its "counter-historical desires," the new historicist anecdote seems to offer queer critics a possibility of adequating between the place of homosexuality as logically prehistorical, as in the major texts of queer theory, and legitimately historical and simply waiting to be recovered, as in most lesbian and gay history. To be fair, many lesbian and gay historians, in specifying the modernity of the homosexuality we think of as ours, have themselves come up against criticism as "social constructionists" who do not believe in any pre-given homosexual identity; and queer theorists have shown a strong commitment to using theories of the presocial mobility of homosexuality to re-inflect properly social and historical forms. There is no absolute line, in other words, between post-structuralist theorists and traditional historians. But no U.S. scholars I know of have tried to write either a history or a historiography of what is proto-historical in homosexuality, desire. That I might try to do so, at least in a "micro-historical" way, is exactly what appealed to me in my materials. And the anecdote, described by Gallagher and Greenblatt, begins to sound like a name for the traffic in and out of history that desire performs.

Indeed, in the writing to which the new historicists are perhaps most indebted, the scholarly encounter with the anecdote takes on the excitement of desire itself. Michel Foucault, in a 1977 essay called "The Life of Infamous Men," recounts his discovery in the Bibliothèque Nationale of a whole archive of eighteenth-century documents that spoke to him like "strange poems," such as hospital internment registers, in which entire lives seemed summarized in a flash of clumsy prose. He becomes aroused:

> I would find it difficult to say exactly what I felt when I read these fragments and many others which were similar to them. Doubtless one of those impressions which one says are "physical" as if it would be possible to have others. And I confess that these "*nouvelles*," suddenly rising up through two and a half centuries of silence, stirred more fibres in me than what one usually calls literature. (77)[10]

Foucault is, of course, the scholar best known for having tried to write a counter-history and historiography of the un- or prehistorical, of sexuality in the protean variety of its productions, and who thereby subjugated "history" as theory's master code to some other term, usually *power*. But this subjugation has taken on the character of a historical master code itself, as his famous assignation of an 1870 birthdate to homosexuality is absorbed into lesbian and gay scholarship (*History of Sexuality* 43). This declaration hinges, first, on an idea that power always breeds its own resistance, which, with deviant sexuality, leads to another famous formulation, where homosexuality, pressed into being by medical and juridical discourse in the nineteenth century, "began to speak in its own behalf"; and second, on a periodization (and, implicitly, an ethnography) that differentiates between societies that regulate themselves primarily through "the deployment of alliance," that is, through kinship systems, and those that have superimposed on this system of alliance another system, "the deployment of sexuality" (106–7). While both this theory of power and this periodization have been immensely congenial to lesbian and gay literary scholars, it has also resulted in exactly the sort of *grand récit* that Gallagher and Greenblatt describe themselves and Foucault as struggling to dismantle. Not only is homosexuality, in this account, a product of modernity, but it veritably represents modernity: it is the example, par excellence, of new forms of power and of new periodizations.

This theoretical privilege gave rise to Eve Kosofsky Sedgwick's 1990 *Epistemology of the Closet,* which, in a dazzling elaboration of Foucault's work, argues that the late-nineteenth-century transformation of homosexuality from a juridical and medical category into a fully ontologized identity ("a species," in Foucault's terms) underwrites a new *episteme* in which cultural distinctions as basic as those between ignorance and knowledge, or culture and nature, owed their coherence to an unacknowledged "open secret" about the existence of homosexuals (11). It is interesting to note, though, that in the midst of this major formulation Sedgwick feels obliged to sketch its own counter-history. Although she places herself squarely in the "constructivist" camp of scholars for whom there is no essential homosexual identity across time, she acknowledges in the introduction to *Epistemology of the Closet* that "essentialist" queer history, rooted in the list-making defiance I describe above, may capture a local, affective dimension of lesbian and gay lives slighted in such global arguments as her own:

> It seems plausible that a lot of the emotional energy behind essentialist historical work has to do not even in the first place with reclaiming the place and eros of Homeric heroes, Renaissance painters, and

medieval gay monks, so much as with the far less permissible, vastly more necessary project of recognizing and validating the creativity and heroism of the effeminate boy or tommish girl of the fifties (or sixties or seventies or eighties) whose sense of constituting precisely a *gap* in the discursive fabric of the given has not been done justice, so far, by constructivist work. (42–43)

The counter-historical resistance to major narratives returns here in Sedgwick's link between "emotional energy" and "historical work," specifically in the form of her description of some lesbian and gay historians' unconscious desire for the unsung, for the study of details undignified by contact with History. Here, interestingly, Sedgwick locates this unconscious desire close to the ground of the inversion model, at the intersection of gender identity and object choice, in the figures of the "effeminate boy" and the "tommish girl" whom "essentialist" historians are not aware of wanting to write about and whom "constructivist" scholars have not yet acknowledged. The explanatory power of the tomboy and the sissy for Sedgwick, in this dream of her own counter-practice, is no less than that of a Jamesonian "political unconscious," a double figure for how particular texts—say, essentialist queer histories focused on luminaries rather than children—repress what they do not have the historical resources to master or organize (*Tendencies* 48–49).

This acute vulnerability of queer texts to what comes after them, their excitation in the matrix of claiming, is why Sedgwick is interested in the possibilities of furnishing the tomboy and the sissy with a historical heroism. It is also, I suggest, why Foucault is moved by the stylistically awkward "infamy" of his archival subjects, and why I have found these foundling texts so compelling. In fact, it is the reason I chose the metaphor of "the foundling" to describe them: the sense of unfinished historical business that close reading can bring, especially the close reading of texts that seem too catachrestic, too counterfactual, too literal-minded or unsophisticated to merit full-scale integration into the story of how we come up with historical periods or theories of history. Here I argue that close readings of Crane, or Cather or muscle magazines or pulp fiction, are of great value because they help us reread U.S. lesbian and gay history against a progressive or liberationist grain, and along the fault lines, instead, of a still-incomplete struggle to adequate inversion and ethnicity, solitude and community, singularity and universality.[11]

When, in her 1903 story "The Making of Americans," Gertrude Stein writes, "It takes time to make queer people" (152), she is trying to describe the development of interesting identities that are neither "bourgeois," that is, undistinguished by any eccentricity, nor "crazy, faddist, or low class," that is, marred by what she sees as an overinvestment in being different from the "normal" world. She is suggesting, I think, that "queer people," the luckily strange people in America, require a particular type of time in order to exist: neither the slow time of conformity to nineteenth-century bourgeois ideals, nor the over-rapid time of adherence to twentieth-century fads, or of abject suffering, caught up in every passing change. The elitist class politics of her distinction, if unhappy for most of us, should nonetheless illuminate what we can gain from reading foundling texts. Because they do not properly belong either to the inert, terminal narratives of inversion or to the triumphant, progressive narrative of achieving ethnic coherence, they suggest another time, a time of expectation, in which their key stylistic gestures, choices of genre, and ideological frames all point to an inaccessible future, in which the inarticulate desires that mobilize them will find some "hermeneutic friend" beyond the historical horizon of their unintelligibility to themselves. The sense that I might be such a "friend" is not only what I consider to be the historical and interpretive bridge between Stein's use of the word *queer* and my own; it is also the main reason I have been so happy to write about these materials. I hope, introducing them to my readers, the feeling will transmit.

The poems of Hart Crane seem like a good place to begin a book about lesbian and gay relationships to history, since Crane was punished early for failing to be "historical." The difficulty of Crane's poems, and their ecstatic lyricism, have produced a body of criticism preoccupied, whether in early dismissals of him or later valorizations, with his unassimilability to literary-historical narration. He is not, in the central accounts, a modernist, despite his chronological placement at the beginning of the twentieth century. His lyrics are famously "opposed" to the ironic, skeptical aesthetic of T. S. Eliot, and their stylistic signature has generally been classified as Elizabethan or metaphysical. This misfit placement in literary history has led to a critical subliming of Crane, a conflation of his person and his poems that are then jointly elevated to the status of aberrant example, hovering immediately outside of history. He is said to "give away the age," in Allen Tate's words, by virtue of embodying "the rootless spiritual life of our time" (121), or to be "the ultimate victim of history," according to Joseph Riddel, by refusing to acknowledge the compromises necessary for a lyric project to survive the modernist truth of pessimism (107). Yvor Winters, an early gatekeeper of critical opinion on Crane, seconds Tate's claim that Crane did not successfully confront the moral truths of the age—mostly meaning the prophecy of human folly visited on mankind in World War I—and describes Crane in a 1930 essay as "hysterical" in his attempt to write his long poem to Brooklyn Bridge, *The Bridge,* at a uniformly high pitch of emotional intensity. Winters, elaborating on this willfulness, calls Crane's poem "a public catastrophe," a fundamental misuse of the means of poetry, and suggests that Crane, by failing to write morally, is merely "a stylistic automaton," trying to stay afloat by sheer personal assertion (105, 107, 108). Hysteric, automaton, victim, hapless giver-away of the age: each characterization is an attempt to keep clean the tableau of literary history by placing the aberrant, immature writings of Crane on its very edge, right next to the void. Tate went so far as to refer to Crane's suicide as "morally appropriate" (Berthoff 58).

These criticisms, with their focus on developmental immaturity and communal disaster, are not hard to decode, in retrospect, as given shape by homophobia. Thomas Yingling, in his book-length study of Crane, makes clear that the poet faced throughout his career a brutal equation of his sexuality with his poetic style, writing as he was among rationalist colleagues for whom homosexuality was a dirty secret and a failure of self-discipline, barely to be tolerated. Crane's correspondence in particular offers a glimpse of the energy he was obliged to spend defending himself as worthy of poetry, despite being a gay man: "One doesn't have to look to homosexuals to find instances of missing sensibilities," he writes Winters in 1927, defending against the accusation that Leonardo da Vinci, and other "homosexuals," lacked the self-discipline to produce moral art—if in fact moral art is what modernity should desire (*O My Land* 338). Other letters make clear the connection between this accusation and others, more "literary," leveled at Crane for his style.

Gay male critics have tried to understand Crane in light of this problem, but there is another critical generation between Crane's contemporaries and the first wave of gay literary criticism. This middle generation of critics, not so invested in the fortunes of English literary modernism as their predecessors, are by and large more sympathetic to Crane's poetry and avoid the lacerating moral judgments that characterize the first round of commentary. What they share with the earlier critics, though, is that they still radicalize Crane—understanding him, if more kindly, as writing at the limits of history.

Allen Grossman's beautiful essay "Hart Crane and Poetry: A Consideration of Crane's Intense Poetics" is a good example of this radical interpretation. Describing Crane as absolutely "authentic" in his commitment to pursue the linguistic promise of poetry—the promise of pure communication among beings—Grossman distinguishes Crane sharply from the English literary moderns by arguing that Crane, unlike Yeats and Eliot, did not believe that poetic style should ironically reflect a notion of "historically irreversible decline." Instead, writes Grossman, "in the name of the poetics of the 'new' he undertook to write *as* his predecessor, ignoring the equally constraining and prudential history of styles, as if he had no body and no unexchangeable place in time" (232). Similarly, Donald Pease writes that Crane, in the dithyrambic flights of *The Bridge,* "revaluates proleptically even the most recent version of modernism," arguing that Crane literally "replaces the Freudian unconscious with what could be called a prophetic unconscious—what Ernst Bloch calls an unconscious of the future" (Yingling 214). In these more sympathetic readings Crane becomes a figure akin to Hegel's Antigone, visited on history, disrupting it ("ignoring" history, in a phrase that is the critical obverse of Winters's "public catastrophe"), and then exhausted and blown apart by it, but not within the compass of its narrative possibilities. Here, imprudent, un-Freudian, and disembodied, Crane's sexuality lurks in the formulations of what makes him so hard to assimilate to literary history—or, more precisely, to a literary understanding of history.

The gay male critics who have written on Crane more recently have not, in illuminating Crane's poems, called this radicalization into question. Indeed, on some occasions they have further specified it, as does Tim Dean when he writes that "Crane preferred poetry over the homosexual subculture of 1920s Greenwich Village because his lyric—rather than his notorious sexual—practices promised freedom from the disabling binary options of closet privacy" (106). Dean's argument depends on reading Crane's lyrics as the true location of his sexuality, sublime and ego-shattering, while dismissing his actual sexual practices (themselves subculturally specific, as in his preference for sex with sailors and for waterfront meeting-places) as merely "notorious"—a gesture that places Crane once again outside history, writing from a jouissance that can have no proper name.

Thomas Yingling's *Hart Crane and the Homosexual Text,* in contrast, offers help in understanding Crane as both ecstatic and historically located. Yingling explains Crane's penumbral status in the American literary canon by pointing out that Crane's poems, "somatic," ecstatic, and "experiential," did not meet the criteria of Eliot's influential practice of historical irony and critical disattachment—by pointing out, in other words, that Crane's poems could not be considered modernist. This maneuver, to repeat, tends to sublime Crane out of literary history, given the broad interpretive power of the Eliot-based definition of literary modernism. But Yingling, alert to the possibility that taking this position might be read as a literary-critical exceptionalism, asserts that if Crane's poems did not fit a definition of modernism, his sexuality certainly did.

> It is important to note that homosexuality was constructed for Crane in such a way that its congruence with more bourgeois, affective modes of bonding was virtually impossible. For Crane, homosexuality initiated what [John] Rajchman calls the peculiar ethics of modernism (modernism defined as a "literature of 'sexuality' that is not love, happiness, or duty but trauma, otherness, and unspeakable truth"). (30)

In Crane's poems, as I show in a later discussion, homosexuality is a scene of both anguish and delight, of code and clarity; and Yingling, exposing the homophobia that produces this anguish, goes a long way toward making it possible to read the poems with an appreciation of the emotional—the "experiential," in his words—breadth they compass. Specifically, by focusing his readings of Crane's poems on rhetorical techniques such as catachresis and morphemic fluidity, Yingling helps us understand that the material experience of homosexuality is reproduced at every level in the poems' linguistic play as a particular and unavoidable gay textuality. This writing, which Lee Edelman calls "homographesis," struggles with the high modernist rhetoric of disembodied impartiality, and with the accusation of gay male narcissism, and it constructs, in response, novel (catachrestic, fluid) forms of identity and difference in the spaces of poems.

Yingling's readings also point the way to reading Crane's poems in the light of something like a foundling imagination. He does this, first, by contextualizing male homosexuality in twentieth-century U.S. culture as an islanded subculture: "The culture [gay men] discover or produce upon coming out—gay subculture—has no relevance to their natal culture; be that upper or lower class, of whatever ethnic extraction or blend" (34). Second, in a close reading of Crane's poem "Recitative," Yingling points out that the poem's difficult images of twisted mirrors and images cut into "Twin shadowed halves" register an attempt to rework a hostile, externally imposed discourse of homosexuality as narcissism—a discourse that depends on dividing genders into "same" and "different," and whose punishments closely correlate to the inversion model of homosexuality, which likewise depends on a notion of the absolute difference between the "opposite" sexes. By linking his sociological observation about gay male separation from home culture to a close reading that reflects Crane's struggle with the gendered question of narcissism (and, implicitly, inversion), Yingling produces the outlines of what I would call a reading of Crane's poem as foundling.

This reading is immensely helpful; but it preserves a distinction between history as framing circumstance and sexuality as framed experience that Crane's poems—like the writing I will consider in chapters 2–4—outmaneuver. While Dean exiles Crane's sex life from his sexuality in order to place his sexuality outside history, that is, Yingling insists on an absolute separation between gay subcultures and their surround, equates modernism with trauma, and makes Crane's sexuality a figure for that modernism. This reading, too, isolates Crane from historical narration: "the utopian in Crane signifies a desire to escape history" (42). But the sexuality we are now able to read in Crane's poems, thanks in part to Yingling, is the engine for a special kind of history writing. Crane is a writer whose sexuality is a major factor in motivating him to be neither elegiac (post-historical) nor "ecstatic" (extrahistorical) but deeply engaged with the question of what history is, how it comes about.

Crane has been accused of believing in a mystical, cyclical idea of history, and this claim has fed on the homophobic accusation that his writing did not achieve a normative "maturity" that would have been marked by a graduation into linear time (Clark 61–63; Riddel 106). But, as Grossman remarks, Crane is no mystic; he is a realist, and the strain on the language of his poems is unimpeachable evidence of a struggle that only a realist could pursue. The question is, what was Crane struggling with? Yingling points to homophobia; but this is only part of the question. I think what Crane wanted was to come up with a better description of how history moves than our clumsy, genetic past-into-present storytelling allows for. As Jared Gardner points out, Crane's being gay meant that some of the basic narrative resources of history writing, especially national and family stories of filial inheritance, were unavailable to him; and his struggle to come up with a narrative of how time and change make history, without making recourse to heterosexual myths, obliges him to hunt in his poems for convincing historical narration in other registers (33). Gardner suggests that what Crane comes up with is a narcissistic myth of American history that begins with the poet himself; I suggest that he produces, instead, what Grossman would call a story of "the fate of structures"—stories, at once intimate and abstract, about the mechanics of change in the world: in soil, in air, in water, in the human body, and in its machines.

I am interested in how Crane's poems sound to us now, at the beginning of the twenty-first century, because I think he is a genius at describing processes that live inside other processes. As we find ourselves, all of us, unable adequately to narrate the nature of the changes late modernity has brought, especially whether small-scale and large-scale changes can correlate to each other in any meaningful way, it is rewarding to read Crane and to discover relationships between the large and the small, or the past and the present, that do not fall into the received categories: parallel, repetition, dimunition, reversal. Crane's poems are too strange for that; they are more like what Deleuze and Guattari would call "desiring-machines," which invite us to envision other modes of relationship between ideas, more idiosyncratic ones, more drawn from the imaginary of physics, of all places—puncturation, swirling, solidification. These are the terms by which Crane tries not to write history exactly but to account for the perpetual origins of historical narrative, in which "history" is some potent relation between the large and the small, the apprehensible and the abstract in experience.[1]

My first aim in this chapter, then, is to read of some of the notoriously "difficult" poems from Crane's first volume, *White Buildings,* with an eye to such dynamic model-making, so as to sketch out how the poems can be read a bit more simply than they have been read to date. I turn next to parts of Crane's long poem of American history, *The Bridge,* to illuminate the historiographical significance of such model-making: what do Crane's allegories of change tell us about the nation, the family, or modernity that more mythologically secure narratives of decline or rebirth, or pendulum swing, fail to tell us? Finally, I consider a posthumously published short poem of Crane's that links his model-making impulse to a specifically gay narrative — not to demonstrate that the story of "the fate of structures" is exclusively a gay story but to show that it is possible for a gay story to yield an invested historical (i.e., not mystical) argument: to show, indeed, that Crane is not "the ultimate victim of history" but a writer of histories whose critical edge has not worn dull.

The Interstices of White Buildings

Taken together, the poems in *White Buildings* suggest that Crane is trying to oppose or overcome misunderstandings about time, desire, and the sensory world. Many of the poems demand that we rethink the significance of such simple, building-block lyric figures as spring or day and night or the mirror or the flame in ways that are not reducible, say, to an Abrams-style division of poetic activity into "the mirror and the lamp," mimesis and creation. On the contrary, the overall effect of the lyrics in *White Buildings* is to suggest that the interstices between moments or sensations or perceptions constitute the realm of experience most worth poetic attention, because those interstices are both mimetic and creative: both difficult to render and, because of that difficulty, the possible source of new and shared knowledge about desire and change. In the section that follows, then, I read a few of these short poems to set up a clear account of Crane's relation to a private, personal experience of time and sensation, as well as his insistence that this experience, however difficult to describe, is communicable. In the longer form of *The Bridge,* Crane translates this drive to overcome misunderstandings about how the private experience of time works into a sustained poetic thesis about the function of the proper name in the more public register of history writing. But that second phase of my argument depends, first, on our reading a few of the lyrics.

The first poem in *White Buildings,* "Legend," begins with the lines, "As silent as a mirror is believed / Realities plunge in silence by . . ." suggesting that our beliefs about "the mirror," in this case the world of presumably docile mimetic representations, are insufficient actually to render experience—which, in "Legend," is an archetypically Crane-like drama of self-expenditure and suffering, endured in order to bring back new emotional knowledge to the world, a "bright logic." The poem:

Legend

As silent as a mirror is believed
Realities plunge in silence by . . .

I am not ready for repentance;
Nor to match regrets. For the moth
Bends no more than the still
Imploring flame. And tremorous
In the white falling flakes
Kisses are,—
The only worth all granting.

It is to be learned —
This cleaving and this burning,
But only by the one who
Spends out himself again.

Twice and twice
(Again the smoking souvenir,
Bleeding eidolon!) and yet again.
Until the bright logic is won
Unwhispering as a mirror
Is believed.

Then, drop by caustic drop, a perfect cry
Shall string some constant harmony,—
Relentless caper for all those who step
The legend of their youth into the noon. (3)[2]

I have come to read this poem as an opening gesture of defiance by a young gay man who has assimilated a certain rhetoric of homosexuality as self-indulgence or failure of will, or personal excess, and who then claims exactly that "failure" as the source of his poetic powers: "yes," the poet seems to be saying, "what I pursue is self-destructive, like a moth's affair with a flame; but the flame desires just like I do, and in any case what I learn from my experience of this desire is a privilege to know." The experience of this unsanctioned desire, which invites the "repentance" and "regret" that the young poet will not accept, is not without its agonies, the "smoking souvenir" and "bleeding eidolon" of a dazed and exhausted aftermath; but they are worth what is "won" from them, an initiation into that number "who step / The legend of their youth into the noon." Those who plunge into the secret life, that is, the world that appears "silent" and "unwhispering" from the outside but which smokes and bleeds and cries and dances once you are on the inside—those who plunge into this world will earn what all poets desire, which is fame, the inscription of their "youth," their rendering of beauty, in "the noon"—the daylight, public world. Homosexuality, in "Legend," is rescued from the accusation of self-indulgence and rewritten as a kind of membership in the sexuality of youth, of energy and delight, which those who never pursue it will never know. A youthful gesture, indeed, to claim youth as one's property; but a gesture, in this dense poem, linked other intuitions, not least the sense that the body's vitality is part of something "constant" and larger than itself.

This intuition provides somatic figures for connectedness to the world throughout *White Buildings*. It is the content of the "bright logic," and it is also the place to begin reading for Crane's relationship to narrative, to understand his attraction to describing the processes of change hidden inside the processes we see. A good and fairly simple example is the four-quatrain poem "Paraphrase," which describes waking up in the middle of the night with the unexpected discovery of another vitality in the interstices of the body's vitality:

> Of a steady winking beat between
> Systole, diastole spokes-of-a-wheel
> One rushing from the bed at night
> May find the record wedged in his soul. (17)

The "steady winking beat" that pulses in between our pulse, and whose motion we notice only in semi-consciousness, recalls the "constant harmony" of "Legend." Here, instead of the docile mimetic "mirror," there are the dismissively rendered "Systole, diastole spokes-of-a-wheel," whose dashes and repeated "-stole" render the poet's impatience with descriptions of the body as merely the vessel for linear movement from one heartbeat to the next. The difference between what the poet senses now and what he normally notices is the difference between geometry and the calculus, between isolated units and fluid continuity:

> Above the feet the clever sheets
> Lie guard upon the integers of life:
> For what skims in between uncurls the toe,
> Involves the hands in purposeless repose.

The one-through-ten integers of toes, protected by the sheets, are nonetheless the conduits for a "skimming" flow that disorients the body, "uncurl-[ing] the toe" and moving the hand to a posture with no purpose. This interstitial life, which in "Legend" describes a homosexuality not outside but hidden within sanctioned experience, is offered here as a key to understanding the relationship between the conscious and the unconscious. If the poem's first two stanzas meditate on what it is like to be awakened for no apparent reason in the middle of the night, that is, the last two consider what is happening when daylight fails to wake us:

> But from its bracket how can the tongue tell
> When systematic morn shall sometime flood
> The pillow—how desperate is the light
> That shall not rouse, how faint the crow's cavil
>
> As, when stunned in that antarctic blaze,
> Your head, unrocking to a pulse, already
> Hollowed by air, posts a white paraphrase
> Among bruised roses on the papered wall. (50)

These stanzas make the best sense if we understand "that antarctic blaze" to refer not to anything in the sleeper's room but to the content of his dream, which produces a bodily response: the sleeper exhales sharply, where his breath, visible in the cold room, harshly meets the "bruised roses"—just as, in the dream, the "blaze" stuns the speaker's dream-self. The elegant thesis of the poem, then, is that the body paraphrases the unconscious; and, more specifically, that we are able to realize this only on strange occasions that invert our sense of the proper relationship of the body to night and day, occasions like waking at night or sleeping through morning. The "steady winking beat" of the poem's first line, then, is the secret vitality that underscores the continuity between the unconscious and its paraphrase, the body, a continuity available only to a speaker who can muster the alienating self-scrutiny to be alert to his body as a "you" who is aware, in failing to wake, that he has failed to wake. Like the speaker of "Legend," alert to the "constant harmony" and "perfect cry" his sexuality can win, the speaker of "Paraphrase" is struggling to communicate a knowledge at once desperately fleeting and continuously powerful, a knowledge that the body's life holds secrets of an intrasomatic vitality whose modes we have only clumsy names for: youth, dreams.

Crane's lyric belief that interstices are more interesting than nodes reaches a crescendo in the middle of *White Buildings*, where in a suite of seven poems he rewrites memory, forgetfulness, lust, drunken transport, and artistic renewal through the lens of the intraprocessual sensitivity that "Legend" and "Paraphrase" first indicate. The most dazzling of these poems is "Lachrymae Christi," in which Crane turns his attention to ancient and Christian myths of spring, as embodied by Dionysus and Christ. As with the earlier poems, Crane takes a standard lyric situation—the contrast between desire and clarity, or between day and night—and emphatically reworks it, not by mere reversal (spring as death, say), but with an attention to what lies within the situation, to how spring *becomes* a lyric subject in the first place. Crane's success in "Lachrymae Christi" is a result of the poem's ecstatic intimacy with its materials—an immersion, in this instance, in dirt. The poem's specific subject is a nocturnal springtime burrowing—a burrowing of worms—that leads us not to contemplation of the past as a deeper layer of the soil but to an enthralled rejuvenation of the past as what lives within the texture of a once-blocked present.

It is a difficult poem. Although nominally it is about a continuity between the figures of Christ and Dionysus, its narrative commitment to making that link is complicated by Symbolist ecstasies ("And the nights opening / Chant pyramids,—"), and, more generally, by Crane's insistence on leaving object-nouns abstract (worms are busy with their "distilling clemencies"). In other words, the poet confounds his reader's two most reflex strategies: first, the narrative approach that would take as the poem's core meaning, Dionysus lives on in Christ, or some variation on that equation; and second, the lyric approach, which expects the satisfaction of the high note hit in song—a note audible only as the outcome of the weave of classes of emblem: soil images, body images, machine images, floral images arranged at the last to give one set musical weight and (therefore) rhetorical priority. But just as the poem swerves violently away from telling any miniature "story" of the continuity of Christ and Dionysus, so do its images range too far afield from one another for their relations to be the basis of the poem's coherence. There is no lyric logic that says, "in this song, soil is like a machine" or "in this song, birds are like the soil." Instead, as with many of Crane's densest, most "intense" lyrics, the images are allowed a wild diversity because they all refer to the same thing: a *process* that is not among the poem's objects but that generates them. And in "Lachrymae Christi," that process is among the most "modest" of possible acts: it is aeration, loosening of the soil. The poem is about aeration as a renewal in spring and as a release for energies blocked by the separation of Christ and Dionysus; and the aeration process quite rigidly governs the otherwise disparate categories of image and levels of concretion and abstraction the poem contains.

True to the project in *White Buildings* of describing the unscrutinized "realities" that "plunge in silence by," the poem's first proposition is that the action of spring takes place at night:

> Whitely, while benzine
> Rinsings from the moon
> Dissolve all but the windows of the mills
> (Inside the sure machinery
> Is still
> And curdled only where a sill
> Sluices its one unyielding smile)
>
> Immaculate venom binds
> The fox's teeth, and swart
> Thorns freshen on the year's

First blood. From flanks unfended,
Twanged red perfidies of spring
Are trillion on the hill. (19)

Spring is an assault, a perfidy or betrayal of dormancy whose "immaculate venom," whose pure life principle "binds" the teeth of predators (not shut but to their gums, it seems; "binds" them into action) and similarly twangs plant life into blossom. And as the spring hillside's "flanks" are "unfended" against this night assault, so are the bricks and mortar of the nearby mills unprotected from the power of the nearly material moonlight, in which they "dissolve" to white froth like so much grease. Only the windows, which deftly sluice the light right through themselves, remain black, passing on the benzine power of the light to the mill's interior—and this elegant (smiling) transparency, which spares the windows dissolution, brings the otherwise obscured machinery to material life, curdles it into solidity out of liquid darkness.

These processes of liquefaction, curdling, and twanging, or assault, linked "whitely" by the sponsorship of the moon, directly benefit from the busy secrecy of night's action and seem (by virtue of their priority in the poem if nothing else) themselves to ignite the poem's next level—a more ecstatic rejuvenation of nature, which takes place close to the earth or just below its surface:

And the nights opening
Chant pyramids,—
Anoint with innocence,— recall
To music and retrieve what perjuries
Had galvanized the eyes.

          While chime
Beneath and all around
Distilling clemencies,— worms'
Inaudible whistle, tunneling
Not penitence
But song, as these
Perpetual fountains, vines,—

Thy Nazarene and tinder eyes. (19)

The stakes of the poem begin to clarify in these two stanzas: the benefit of night is that its surface stillness allows attention to its "inaudible" but multi-form activity—a chorus of small openings that, in their perpetuity, readjust perception to their fine grain. The too-large, blockish sense-perceptions of the daylight (recall "Paraphrase" with its "systematic morn"), which "[gal-vanize] the eyes" to a blindness of mere intake, dissolve here like the mill that operates in daylight; and the night observer, the as-yet disembodied speaker of the poem, feels in the restoration of that finer grain an "inno-cence," veritably a clemency, granted not because of an act of penance for some crime but as the organic gift produced by "tunneling," by the worm-blind but dead-certain activity of subterranean motion—which, gloriously, aerates the soil.

We might pause over two effects produced by this happy aeration, born of spring's assault: first, we see generated a small cluster of nonconcrete images, the pyramid, the fountain, the vine, which are literally the poem's fruits. In their capacities to preserve, to launch, and to connect, each object is valuable much as a machine part would be—for its "perpetual" function-ing, its reliability as a piece of energy in the act of creation. And, I would argue, their three-dimensionality, their capaciousness for the speaker's next demand is earned by the double-verbing by which the poem creates them: the "nights," while "opening" like the trillion buds, "chant" the pyramids hyper-transitively into being, while the worm's whistle chimes through the soil, "distilling" its clemencies to the day-perjured perceiver. The phrases "opening / Chant pyramids" and "chime . . . Distilling clemencies" attempt a syntax of pure effectiveness, in whose foregrounded transitivity lies Crane's ethos of production: in the context of night, music makes objects. It ma-terializes promise.

Second, the pyramid, fountain, and vine make visible the "Nazarene and tinder eyes" of the spring-principle itself, Christ-Dionysus. This person-principle provides the poem an object of address—in fact produces that address out of its subterranean and wormlike micro-processes. The appear-ance of the figure will give the poem momentum to carry through to its as-tonishing conclusion, in which the poet calls forth the figure out of flames. First, though, we approach the broader implications of these processes for Crane: for one thing, they facilitate blocked speech. Within parentheses, he steps in for a moment:

(Let sphinxes from the ripe
Borage of death have cleared my tongue
Once and again; vermin and rod
No longer bind. Some sentient cloud
Of tears flocks through the tendoned loam:
Betrayed stones slowly speak.) (19–20)

Having failed, it seems, to answer successfully the riddle of his art in some previous, enwintered attempt, our speaker in this aside asks for one more chance in the odd imperative past-perfect that wobbles between command and prayer: "Let it have been done (by those forces)." The greeny sphinxes, the speaker beneath their feet in the dirt, give him his spring's reprieve, and he unburies himself sufficiently to move through the freshly loosened soil, in or as the "sentient cloud / Of tears," the Christ-tears, whose way has been opened by the worms. "Betrayed stones slowly speak" is almost anticlimactic here.

The liberation of release from burial allows the poet to proceed to his real goal: address to the deity. The remaining three stanzas are devoted to encouraging the figure, who becomes more Dionysus than Christ, to "lift" itself up and face the spring. In this closing address we see exactly what the poem has been aiming, this moonlit spring night, to recover:

Names peeling from Thine eyes
And their undimming lattices of flame,
Spell out in palm and pain
Compulsion of the year, O Nazarene.

Lean long from sable, slender boughs,
Unstanched and luminous. And as the nights
Strike from Thee perfect spheres,
Lift up in lilac-emerald breath the grail
Of earth again—

Thy face
From charred and riven stakes, O
Dionysus, Thy
Unmangled target smile. (20)

Insofar as "spring," in this poem, has the attributes of a verb, its prefix must be "Un-." The effect of this night's renewal, of the tendoning of the loam, its preservation, launching, and connection, is to "unmangle" the smile of the god whose face, previously obscured, now serves as night's gong, his eyes "undimming," his spirit "unstanched." And "Names peeling" from the god's eyes with every blow allow at last the "spelling" of the year's "compulsion," give it language. As music is the principle of the aeration in the middle of the poem, so, in turn, the closing by-product of that music is a name; as the poem's micro-processes emerged into form as a song, so, at last, does the life-drive of the poem's occasion shudder into speech. The "un," in other words, is the poems' goal: un-betrayal, un-galvanization. And, finally, "the grail / Of earth," which is the deity's very face, "unmangled."

A brief contrast may be helpful here. T. S. Eliot writes about the grail legend in *The Waste Land,* and in the final section of that poem, the part called "What the Thunder Said," he writes a similar description of moonlit renewal. Synthesizing (as his notes suggest) the Biblical story of the disciples encountering the resurrected Christ in Emmaus and the Arthurian episode of the Chapel Perilous in which Lancelot inadvertently raises the dead, Eliot deploys contrasts between night and day, and dry and wet to prepare readers for the arrival of his Sanskrit "thunder." But where Crane stays within his materials, fascinated by their generative possibilities, Eliot uses his as a way of getting a leg up on their content, merging and overlapping them to arrive at a single, mighty enunciation that can make the history of Western culture legible from without. Two relevant stanzas:

> A woman drew her long black hair out tight
> And fiddled whisper music on those strings
> And bats with baby faces in the violet light
> Whistled, and beat their wings
> And crawled head downward down a blackened wall
> And upside down in air were towers
> Tolling reminiscent bells, that kept the hours
> And voices singing out of empty cisterns and exhausted wells

> In this decayed hole among the mountains
> In the faint moonlight, the grass is singing

Over the tumbled graves, about the chapel
There is the empty chapel, only the wind's home.
It has no windows, and the door swings,
Dry bones can harm no one.
Only a cock stood on the rooftree
Co co rico co co rico
In a flash of lightning. Then a damp gust
Bringing rain (67–68)

Eliot's poem has several things in common with Crane's: they both choose moonlit night as the moment of hybrid pagan-Christian augury; they both draw our attention to recessed activity of night creatures—bats, here, to Crane's worms—and they both imagine the scene as producing a song. Indeed, given the avid attention Crane gave *The Waste Land* when it was published in 1922, we may justifiably imagine this section of the poem as a source text, conscious or not, for the 1924 "Lachrymae Christi." In any case, Eliot's poem handily illuminates some key differences between his poetic grasp of history and Crane's—and not the reductive difference between some poetic "pessimism" of Eliot's and Crane's "optimism," however Crane himself might have imagined the difference that way. It is true that Eliot's setting is a graveyard, and Crane's is a field beside a factory—a contrast that suggests two obviously divergent views of modernity—but the interesting difference between the two poems lies in which vantage each poet chooses to tell the story of renewal.

Both poems, to repeat, imagine the portentous night as a song: Eliot hears "voices singing out of empty cisterns," while Crane's "nights opening / Chant pyramids." But for Eliot, modern song is the result of a hollowing out, not an aeration: modernity has hollowed out experience, the poem tells us, but the one thing a hollow can do is produce a wail, or an echo. His poem, that is, relies on the romantic convention of the animating wind to make meaning (and song) out of his "decayed hole." What follows this wailing is the lightning, rain, and declaiming thunder, whose famous "Datta/Dayadhvam/Damyata" and "Shantih shantih shantih" are its redemptive message. The poem's message, concluding as it does with speech imported from without, seems to be that human history has hollowed itself out sufficiently to become the echo chamber the gods have been looking for: we can really *hear* what the thunder says, now, because, like Tiresias, we have been cast from the texture of history and into a place of pure audition.

This is a complex gesture, whose ambivalence—are we raising the dead, who will devour us, zombie-like, or are we witnessing the resurrection?—may or may not justify the stagy deus ex machina arrival of a storm, depending on how generously we read Eliot. My point, here, is simply to demonstrate that Eliot prefers to tell the story of how history happens from outside history, summarizing it, synthesizing it, echoing it. History empties itself out. In "Lachrymae Christi," by contrast, Crane nests several figures for change, night-to-day, winter-to-spring, ancient-to-Christian, and builds on them from the inside out, starting with the operation of the worms and culminating in the address to the grail-bearing deity whose promise of renewal is the outcome of the aeration, as well as its repetition. Another way of saying this is that the worms' burrowing is both a miniature of, and necessary condition for, Dionysus's exhumation. The poem is a scalar repetition of itself whose triumphant striking of the note of closure ("And as the nights / Strike from Thee perfect spheres, / Lift up in lilac-emerald breath the grail / Of earth again") is sounded by the contact between the large and the small, the touch of the worms' "inaudible whistle" and the "names peeling" from the deity—the place where we see the large historical narrative of renewal, the recovery of the grail, meet its preconditions in the micronarrative, the subhistorical but necessary humus. This poem, more than any other in *White Buildings,* is a demonstration of how Crane prefers to read history: not by hunting the past to find, in its echoes, the signs of the future, but by becoming aware of the conditions producing history at every turn.

The Bridge *and "the Names of History"*

Warner Berthoff, in his fine and briskly comprehensive reading of *The Bridge,* suggests that criticism of the poem has by and large been caught up in two assumptions that have blocked the possibility of its enjoyable interpretation. The first, following on Tate's and Winters's contemporary assessments, is the notion that Crane's poem is a "failed" epic, unable to muster an organic connection to a fractured culture, or even to muster the mature masculine awareness of the impossibility of such an endeavor. The second assumption is that Crane, although he dabbles in what he thinks is "history" in *The Bridge,* is actually just writing about facets of himself, so that the whole poem becomes an allegory of Crane's private struggle to create a global self through his art. These two criticisms are linked to homophobic knowledges about homosexuality as developmentally stalled or narcissistic (Yingling 20). But, to his credit, Berthoff manages to suggest another critical vocabulary for reading the poem. While acknowledging that there is occasional "evidence" for the "failed epic" and the "self-questing" readings of *The Bridge* in Crane's letters, Berthoff does not take the poet at his sometime word, arguing instead that we focus on the poem's "performative logic" and recall the regularly "delivered eloquence" of Crane's phrases, lines, and passages (84–85, 109).

Berthoff's suggestion goes a long way toward clearing ground from which we might be able to read *The Bridge* apart from the failure effect that has been thrown up around it: once that ground is clear, one of the first things we are able to see is a continuity of the impulse, from *White Buildings* to *The Bridge,* to track the conditions that produce history, rather than to tell a historical story. It is true that Crane wrote to Gorham Munson describing *The Bridge* as "a mystical synthesis of 'America'"—a phrase quoted constantly in the criticism—and that there runs throughout the poem the typically turn-of-the-century theme of the late and the new. But these frames, while necessary, are exactly that, frames: designed to assert the presence of art and to be held onto and forgotten during the course of the "performance." To hunt for "America" in the poem, if this is in fact its synthetic and entire aim, takes mere moments: there is Whitman, there is Poe; there are Melville, Dickinson, the Wright brothers, Pocahontas and Captain Smith. This array, if we read it as Crane's claim for the "American-ness" and therefore the literary worth of his poem, keeps us squabbling in what Yingling calls "myth-criticism," which is at once a counterfactual and a canonical debate: why no Thoreau? I prefer to take us through *The Bridge* with an eye for how the proper names that circulate within it are the sites of poetic knowledge about the birth of history, much as the worms are in "Lachrymae Christi." Indeed, I hope to show that Crane's long poem is an elaboration of that shorter lyric's charted path between the "inaudible whistle" and the resonance of the proper name.

To follow this path in *The Bridge* between the inaudible and the pronounced is not to look for Crane's inspirational "sources"—that is the project of a myth criticism whose function would merely be to determine the authenticity of the poem's "American-ness." As Berthoff points out, the "authority" of Crane's poem depends not on its authenticity as epic or as history but on whether it has wormed its way into our sense of language's possibilities or has "become an available and availing part of our own language-framed apprehension of things" (109). I will argue that Crane's traffic between the inaudible and the named is not the tracery of an epic or a quest designed to carry him from anonymity to authority but an exploration of how history is made up of effects generated by that traffic.

Another way of saying this is that the movement between the unnamed and the proper name in *The Bridge* is less the search for a national patronym, but rather, as Grossman would say, the search for "hermeneutic friends" whose names are condensations of the processes—especially those of silent, continuous vitality—Crane wants us to become alert to. If in the poems in *White Buildings,* that is, Crane tries to draw our attention to such processes by aggressively reworking conventional poetic figures—the mirror, the arrival of spring, sleep and waking—in *The Bridge* he turns to historical figures to do the same thing: to point out what complex code for the traffic between the large and the small, the inapprehensible and the concrete, the proper names compress. Indeed, it is his sense of their vivid proximity to this movement, and not their abstract cultural worth, that makes Crane choose his "friends": "Not greatest, thou—not first, nor last,—but near," he writes, addressing Whitman.

Gilles Deleuze and Félix Guattari provide a similar (and wonderful) rendition of the role of the proper name in history in *Anti-Oedipus:*

> The theory of proper names should not be conceived of in terms of representation; it refers instead to the class of "effects": effects that are not a mere dependence on causes, but the occupation of a domain, and the operation of a system of signs. This can clearly be seen in physics, where proper names designate such effects within fields of potentials: the Joule effect, the Seebeck effect, the Kelvin effect. History is like physics: a Joan of Arc effect, a Heliogabas effect—all the *names* of history, and not the name of the father. (86)

The patronymic theory of the name as merely the site of propriety (however virtual, recursive, or cunningly disavowing) is exposed, in this helpful reading, as a sorry tool indeed for coming to grips with the "effects" Crane wishes to attend to: the interiors of the social bonds that make up "American history," and not the abstract idea of their realization in the past. The value of reading *The Bridge* as a "queer" poem, then, as a poem born of unsanctioned experience, is significant: such a reading opens us to the full effect of Crane's intense apostrophes, of the poem's "delivered eloquence."

Where to begin? A brief map of the poem might help. *The Bridge,* which was published in 1930, comprises a proem and eight sections. The first part, "Ave Maria," is spoken by Christopher Columbus, sailing back to Spain after his first encounter with North America. The second, longest part of *The Bridge,* "Powhatan's Daughter," is a suite of five poems that offer a sharp contrast to Columbus's flush of success: with a mythical Pocahontas watching over the speakers of each of the five sections, these poems meditate on the twentieth century's sense of itself as belated, and on the "lost" heritage and inarticulate lives that haunt it. "Powhatan's Daughter" is followed by a single-poem section called "Cutty Sark," in which the speaker, now recognizably a contemporary lyric poet, encounters a Melville-like sailor in a waterfront bar in New York. The next poem, "Cape Hatteras," is perhaps the most famous section of the poem. It is a sustained rhapsody on Whitman and his vision of an American brotherhood, focusing by turns on the Civil War and World War I, through which "fraternal massacres" Whitman (and, through Crane, his spirit) manages to speak hopefully of the future nonetheless.

This ode to American brotherhood is followed by a fifth section called "Three Songs," in which the poet tries to find, in awestruck, burlesque, and lighthearted descriptions of American femininity, the traces of the Pocahontas myth; and then by "Quaker Hill," which returns us to a notion of lateness, this time through images of real-estate development in what was once a Quaker settlement. The penultimate section, "The Tunnel," uses the figure of the subway to imagine Poe apparitionally guiding the poet on a passage through hell; and the closing piece, "Atlantis," is a triumphant evocation of the Brooklyn Bridge itself, in its power to act as an historical lyre, weaving from earthly events a song that moves in and out of time.

I do not presume to lead my readers sequentially through the entire poem; instead, I focus briefly on three places (roughly the poem's beginning, middle, and end) where we can see Crane working with the tension between the historical name and the inarticulate silences around it, and on how, across these three sections, we see the poem as a whole tending toward a poetically sure statement about the relation between those two limits of linguistic reach. My readings are not designed to highlight the homoerotic content of the sections, to show that Crane's homosexuality makes him able to render an especially convincing Columbus or Whitman, but rather to develop a knowledge of Crane's homosexuality as shaping a poetic interest in the character of the name that does more than merely correspond to its representational status. I do hope to show that his being gay led him to a curiosity about what, besides authenticity, proper names promise history.

Certainly Crane has some investment in history as a source of authentic (as opposed to viable) meanings. But this is not the most poetically interesting or successful project of *The Bridge*. When Crane presumes a bond among his readers, instead of exploring its possible conditions, the poem falls flat and suffers politically in terms of race and gender. When he addresses Whitman in "Cape Hatteras," thanking him for his ability "to bind us throbbing with one voice, / New integers of Roman, Viking, Celt—"; or when, in the "National Winter Garden" part of "Three Songs," he dismisses a vaudeville dancing girl for performing a "burlesque of our lust," we can easily feel the lie of the first-person plural, embedded in the imperial cliché of racial inheritance and in the sexist misprision. Such moments suggest that the failures of Crane's poem lie exactly in its attempts to oblige a historical poetics of authenticity: a poetics of the true nation and the virile, virtuous man. These are the places where Crane plays into the hands of his critics, who link his sexuality either to a failure to write epic (as with Winters and Tate), or to a distasteful politics (as with Gardner). But these are the failures, and not the foundations, of the poem—to which I now turn.

"Ave Maria" sets *The Bridge* in motion with Columbus's address to the heavens, thanking them for his success as he returns to Spain after his first voyage to the New World: the precise object of his speech hovers, in the style of "Lachrymae Christi," between the saints, Mary, and a God whose names vary throughout the poem. What the entire apostrophe shares, though, is a (proleptically) Baconian enthusiasm for the coherent complexity of the natural world, the solving of whose mysteries is a continual act of religious praise. And what the address settles on is a rhapsody over earth's magnetic field, and the invention of the compass. The penultimate stanza:

> Of all that amplitude that time explores,
> A needle in the sight, suspended north,—
> Yielding by inference and discard, faith
> And true appointment from the hidden shoal:
> This disposition that thy night relates
> From Moon to Saturn in one sapphire wheel:
> The orbic wake of thy once whirling feet,
> Elohim, still I hear thy sounding heel! (49)

This science in the service of faith "yield[s]" an echo of the dance that created the world. Still in range of the "sounding" feet whose percussion against earth created the magnetic field he now relies on, Crane's Columbus discovers not so much the New World as an "appointment" and a "disposition" (both names for magnetism) toward the "north" of a knowledge that reveals earth and humans to be built the same way, around a warm and cooling center. The poem ends:

> White toil of heaven's cordons, mustering
> In holy rings all sails charged to the far
> Hushed gleaming fields and pendant seething wheat
> Of knowledge,— round thy brows unhooded now
> —The kindled Crown! acceded of the poles
> And biassed by full sails, meridians reel
> Thy purpose—still one shore beyond desire!
> The sea's green crying towers a-sway, Beyond
>
> And kingdoms
>
>   naked in the
>
>   trembling heart—
>
> Te Deum laudamus
>
>   O Thou Hand of Fire (49–50)

The magnetic "holy rings" reveal earth's shape, making it navigable, and capitalize the "Beyond" that serves as placeholder for the name of God. The figural traffic of magnetism-as-code, sustained here both in the "holy rings" and in the "meridians" that "reel," culminates in a higher-order comparison of the earth to the human body, whose "trembling heart," exposed to the super-heated "Hand of Fire," is left to cool and become a magnetic clue to the shared creation of earth and man, spinning off four extra lines of text as the figural whirling subsides. The Columbus-effect, then, is the repetition of the cooling of the earth in the cooling of the body, as the "Hand of Fire" withdraws, leaving certainty behind. The figural stacking of earth-as-magnet and body-as-earth is the shape and content of that certainty, built from the quiver of a compass needle.

This triumphalist certainty of historical purpose does not last throughout *The Bridge;* it is meant as a high-water mark. Before turning to the poem's lower tides, though, I would like once more to provide a brief contrast to Crane's play on the proper name. Berthoff reminds us that Crane's generation, writing in the immediate aftermath of World War I, seems in retrospect almost uniformly enthusiastic about conducting a "national self-audit" in the service of refining the thesis of American exceptionalism—and William Carlos William's *In the American Grain* (1925), which Crane read while working on *The Bridge,* is the closest cousin to Crane's attempt at this project (Berthoff 89). Like *The Bridge,* Williams's book also meditates on the play in American history between the proper name and the nameless forces that surpass it: *In the American Grain* is a series of essays on historical persons, arranged chronologically from the Viking "Red Eric" to "Abraham Lincoln," that are meant to burnish what history has dulled, specifically the names of those whom we understand to have shaped America.

But unlike Crane, Williams is interested in these names more as a historian than as a poet, which is to say, he is primarily interested in restoring their authenticity—in making Benjamin Franklin, for instance, as Franklin-like as possible. In an introductory note, Williams writes, "In these studies I have sought to re-name the things seen, now lost in chaos of borrowed titles, many of them inappropriate, under which the true character lies hid" (xxi). This search for "true character" leads Williams, like Crane, to look at primary sources (both of them read Columbus's journals). But with Williams, the result of research is a prose narrative whose "re-naming" involves obliging readers to read the story of the "discovery" of America *after* they have read Williams's account of Columbus's political disposability to the monarchs of Spain, who grow rich on his discovery while grinding him into poverty and obscurity. Columbus, for Williams, is a perfect (if slightly lesser) example of Hegel's world-historical man, who brings something new into history and is tossed aside by it. The resulting figure is somewhere between exiled Adam and Napoleon at Elba.

> There is no need to argue Columbus' special worth. As much as many another more successful, everything that is holy, brave, or of whatever worth there is in a man was contained in that body. Let it have been as genius that he made his first great voyage, possessed of that streamlike human purity of purpose called by that name—it was still as a man that he would bite the bitter fruit that Nature would offer him. He was poisoned and his fellows turned against him like wild beasts. (11)

We might say that Williams's attention to the political surround of the voyages of discovery makes his account of Columbus more "realistic" than Crane's, since it so heavily occludes the aspect of triumph on which "Ave Maria" remains focused; but this reading would prevent us from seeing that Williams's attempt to balance greed and honor, discovery and the horror of empire, leads him out of history and into myth: Columbus is an Adam, brought low by a perversion in the universe whose incidental form is men's greed. The figure of "the bitter fruit," in fact, opens the Columbus essay: Williams describes America as

> a predestined and bitter fruit existing, perversely, before the white flower of its birth. . . . It is as the achievement of a flower, pure, white, waxlike and fragrant, that Columbus' infatuated course must be depicted, especially when compared with the acrid and poisonous apple which was later by him to be proved. (7)

In other words, Williams's commitment to understanding history within the framework of the authenticity of names (rather than their effects) leads him to extra-historical explanations for colonial greed and for the destruction of great men: he is obliged to write figures of temporal reversal, the flower before the fruit, in order to include Columbus in "the American grain," now shaping up as a story of purity and perversion. Williams's "time-reversal that reveals perversion" is to Crane's "cooling-off that reveals a lucidly coded natural world" as Eliot's millennial echo-chamber is to Crane's modestly aerated soil: a more "major," metaphysical, and abstract attempt to navigate between the large and the small. In "Ave Maria," meanwhile, whatever its triumphalism, it is not so much the dulling of "true character" that excites Crane as it is the exploration of possibilities that lie unfinished in the name.

The colonial glee of "Ave Maria" itself cools off in the next section of *The Bridge:* the five poems that make up "Powhatan's Daughter" are concerned to find the traces of the proper name in the midst of a modern namelessness very far removed from Columbus's voyage. The poems thus focus on half-sleeping, anonymous lovers ("The Harbor Dawn"); on a disoriented old man who turns out to be Rip Van Winkle ("Van Winkle"); on the silent movements of hobos across the continent ("The River"); on the supposedly "lost" Native American spirit of the land ("The Dance"); and on a poor white woman's attempt to contact her sailor son, long disappeared from her prairie home ("Indiana"). Strung along the margins of these five poems is an italicized parallel text that frames the whole section with a story of the workings of the name of "Pocahontas" in the twentieth century.

"The River" is the most complexly satisfying poem in the section. In this piece Crane tries to draw links among different speeds of time, beginning with the accelerated experiences of the telegraph and the railroad, then moving from the railroad to a vision of the hobos who live in its underbelly, idly crossing the continent and reminding the poet of a slower, more quiet relationship to time, reflected both in his own childhood and—more important—in the obscured spirit of Pocahontas, whose body Crane figures as the body of the land itself. The last shift in description is to what Crane called a "River of Time," in which a "you," presumably the poem's American reader, is made to feel the utter anonymity and silence of history, in the flow of which the poet nonetheless senses a vast song. The poem is interesting for our purpose here both because the social relationships Crane sketches in the poem are more concretely rendered than almost anywhere in his work and because it is the nadir of the proper name in *The Bridge,* the anonymous counterpoint to the high certainty of "Ave Maria." It feels, in other words, like the poem's resonant middle.

From our twenty-first-century perspective, there are political problems in the poem: an easy analogy between the wanderings of the young poet, a factory owner's son, and the hobos; the cliché of describing a body of land as a woman's body; and the sorry if typical early-century use of "niggers" to describe the vital undercurrent of American life. All of these problems dim the poem's attempt to take on the very difficult task of simultaneously describing the dissolution of personhood in the movement of history and presenting history as a generator of vocalizable names, because they are each metaphysical abstractions that get in the way of what is usually Crane's quite physical attention. So the attempt wobbles: but in the closing stanzas of the poem, Crane manages to figure "the river" so that it remains in keeping with his project of reading history as the story of the unfulfilled aspects of the name.

The poem opens at top speed, with the placards on railroad cars, the texts of telegrams, and the voice of radio news flying capitalized and head-long into the lowercase details of the speaker's own commentary. He tries to watch the train tracks

> —while an EXPRESS makes time like
> SCIENCE—COMMERCE and the HOLYGHOST
> RADIO ROARS IN EVERY HOME WE HAVE THE NORTHPOLE
> WALLSTREET AND VIRGINBIRTH WITHOUT STONES OR
> WIRES OR EVEN RUNning brooks connecting ears (57)

This figure of the radio "connecting ears" without apparent material seam is what, later in the poem, sponsors Crane's ability to plunge forward into the idea of the silence of history: just as radio waves are not percussive instruments or conduits for electricity or human bodies (the "stones" and "wires" and "brooks" of earlier forms of communication) but nonetheless convey a sound, so too will "the river" produce song from nothing. The coherence of the relationship between these first and final figures depends on the hobos, who figure for Crane the relationship between the small and the large, the silent and song, as a lumpen nomadism:

> Behind
> My father's cannery works I used to see
> Rail-squatters ranged in nomad raillery,

The ancient men—wifeless or runaway
Hobo-trekkers that forever search
An empire wilderness of freight and rails.
Each seemed a child, like me, on a loose perch,
Holding to childhood like some termless play.
John, Jake or Charley, hopping the slow freight
—Memphis to Tallahassee—riding the rods,
Blind fists of nothing, humpty-dumpty clods. (58–59)

In this rendering the hobos subsist beneath the register of the proper name: children with no adulthood to look forward to, without wives or families, their names—"John, Jake or Charley"—are interchangeable to the middle-class boy observing them. But the "loose perch" of their personhood is attractive to the poet—not least, we should notice, because his homosexuality will pre-empt wife and family and even middle-class adulthood. So, although they are "blind fists of nothing," their wanderings are not pointless:

Yet they touch something like a key perhaps.
From pole to pole across the hills, the states
—They know a body under the wide rain;
Youngsters with eyes like fjords, old reprobates
With racetrack jargon,—dotting immensity
They lurk across her, knowing her yonder breast
Snow-silvered, sumac-stained or smoky blue—
Is past the valley-sleepers, south or west.
—As I have trod the rumorous midnights, too,

And past that circuit of the lamp's thin flame
(O Nights that brought me to her body bare!)
Have dreamed beyond the print that bound her name. (59)

The "inaudible whistle" of worms tunneling earth slowly to produce the name of Dionysus reappears here in "the key" the hobos touch, "dotting immensity" with their errant paths across the continent and unknowingly producing Pocahontas's name, the name of the continent "unmangled" by a merely clockwork "time like / SCIENCE" (recall the dismissed "spokes-of-a-wheel" in "Paraphrase"). This description actually calls to mind a remark of Williams's about the greed of the colonizers of the New World, who could not see themselves, in the vast workings of their colonial project, destroying what they sought: "Such things occur in secret" (27). Crane's valorization of Pocahontas as an organic, feminine principle of the land, that is, if tedious to us as feminists or as antiracist thinkers, is not quite so simple as an opposition of the resplendent primal whole to the sullied, historical particular. His use of the myth is, rather, an attempt to point out that history contains its secret, which is the traffic between the whole and the particular: a traffic always in danger of being written out of history and replaced with either the idea of the pointlessness of human life in the face of immensity or the identity of human life with immensity. Instead, in Crane, human life "dots" it. This is one of the delicate but important places in *The Bridge* where those of us interested in lesbian and gay theory can perceive an open passage between the secrecy that homosexuality entails and the "secret" that history withholds from representation—both of them suggesting to those who will listen that the proper name, the "name of the father," fails to describe experience, since it is so preoccupied with seeking out its authenticity. Homosexuality is too cast-off for the proper name; history too large.

This namelessness produces, at the close of "The River," the figure of moving water as the ultimate sign of the unknowingness the secret entails:

> The River lifts itself from its long bed,
>
> Poised wholly on its dream, a mustard glow
> Tortured with history, its one will—flow!
> —The Passion spreads in wide tongues, choked and slow,
> Meeting the Gulf, hosannas silently below. (61)

There are three forces at work here: the dumb life of the river, its "dream," flowing beneath the name; the middle terrain of "history," which strikes— "tortures"—the fluid surface of that unnameable flow and produces the third part, which is song: the "hosanna" of the river, "silent" except to those who are willing to understand "history" as not the limit but the occasion of human experience. The Christological trio of torture, suffering, and praise is one shorthand by which to place the name at the center of a set of forces that, on one hand, impel it to pronounce itself, and on the other, speak back to it: a set of forces from within whose net it is no longer possible to read the "reality" of the name as its primary function. The close of the poem is not, then, a vain attempt to see "the Word made flesh," as so many of Crane's critics (sympathetic and otherwise) are wont to see him struggling in—it is, in fact, an attempt mimetically to render the circuit in which the "Word" is placed.

This three-part play of forces among the dumb "dream," the "history" that strikes it, and the song the striking makes is brought to a high sheen in "Atlantis," the final section of *The Bridge,* in which Crane dithyrambically assaults the Brooklyn Bridge itself so as to sound as many names as possible off its surface, returning again and again to musical figures whose "merely" metaphorical work is only one-half of an autonomously musical cascade of praise. In an early stanza, observing the bridge's wire cables, Crane repeats the trio of dream, history, and song:

> And through that cordage, threading with its call
> One arc synoptic of all tides below—
> Their labyrinthine mouths of history
> Pouring reply as though all ships at sea
> Complighted in one vibrant breath made cry,—
> "Make thy love sure—to weave whose song we ply!"
> —From black embankments, moveless soundings hailed,
> So seven oceans answer from their dream. (105)

The bridge here is the musical hollow through which oceanic silence must flow until, "mouthed" by history, it generates the "song" of pure reply to form: "Make thy love sure!" Crane is not interested in logical tautology, but in physical relationships:

> O Thou steeled Cognizance whose leap commits
> The agile precincts of the lark's return;
> Within whose lariat sweep encinctured sing
> In single chrysalis the many twain,—
> Of stars Thou art the stitch and stallion glow
> And like an organ, Thou, with sound of doom—
> Sight, sound and flesh Thou leadest from time's realm
> As love strikes clear direction for the helm. (106–7)

The "lark's return," the "lariat sweep," the "stitch"—the bridge "commits" the poet to describe its principle, which is a circuit: from namelessness through history to song and back again. Here we have pure allegory, or what we might call the effect-effect: the code out of which all other effects—the certainty of the compass, the nomad dotting of immensity, the worms aerating soil—are to be generated. Crane's struggle in these amazing lines is the struggle to describe the sheer plenitude of form as it is happening, at the speed of form; it is not the struggle to repress the truth that form conceals an absence. He is not, in other words, desperately staving off the adult knowledge of the finitude of built forms; he is battling with something much more worldly and precise, which is the inability of the mind to survive long at the speed of the universe, without the membrane of language to slow things down beneath sublimity.

His figure for this struggle, strewn throughout *The Bridge*, is appropriately scientific—the flooding of a point of light with light whose source we cannot singly locate. In "The Harbor Dawn" it appears as a star that "Turns in the waking west and goes to sleep," awaiting the poet at the other end of the poem. Along the way, in "The Dance," this star is recalled in a past morning in which "immortally, it bled into the dawn"; and again, in "Southern Cross" (one of the "Three Songs"), the poet, sailing all night, watches the constellation sink into the sea and obscure the froth of phosphorous flecks (here figured as dim children of stars) his ship has kicked up: "Light drowned the lithic trillions of your spawn." In the final stanza of "Atlantis," the figure of the star flooded by day is altered to fit the architecture of the bridge, itself a form of daylight.

> So to thine Everpresence, beyond time,
> Like spears ensanguined of one tolling star
> That bleeds infinity—the orphic strings,
> Sidereal phalanxes, leap and converge:
> —One Song, one Bridge of Fire! (107–8)

I catalog the appearance of this motif because it is the strongest figural signal that Crane is not struggling to deny the "reality" of lack in experience but rather to collate its superabundance. The name, the star, will always turn out to be part of a constellation, or circuit, whose entire light will flood perception, leading the poet right back to another round of attempt, another star—during which it will collapse back into the particular thing he has produced, like some fragrant incense, a song: a poem.

If the poems in *White Buildings* begin to advance Crane's poetic probe of what lies between sanctioned experience, then, the sections of *The Bridge* now take that concern directly into the realm of the historical by unraveling and reconstructing its names, like enzymes. What appears in this attempt is a sense of all the processes that names can code, as well as a deeper statement that names are not merely undelivered notes to authenticity but are courtesies and challenges to the mind that braves abundance. This is truly bold. A vision (a knowledge) of the absence of lack implies no justice, no morality, no peace in particular: it is simply a fact of the poetry. Crane's message is also bold because it is so abundantly punishable, so perpetually rewritten as an Icarian tragedy of over-reaching, in order to muffle the signal it gives about the social body, which is that it is moving too fast ever to be authentic. Instead he is written as having moved too fast for history.

This misperception has enabled both the homophobic punishments of Crane, and some of the gay valorizations of him. He reached outside of language and history, the argument goes, because he could not endure the truth of emptiness: he wanted more poetry than it could give; he is a child, a narcissist. Or: he is writing a jouissance, his own death; he is a subversive Blakean madman. In fact Hart Crane was a scientist, a physicist-historian. He was concerned with "the fate of structures," because in their fates lie flickering the codes of the history it is claimed he never understood, or cared for. His great gay patience with low speed and distant sound is more exciting than subversion, and worth far more than modernist embarrassment.

Coda: "Reply"

In my interpretation of Crane as a historian of the name I focus primarily on the historical and mythological names of his famous poems; but I close here with a short poem in which the issues I have been discussing resolve into clarity around the proper name of the poet himself. This poem, given the title "Reply" by Crane's literary executor Samuel Loveman, was published in *Poetry* in 1933, a year after Crane's death.[3] Its idiom is different from that of the poems I focus on above, mostly because it is not written in Crane's exclamatory style: it is a cool, measured poem in three quatrains, with a clear A-B rhyme scheme, and none of the unexpected turns of syntax, or striking word choice, of the more famous lyrics. But it has uncanny power, not least because it is written as if from beyond the grave. The poem:

Reply

Thou canst read nothing except through appetite
And here we join eyes in that sanctity
Where brother passes brother without sight,
But finally knows conviviality . . .

Go then, unto thy turning and thy blame.
Seek bliss, then, brother, in my moment's shame.
All this that balks delivery through words
Shall come to you through wounds prescribed by swords:

That hate is but the vengeance of a long caress,
And fame is pivotal to shame with every sun
That rises on eternity's long willingness . . .
So sleep, dear brother, in my fame, my shame undone. (Weber 177)

It is chilling to think of the knowledge with which Loveman (a gay man) attached the word "Reply" to this poem, writing back as it does to the entire ethic and philosophy of history by which Crane's heterosexual critics and friends so roundly punished him. Safely escorted to the pages of *Poetry,* it became what I believe to be the first lyric denunciation of homophobia in American letters.

The poem's first line proposes that literature and desire are not to be held apart from one another, that literature is not the release from personality but—as the next three lines show—a model for fraternal social relationships. Having "joined eyes" on the page—the poem looking out, and the reader looking in—the "brothers" no longer see one another as they move about, because they are watching the same thing: the movement of the poem. In a "finally" that is not so much utopia as simple relief, the poem becomes the site of "conviviality."

This belief of Crane's in the fraternal power of poems is not new to anyone who has ever read the ode to Walt Whitman in "Cape Hatteras"; but the second stanza is unprecedented in Crane's poetry. With "Go then, unto thy turning and thy blame. / Seek bliss, then, brother, in my moment's shame," the poet rewrites criticism as submerged desire—the critic's "bliss" in the poet's "shame"—and then shrugs it off as fleeting. His next remark, "All this that balks delivery through words / Shall come to you through wounds prescribed by swords," is a way of suggesting to these hostile readers that, even if they imagine literature as protected by cool maturity from raw "appetite" and its indescribable pull, "appetite" will visit itself on them anyway and carry with it a decodable message. You think what's described in my poems is too fleeting, the poet says; just wait until it becomes too painful. "Then," he writes, your "wounds" will have exactly the legibility that you have refused to acknowledge in my poems.

What is revealed in the "wound" (delivered to the punishing mind, at last run down by "seeking bliss" in other's "shame") is the connection between punishing violence—"hate"—and the homosexual "caress" whose "long" duration, elaborated two lines below into "eternity's long willingness," suggests that what is intolerable about male homosexuality is its easy habitation of eternity: its connection to time as "willing," as a partner. This "caress[ing]" relation to time implies no vigor, no foundation, in short, no *work:* I think it is this laborlessness that Crane knew his rationalist critics despised.

This circuit of pleasure and punishment is not in our current vocabulary for understanding homophobia. We stop at saying that homophobes despise "femininity" in men, or are physically disgusted with gay male sexual acts themselves; but those explanations never quite seem to touch the electric ground of the problem, partly since sexual acts and gendered affect are so slippery and can be seen to overlap so widely between straight and gay people. What seems truly appalling, and what Crane reminds us in "Reply," is the possibility that homosexuality might lay claim to earthly bliss without agreeing to suffer for it.

Perhaps this sweet temporality, the "long caress," would be inoffensive to the shame-seeking brothers if it could be written as a deep, immobile passivity; but this poet has not eaten the lotus. He wants "fame" and believes that "eternity's long willingness" is more than a recumbent relation to time: he believes it is the hinge on which poetic glory swings. "And fame is pivotal to shame with every sun." And this is where Crane brings his own name into historical play: "So sleep, dear brother, in my fame, my shame undone." The tell-tale prefix "un-" makes its appearance here in a prefiguring of Dionysus's "unmangled" smile: the function of Crane's own name, he suggests, will be to serve as a historical house for the eventual quiet of his critics, whom he welcomes with unearthly generosity into its rooms. His name, then, has the function of a pivot that literally makes open to others what was closed: the "long."

This gesture, especially in a poet only twenty-five years old, might come off as simply young bravado: "I will outlive you all." I hope, though, that the readings I offer here will shift the vantage on Crane enough to make audible another tone—his desire, regardless of criticism, or his own gambit for immortality, to communicate to readers a knowledge that the "names of history" have the heft and temporality not of nouns but of prepositions: we move through them, into them, around them. This distinction, which we might call the distinction between history and genealogy, I would actually prefer to read as the genealogy of history, perpetually reworking it in what sounds like silence. His practice of this historical aeration, conducted in such good faith, has kept Hart Crane patiently waiting on the outer limits of our literary sense of the historical, among the mystics and Romantics; perhaps it is time to let him in.

chapter two

FEELING AND

AFFILIATION IN

WILLA CATHER

In 1977 the violinist Yehudi Menuhin published a memoir, including this fond reminiscence of Willa Cather:

> Willa Cather was the embodiment of America—but an America which has long ago disappeared. . . . Only recently has the United States become a society of abstractions; no doubt the abstraction of the pursuit of happiness existed then, but happiness itself had not become an abstraction and was still rooted in the earth, as Aunt Willa was herself. . . . It is not too much to say that she revealed a face of America to us youngsters who were growing up among adults largely born abroad. Her mannish figure and country tweediness, her let's-lay-it-on-the-table manners and unconcealed blue eyes, her rosy skin

and energetic demeanor bespoke a phenomenon as strangely comforting to us as it was foreign, something in the grain like Christian Temperance or the Girl Scout movement. (128–29)

I delight in this description for two reasons. The first is that Menuhin manages to make Willa Cather, in his rendering, sound like a character in a Willa Cather novel; the second is that Menuhin, falling under Cather's imaginative sway, also conveys her lesbianism without resorting to the major languages for homosexuality, of either the 1930s, which he is describing, or the 1970s, when he is writing. Menuhin, whose family befriended Cather when he was a small boy, saw Cather with a child's eyes, and he recalls his Aunt Willa neither as an invert, living the wrong gender, nor as a bohemian, testing the mores of the day (both early-century figures for homosexuality); nor, certainly, as an early example of a woman-loving-woman (the 1970s version), despite the fact that his childhood contact with Cather meant witnessing her domestic life with her partner, Edith Lewis. Only the crucial word "mannish" signals to us that Menuhin understands Aunt Willa is different, somehow; but the word, which mildly suggests a gender inversion of some kind, is quickly subsumed into the stream of Menuhin's paragraph, which animates Cather just as she always animated her characters: through a description that mutually implicates her body and her relationship to history. Cather's "rosy skin" and "unconcealed blue eyes" are not abstract: they are "rooted in the earth," and this description is particularly striking since abstraction, for Menuhin, can be assigned a historical period—it is "only recently" a characteristic of American life. If Cather is an invert, then, and if that inversion is written on her body, it is nonetheless a historical and not a gender inversion she projects. Or rather—and this is the focus of my discussion—Cather projects a gender inversion that can be understood only as a relationship to history, usually a nostalgic and primitive one, occasionally a "new" one, but a relationship significant at every turn for being out of step with modernity.

Indeed, Menuhin praises his Aunt Willa for something like an antimodernism, noting her aversion to mass culture and her loyalty to an idea of America's traditional, European roots:

> There were abuses and vulgarities she refused to tolerate, such as exposure in newspapers or on radio. She had a contempt for anything

too much owned or determined by mobs, reserving admiration for high individual endeavor, withdrawing more and more from society even as she drew closer to us. . . .

She adored what she felt had not been her birthright—the old, the European, the multilayered, and above all music. (129)

Menuhin's remarks suggest that, not surprisingly, Cather resented mass cultural forms because they implied uncontrollably wide distribution and casual consumption. But describing what Cather "adored," the "old," the "multilayered," and "music," Menuhin also suggests that what was missing for Cather in the languages of mass distribution was implication—recess, secrecy, all the tools of the closet that a lesbian might need in the early twentieth century. The "high individual endeavor" she admired required a small stage, rich in the allegorical language of art—which the young Menuhins, who served as her adoptive children in the waning years of her sixties, were happy to provide.[1]

Cather's refusal of the trappings of mass culture, and of the literary strategies modernist writers were developing in response to it, sets her apart from her literary and her lesbian contemporaries: she makes recourse neither to the strategies of irony so many of them embraced nor to the new explicitness about sex. Radclyffe Hall, although similarly sincere, is of course writing directly about lesbians in *The Well of Loneliness* (1928), and Djuna Barnes's dithyrambic *Nightwood* (1936) reads light years away from the measured prose of *Lucy Gayheart,* published the year before. Of course, one difference between Cather and Hall or Barnes is that Cather wrote about rural people of little means, while Hall and Barnes, whatever their innovations in sexual subject matter or literary style, were still firmly rooted in the tradition of writing about the rich, or at least the glamorously mobile. This difference reflects a class difference between Cather and the other literary lesbians of the period, such as Hall or Barnes or Edna St. Vincent Millay, all of whom were either born into privilege or privately educated. Cather, born on a farm and enrolled in a state college, seems in retrospect all the less likely to incorporate her lesbianism either mimetically, into her writing, as did Hall and Barnes, or publicly, into a bohemian life, as did Millay. Barnes, Hall, and Millay all embraced the age as the age of sex, either according to Freud or according to the sexologists (in Hall's case)—an embrace that would have appalled Cather, in whose novels sex is never narratively rendered.

I think the writer whose dilemmas and strategies Cather most resembles, oddly, is Hart Crane, whose ecstatic embrace of the machine age is the living opposite of Cather's ruralism but whose eager sincerity with regard to the question of modernity, in the abstract, marks him as Cather's companion. Crane's not-quite-modernist practice of celebratory apostrophe, while utterly different in tone from the isolated yearnings Cather depicts, nonetheless shares a certain sincerity with Cather's writing that keeps them aslant the major currents of English-language modernist innovation. Crane wrote half a generation later; but he and Cather met with similar critical response during their careers: both were praised early and summarily dismissed. And the grounds for dismissal are uncannily alike, phrased as they are as accusations of failed heterosexuality.

Cather's critical fortunes, it has been pointed out, have been strange: claimed by many different readerships over the past seventy years, she has been upheld and reviled for the same features of her writing, praised by the likes of H. L. Mencken for her focus on rural poverty, then damned by Edmund Wilson for an inability to address truly modern concerns, such as World War I; championed by Catholics, Nebraskans, feminists, and lesbians and ignored by the New Critics and the theorists of modernism (Acocella; Carlin). At the end of the twentieth century, two features of the response to Cather stand out: first, the persistence of her characterization as somehow antimodern, or nonmodernist, and second, the long-overdue acknowledgment of her lesbianism. I suggest that these two features are related and that Cather's lesbianism, as it shapes her fiction, is to be understood as a resistance to certain modern pressures, such as the pressures of mass culture, which she uses, further, to outmaneuver another imperative placed on novelists, to create a heterosexually binding narrative by writing marriages and childbirth and inheritance into novels, no matter what their subject.

Lionel Trilling is exemplary in linking these two features of Cather's writing. In a 1937 *New Republic* essay, he accuses Cather of relying on myths of the land because she cannot produce heterosexual narrative: "It has always been a personal failure of her talent that prevented her from involving her people in truly dramatic relations with each other. (Her women, for example, always stand in the mother or daughter relation to men; they are never truly lovers)" (13). In one sense Trilling is correct: it cannot really be said that Cather wrote dramatic fiction, if by that designation we mean novels organized around a marriage plot. Marriage in Cather's novels is never the consummation of narrative drives—more often, indeed, characters start out married and conveniently suffer separation from their partners. This convenience applies to familial bonds as well: even those of Cather's young protagonists who develop their characters, early on, through their relations with parents and siblings, as in *The Song of the Lark, One of Ours,* and *O Pioneers!*—novels of genesis—those protagonists abandon familial relations in favor of another drive, say, to art or war or to the land.[2]

There is a question, of course: is it only in heterosexual relations that narrative becomes "truly dramatic"? Elsewhere in his essay Trilling sharpens his accusation against Cather, denouncing her elevation of pioneers and singular (if not always single) people as regressive nature-myths: *The Professor's House,* for instance, "epitomizes as well as any novel of our time the disgust with life which so many sensitive Americans feel, which makes them dream of their preadolescent integration and innocent community with nature" (152). The problem with such willful regression, Trilling concludes, is that its expression as fealty to old ways is an "implied praise of devitalization. She can recognize the energy of assiduous duty but not the energy of mind and emotion. Her order is not the channeling of insurgent human forces but their absence" (12). Such a description of Cather's work leaves unexamined a connection that, for those of us reading Cather at the end of the twentieth century, seems very urgent: what is the relationship between a resistance to "channeling of insurgent human forces," here a synonym for heterosexuality, and a resistance to mass culture, urbanization, and literary modernism? If Cather is willfully resisting an idea that time must move forward, is she trying to come up with some other notion of history that would explain and justify her fictional practice and, implicitly, her lesbianism? Lesbian and gay critics nowadays, as part of a generation wielding the tools of identity politics to explain literary motivations, find themselves facing the difficult question whether, if lesbian and gay writers use particular ideas of history to explain or contextualize themselves, we may invert the question and read their strategies of closeting and exposure as explanations of how history works. It is persuasive that Cather's "praise of devitalization," or her "contempt for anything too much owned or determined by mobs," linked as they are to nondramatic male-female relations and to a shunning of publicity, signal and shape her lesbianism. But does her lesbianism, once we understand it this way, tell end-of-the-century readers anything about the sources of history, of "truly dramatic relations" not limited to heterosexual marriage?

I think it does. Cather is suspicious, in the early part of the century, of two historical categories that have come under great scrutiny in subsequent decades: the nation as an instance of modernity, and the nuclear family as its locus of intimate meaning. There is a reason, in other words, that Cather wrote about vast, empty places and about young people fleeing their families. She explains herself with particular clarity in her 1936 collection of essays, *Not Under Forty,* which contains, among other things, an illuminating discussion of Katherine Mansfield's domestic fiction. Cather clearly saw a commonality between the isolation of her Nebraska youth and of Mansfield's New Zealand, and the paradoxical sense of crowding those quiet places create. She writes:

> I doubt whether any contemporary writer has made one feel so keenly the many kinds of personal relations which exist in an everyday "happy family" who are merely going on living their daily lives with no crises or shocks or bewildering complications to try them. Yet every individual in that household (even the children) is clinging passionately to his individual soul, is in terror of losing it in the general family flavour. As in most families, the mere struggle to have anything of one's own, to be one's self at all, creates an element of strain which keeps everybody almost at the breaking-point.
>
> One realizes that even in harmonious families there is this double life: the group life, which is the one we can observe in our neighbour's household, and, underneath, another—secret and passionate and intense—which is the real life that stamps the faces and gives character to the voices of our friends. Always in his mind each member of these social units is escaping, running away, trying to break the net which circumstances and his own affections have woven about him. One realizes that human relationships are the tragic necessity of human life;

that they can never be wholly satisfactory, that every ego is half the time greedily seeking them, and half the time pulling away from them. (135–36)

For Cather, then, the promise of individuation is to be found neither in the contemporary urban mob, with its "dramatic" heterosexual pressures, nor in the family, which, although a "tragic necessity," is also a "social unit"—which cold phrase precisely communicates its function: to inhibit "passion." It is friends, each of whose "secret, passionate, intense" attempts to have an ego "stamps" her "face" and "gives character" to his "voice," who provide an escape from this airtight "unit." Cather places the highest value on the bodily production of intensity she sees in friends: it is "real," it is "the real life." And its reality is an evanescence: "Always in his mind" each companion "is escaping, running away."

It is to the passion of these perpetually vanishing friends that Cather was attracted, and it was to them she dedicated *Not Under Forty*.

The title of this book is meant to be "arresting" only in the literal sense, like the signs put up for motorists: "ROAD UNDER REPAIR," etc. It means that the book will have little interest for people under forty years of age. The world broke in two in 1922 or thereabouts, and the persons and prejudices recalled in these sketches slid back into yesterday's seven thousand years. . . . It is for the backward, and by one of their number, that these sketches were written. (v)

There is a community, then, "secret, passionate, and intense," neither nation nor family, for whom Cather is able to imagine herself writing, even in the face of criticism from the likes of Trilling and his peers. They live, even in the present, in "yesterday's seven thousand years"; they are a community whose very atavism is the mark of their pride and passion. Born of the domestic scene but by intense struggle removed from it, they constitute a tribe, a "number." In Cather's novels they are to be found among the artists, the soldiers, the pioneers, the colonizers—all the people whom susequent critics have recognized as "queer," as somehow gender-inverted or evasive of heterosexual "drama." Indeed, Menuhin himself registers the existence of such a "number" when he compares his Aunt Willa's presence to that of "Christian Temperance or the Girl Scout movement"—suggesting that, if she was not exactly a family woman, and if her American-ness, however deep, was actually built on an outmoded form of national identity, then her modernity (her presence) lay in something somewhere between family and nation—a movement.[3]

Two things about Cather's fiction, then, are of interest to me. The first is the way Cather—who understands homosexuality on the model (contemporary to her) of gender inversion—rewrites gender inversion as historical "backwardness." The second is the way Cather, shunning the modernity of nation (its mobs) in favor of its ethnicized, embodied "number" (its "character," its "voice"), and shunning the family in favor of its runaways, confronts a question haunting our much later generation: what sodality or affiliation will give sense to late modernity, scene of clamoring nationalisms and mutating family structures?

I do not think Cather previews a "correct" answer to the problem of not knowing what a habitable human bond is, especially because her desire to read the "real life" on the bodies of her characters is too private somehow. The fictional project of determining which bodies are good and which are bad involves too many of Cather's particular prejudices. But if I do not want to read Cather as a lesbian sibyll, prophetically solving the problems of late modernity for us by virtue of having refused some of its early trappings, neither do I want to read Cather's fiction as merely a symptom of the closet or of her personal dislikes. It is exactly because of the sustained determination, the stubbornness, of her eccentricity that her fiction becomes not only a puzzle but a kind of answer. Cather's insistence that the "real life" is to be found on bodies and in voices, and not in "social units," offers a startling and strangely exhilarating discovery, which is just how far the allegory of history-as-body, as morphology, can go before it collapses. This middle-term success, registered in the surprising fictional viability of Cather's characters, may turn out to tell us more clearly than current body theory, or queer theory, just how much explanatory weight our bodies can carry, in a time when we cannot be sure which "social units"— the nation, the nuclear family—will survive our era. "History is what hurts," writes Fredric Jameson, referring to exactly this gap beween lonely solitude and vast impersonal change (*Political Unconscious* 102); and we will see how Cather hurts her characters with history, repeatedly, lovingly, and makes that hurt the basis for a bond with other pioneers, other outcasts, other closeted idealists. It is feeling, "written on the body," and not family or the nation or even the romantic couple, that links her lonely dreamers; and her dreamers keep attracting readers.

The Song of the Lark *and the Pride of Secrecy*

The Song of the Lark (1915) is widely regarded as Cather's "autobiographical" novel, the retelling of her own artistic development through the story of Thea Kronborg, a Swedish American girl from Moonstone, Colorado, who grows up to be a world-class opera diva. As a tale of "high individual endeavor," it is unsurpassed in Cather's work: on her way to the top, Thea must at one point or another forsake family, teachers, friends, and even, at last, her lover. But *The Song of the Lark* is a novel of wish fulfillment, and in the end, no one begrudges Thea her journey toward high art. Along the way, Cather makes particularly clear that Thea could not possibly have married; indeed, Thea's lover, Fred Ottenberg, tells her himself exactly why.

> Don't you know most of the people in the world are not individuals at all? They never have an individual idea or experience. A lot of girls go to boarding-school together, come out the same season, dance at the same parties, are married off in groups, have their babies at about the same time, send their children to school together, and so the human crop renews itself. Such women know as much about the reality of the forms they go through as they know about the wars they learned the dates of. They get their most personal experiences out of novels and plays. Everything is second-hand with them. Why, you *couldn't* live like that. (319)

Women's heterosexuality, in other words, is about consuming culture, reading "novels and plays," idly observing "the forms"; there is no room in it for them to become producers themselves. This rejection of feminine heterosexuality as de-individuating runs parallel to feminism, and this has been duly noted by Cather's feminist readers. But it is not Cather's desire, particularly, to rescue those women trapped renewing "the human crop."[4] For her, the reproduction of the family, and women's role in it, is too closely tied to the blind consumption of mass culture, to "second-hand" life, and she dismisses it out of hand. She is interested, rather, in affiliating Thea with high art—with making Thea seem naturally, congenitally an artist. Consider this early scene in which Thea's piano teacher, Andor Harsanyi, hears her singing for the first time:

> It was like a wild bird that had flown into his studio on Middleton Street from goodness knows how far! No one knew that it had come, or even that it existed; least of all the strange, crude girl in whose throat it beat its passionate wings. What a simple thing it was, he reflected; why had he never guessed it before? Everything about her indicated it—the big mouth, the wide jaw and chin, the strong white teeth, the deep laugh. The machine was so simple and strong, seemed to be so easily operated. She sang from the bottom of herself. Her breath came from down where her laugh came from, the deep laugh which Mrs. Harsanyi had once called "the laugh of the people." (171)

This passage is designed to place Thea all at once in the community of artists, to give her a *place,* even to the point of insisting that her voice is the result of racial characteristics—her jaw, her mouth, her teeth, her laugh: "Everything about her indicated it." And that place, deep down in her breathing, is with "the people," whose laugh she laughs. Not exactly Swedish, despite her Swedish face, or Czech, despite the phrase, Thea's voice projects the laugh of "the" people *as* people, as collectivity. And by conducting through her voice the vastness of a population, Thea earns an invitation to her individuality: the experienced observer, Harsanyi, recognizes her as one of those capable of consolidating "the people" in her one person and accepts her arrival in the kingdom as a natural extravagance, like the entrance of a "wild bird."

Because the artistic potential of Thea's voice is so vast, it is also, necessarily, a secret—much in the way the personhood of any adolescent is a secret, until events prompt it to unfold. But that secrecy sticks with the artist, Cather believes: attention merely shifts from, where did she come from? to, how does she do it? Near the end of the novel, when Thea's friends from far and wide are in New York to witness the now-renowned diva's performance in *Die Walküre,* Fred Ottenberg asks Harsanyi what Thea's "secret" is. Harsanyi responds impatiently: "'Her secret? It is every artist's secret'— he waved his hand—'passion. That is all. It is an open secret, and perfectly safe'" (409). That "passion" distinguishes not only the presumably bland adulthood of many operagoers from the prolonged adolescence of the artist's life but also the striking individuality of the artist from the anonymity of the consumer. The secret of art is "perfectly safe," as Harsanyi irritatedly remarks, because it is inaccessible to the onlooker: artists, in Cather's world, are simply another type of person altogether.[5]

They remain distinctly American, however. For if she wants to extract Thea from the demands of market-driven female heterosexuality, Cather also reinserts her, protected by her "secret," into a national register. In this passage, another early one, Thea's incipience carries no less than a manifest destiny—speeding westward home on a train to Colorado after her first glorious season as an apprentice in Chicago, she senses the difference between herself and the other young dreamers of her generation.

> She put her hand on her breast and felt how warm it was; and within it there was a full, powerful pulsation. She smiled—though she was ashamed of it—with the natural contempt of strength for weakness, with the sense of physical security which makes the savage merciless. Nobody could die while he felt like that inside. The springs there were wound so tight that it would be a long while before there was any slack in them. The life in there was rooted deep. She was going to have a few things before she died. She realized that there were a great many trains dashing east and west on the face of the continent that night, and that they all carried young people who meant to have things. But the difference was that *she was going to get them!* (197)

This violent articulation of "the difference" links adolescence, artistry, and individuality together in a deeply American vision of "destiny," single-minded and impatient. Like her singing voice itself, this destiny is a physical sensation, a feeling of interiority; and it is has all the efflorescence of the true secret, barely to be contained: "She smiled—though she was ashamed of it." And, paradoxically, we may understand the distinction between Thea and the other youngsters traveling the railways of America that night to be that Thea, alone, will fulfill the metaphysical as well as the geographical imperative of manifest destiny: she, alone, will become an American self. To do it, however—to secure her individuality once and for all—she must first brush up against the "savage."

The defining episode of *The Song of the Lark* takes place in Panther Canyon, Arizona, where Thea spends a rejuvenating summer amid the abandoned cliff dwellings of an "ancient people." A winter's apprenticeship in Chicago has exhausted her voice and left her uncertain of her own artistic future; but in the canyon to which her suitor, Fred Ottenberg, has brought her, Thea makes contact with the spirit of the "extinct" people who once occupied the cliffs, and through that contact refashions her idea of song. At once, Thea's identification with the ancient people—especially the women—animates her body.

> On the first day that Thea climbed the water-trail, she began to have intuitions about the women who had worn the path, and who had spent so great a part of their lives going up and down it. She found herself trying to walk as they must have walked, with a feeling in her feet and knees and loins which she had never known before—which must have come up to her out of the accustomed dust of that rocky trail. She could feel the weight of an Indian baby hanging to her back as she climbed. (271)

And, later:

> It seemed to Thea that a certain understanding of those old people came up to her out of the rock shelf on which she lay; that certain feelings were transmitted to her, suggestions that were simple, insistent, and monotonous, like the beating of Indian drums. They were not expressible in words, but seemed rather to translate themselves into attitudes of body, into degrees of muscular tension and relaxation. (272)

Thea's time in Panther Canyon firmly attaches her to the ghosts of the cliff dwellers, in whose city "along the trails, in the stream, under the spreading cactus, there still glittered in the sun the bits of their frail clay vessels, fragments of their desire" (288). The ancient people, in other words, are busy here initiating Thea into a secret, cross-racial nationality of art, of desire expressed as a secret but confirming genealogy: the physical sensations, too deep for words, that "she had never known before," the "certain" understanding of the disappeared Indians, its specialty and privacy—these attune Thea to the artistic production of her forebears, whose pottery remains scattered through their city, "fragments of their desire," perceptible to the watchful, the filial eye.

Cather does not include the canyon dwellers in *The Song of the Lark* merely to rejuvenate Thea, however; they have a task to perform in the novel, which is to make clear that she should not marry. The episode in Panther Canyon is designed to demonstrate that Thea is more ancient than modern—and, apparitionally, more boy than girl.[6] That is, her affinity with the Indian women mutates, as her courtship with Fred Ottenberg builds to a pitch, into an affinity with Indian boys, one of whom she comes to resemble. Not only does she see, atop one promontory, "the coppery breast and shoulders of an Indian youth there against the sky" but, later, her benefactor, Mr. Biltmer, observes her and Fred on the same height and thinks to himself that they look, for all the world, like two boys together (272; 278).

Indeed, Thea's time with Fred resembles what Eve Sedgwick might call a "homosocial romance." Thea and Fred compete in fencing and in rock-throwing; they straggle together over the dangerous twists of a rain-drenched rock trail after a sudden thunderstorm strikes the canyon. Even Fred's attraction to Thea is to her masculinity, and it redounds on Fred's own sexuality—if Thea's attractiveness is a boyishness, then Fred, for his part, is just not like other guys. When she tells him she's been "drifting" in the time they spend together, he answers, "'Yes, you drift like a rifle ball, my dear. It's your—your direction I like best of all. Most fellows wouldn't, you know. I'm unusual'" (283).

In the culminating scene of Fred and Thea's seduction, Fred is moved while they play at throwing stones to try to kiss her—and here, in the moment of impulse, Cather makes clear that Thea is not available for wooing; that she is, in fact, a "savage."

> She was breathing hard, and little beads of moisture had gathered on her upper lip. He slipped his arm about her. "If you will look as pretty as that—" He bent his head and kissed her. Thea was startled, gave him an angry push, drove at him with her free hand in a manner quite hostile. Fred was on his mettle in an instant. He pinned both her arms down and kissed her resolutely.

When he released her, she turned away and spoke over her shoulder. "That was mean of you, but I suppose I deserved what I got."

"I should say you did deserve it," Fred panted, "turning savage on me like that! I should say you did deserve it!"

He saw her shoulders harden. "Well, I just said I deserved it, didn't I? What more do you want?"

"I want you to tell me why you flew at me like that! You weren't playing; you looked as if you'd like to murder me."

She brushed back her hair impatiently. "I didn't mean anything, really. You interrupted me when I was watching the stone. I can't jump from one thing to another. I pushed you without thinking." (279–80)

Haunted by the ancient people who occupy her boyish body, Thea has no agency in this seduction—or has rather the agency of the "savage," who acts instantaneously and in keeping with the demands of the ancestors. Thea is not "playing"—her murderous impulse emerges as a reflex against Fred's "interruption" of her concentrated efforts to throw the stones like him, like another boy. So the Indian ghosts defeat Fred, cutting off the game that was building to the kiss: "They left the stone-pile carelessly, as if they had never been interested in it, rounded the yellow tower, and disappeared into the second turn of the cañon, where the dead city, interrupted by the jutting promontory, began again" (280). The interrupted kiss does not, technically, impede the movements of the marriage plot: if we read carefully, we find that Fred and Thea marry at the end of the novel. But we have to read carefully; Cather has no interest in the marriage. Indeed, Cather makes Fred heir to a midwestern brewery fortune, which taints the old-fashioned privacy and secrecy she prizes: "When your visiting-card is on every beer-bottle," Fred complains to Thea, "you can't do things quietly. Things get into the papers" (295). Cather indifferently marries Fred and Thea, then, but Fred is simply too mass distributed to be Thea's match.

One of Ours: *Idealism and the Uses of Shame*

If in *The Song of the Lark* an affinity for things ancient thwarts the modern marriage plot, in *One of Ours* (1922) Cather's sense of a new age dawning with World War I serves as carapace for secret sexuality. The novel takes the war as an opportunity to tell the story of what world-historical events can mean to small-town farmboys, when suddenly they find themselves participating in History. Even in the face of the war's unprecedented technological brutality, the book is a bildungsroman, a Hegelian romance in which young Claude Wheeler, son of a prosperous Nebraska farm family, suffers mutely the smallness and backwardness of the little town of Frankfort, until he finds himself a hero upon enlisting for the war in France: he dies, as one character puts it, "to bring a new idea into the world" (331).

Although it won a Pulitzer Prize, *One of Ours* was widely denounced by the major critics of the day, who without exception saw the book as having two distinct halves: the first, an expert and typically Cather-like depiction of the hidden passions of the American interior plains; and the second, a hopelessly romantic, whitewashed, and blindly patriotic depiction of the war, the naïveté of which marked it instantly as the writing of a woman. The most brutal assessment came from Ernest Hemingway, who wrote privately to Edmund Wilson: "You were in the war weren't you? Wasn't that last scene in the lines wonderful? Do you know where it came from? The battle scene in *Birth of a Nation*. I identified episode after episode. Catherized. Poor woman she had to get her war experience somewhere" (Lee 167). H. L. Mencken similarly referred to the novel's battle scenes as taking place "on a Hollywood movie lot" (12); Sinclair Lewis's judgment was that Cather "disastrously loses [the truth] in a romance of violinists gallantly turned soldiers, of self-sacrificing sergeants, sallies at midnight, and all the commonplaces of ordinary war novels" (33).

The stumbling block for these critics is the novel's political idealism, or what Mencken calls its "underlying unreality"; but in each case, the evidence they use to indicate that unreality is not drawn from battle episodes — they point instead at the failure of the novel to fulfill its heterosexual imperative. Mencken's example of a "real" moment in the novel is an early episode in which a visiting opera diva flirts shamelessly with Claude: "She is there but a day or two," writes Mencken, "but when she passes on she remains almost as vivid as Claude himself" (12). Wilson and Lewis, meanwhile, both balk at a crucial dynamic in the novel's first half: the failure of Claude's marriage to Enid Royce, the cool, independent Prohibitionist who flees to China to help her missionary sister before the war begins. Wilson writes: "Even in incidents that might be convincing—as in the first night of

Claude Wheeler's wedding trip, when his new bride coldly tells him she is ill and requests him not to share her stateroom—the emotions of the hero are not created: we do not *experience* the frustration of Claude when his wife will not return his love" (26). Lewis believes in the local reality of Enid's rejection of Claude—he quite clearly identifies with it—but he nonetheless finds it grounds for a similar complaint:

> The most important defect is that, having set the Enid problem, she evades it. Here is young Claude Wheeler, for all his indecisiveness a person of fine perceptions, valiant desires, and a thoroughly normal body, married to a bloodless, evangelical prig who very much knows what she doesn't want. The scene of Enid's casual cruelty on the wedding night is dramatic without affectation—a rare thing in domestic chronicles. . . . But Miss Cather throws it away. With Claude's relations to Enid unresolved, the author sends Claude off to war. She might as well have pushed him down a well. (31–32)

What unites Lewis's and Mencken's and Wilson's frustration about being denied access to Claude's heterosexuality is that they experience no agency in him: there is no "created" emotion; he might as well be dead; he is not "vivid." Despite a "thoroughly normal body," then, he is not really alive— he has passions, but his wife does not excite them.

The problem, of course, is that it is not a matrimonial bond that motivates Claude's narrative. There are other bonds, and they form the coherent heart of the novel: the tormented, at-cross-purposes passion between Claude and his mother, the transport Claude feels in the vicinity of the idea of war, and—ultimately—the competitive, half-embarrassed love he comes to feel for his fellow soldier David Gerhardt. More explicitly than in *The Song of the Lark*, the erotic drive of *One of Ours* is homosexual: the all-male U.S. Army infantry supplies the context for a male bonding unparalleled in her fiction. But as with the other novel, the relative explicitness or implicitness of homosexuality is secondary to its theoretical vehicle. And whereas in *The Song of the Lark* that vehicle is nostalgia, in *One of Ours* it is idealism— both in the early-twentieth-century American sense of support for World War I as just and in at least one German sense, the sense in which it is geist that moves the world. Clearly Cather saw the subsumption of one boy's life into the flux of the new age as her theme in *One of Ours:* in the novel's third section, as Claude crosses the Atlantic with building excitement, he wonders why he did not quit the farm much earlier, why he had not dived immediately into war:

> Well, that was not "the Wheelers' way." The Wheelers were terribly afraid of poking themselves in where they weren't wanted, of pushing their way into a crowd where they didn't belong. And they were even more afraid of doing anything that might look affected or "romantic." They couldn't let themselves adopt a conspicuous, much less a picturesque course of action, unless it was all in the day's work. Well, History had condescended to such as he; this whole brilliant adventure had become the day's work. . . . Three years ago he used to sit moping by the windmill because he didn't see how a Nebraska farmer boy had any "call," or, indeed, any way, to throw himself into the struggle in France. . . .
>
> But the miracle had happened; a miracle so wide in its amplitude that the Wheelers,—all the Wheelers and the rough-necks and the low-brows were caught up in it. Yes, it was the rough-necks' own miracle, all this; it was their golden chance. (252–53)

This passage hints at the major affective chord of the novel: shame, and the flight from it. The Wheeler terror of exposure, of conspicuousness, of "romance" is distilled in Claude to a clarity that motivates his entire character and that entirely motors the novel. With a loving and sadistic persistence Cather pricks Claude from scene to scene through his story, from small humiliations of dress, carriage, and behavior in his early days to the more acute despairs of youth and love in the novel's middle. Shame is virtually Claude's continuous emotion; and his ignorance of his own breathtaking beauty is Cather's continuous tenderness. She describes his lovely body as he bathes in his childhood home; she has him submit to a college sweetheart's demands and pose nude for her drawing class. These small features of the novel, if they do not surface in its major reviews, are nonetheless metabolized into them. Sinclair Lewis is able to notice Claude's "thoroughly normal body" as a feature of his character because Cather makes use of his gorgeous physicality to eroticize his shame. If Thea Kronborg's incipience is phrased as discovery, as the glorious assumption of artistic talent, Claude's is set forth as the tentative motion by which extreme inarticulateness and embarrassment find an arena in which to move at last unnoticed; in which the "romance" of a History motivated by ideas and by heroism can become "the day's work."

"Lost Americans": The National Society of Shame

As for Thea in *The Song of the Lark,* Claude's coming-of-age has a genealogical stamp: his birth into the world of ideals is a birth into a chain of unnamed ancestors. While Thea's artistic racial-nationality was merely secret, however, Claude's is both secret and imprisoned: and that imprisonment out of which he is constantly beginning to rise gives the novel all the emotional "reality" that the critics of the "lost generation" are unable to locate. In one passage, the newly married Claude consoles himself at evening with a soak in the tin horse tank near the farmhouse. He has been working all day, and Enid is away promoting her Prohibition literature. Idly playing with the water, he relishes the flicker, on its surface, of the moon:

> For some reason, Claude began to think about the far-off times and countries it had shone upon. He never thought of the sun as coming from distant lands, or as having taken part in human life in other ages. To him, the sun rotated about the wheatfields. But the moon, somehow, came out of the historic past, and made him think of Egypt and the Pharaohs, Babylon and the hanging gardens. She seemed particularly to have looked down upon the follies and disappointments of men; into the slaves' quarters of old times, into prison windows, and into fortresses where captives languished.
>
> Inside of living people, too, captives languished. Yes, inside of people who walked and worked in the broad sun, there were captives dwelling in darkness,—never seen from birth to death. Into those prisons the moon shone, and the prisoners crept to the windows and looked out with mournful eyes at the white globe which betrayed no secrets and comprehended all. . . . The people whose hearts were set high needed such intercourse—whose wish was so beautiful that there were no experiences in the world to satisfy it. And these children of the moon, with their unappeased longings and futile dreams, were a finer race than the children of the sun. (170–71)

These sublunar "children," then, owe their muted glory to the pale illumination of a secret history of slaves, captives, prisoners—incarcerated souls whose very "secret," kept with absolute discretion by the supervising moon, is that they are a race. They do not "rotate about the wheatfields"—the repetition of their experience is a tradition, not a dumb cyclicality. And the pathos of their "intercourse" is its historicity, the sense of dilation or amplitude around the bodies of the lunar children that alerts them to their silent participation in something larger, that compels them like a tidal pull. That painful free fall is not only what makes them a "finer race" than their solar counterparts; it is what makes them a race in the first instance.

That fineness, though, is marked with failure, with "follies and disappointments." And lest it be unclear what sorts of follies Cather means, let us read for a moment this companion passage, in which young Gladys Farmer, Claude's only spirited companion, laments his upcoming marriage—which she knows will wring the life out of him. The other local "failures," with whom Gladys groups Claude, are all noninstrumentals, homosexuals:

> There were people, even in Frankfort, who had imagination and generous impulses, but they were all, she had to admit, inefficient—failures. There was Miss Livingstone, the fiery, emotional old maid who couldn't tell the truth; old Mr. Smith, a lawyer without clients, who read Shakespeare and Dryden all day long in his dusty office; Bobbie Jones, the effeminate drug clerk, who wrote free verse and "movie" scenarios, and tended the sodawater fountain. (129)

With this sad patchwork of local identities we see in miniature exactly the strategy that motivates the novel as a whole: sexuality is figured as an affiliation. Here the affiliation is a loosely literary habit, found in cultural commitments to the nonliteral, the fantastic: movie scripts, free verse, English literature, compulsive tale-telling. To be a homosexual is to be part of the race of dreamers.

But in Cather there are always two kinds of homosexuals: the failures, especially effeminate men whose flaw is passivity, stupidity, reflex sensuality, and the vigorous dreamers, the malcontents who are moved to wrestle with their odd position. Thea Kronborg is the archetype of this young character in Cather's fiction; she earns her stripes as a good secret-bearer by being a fighter, by her stubbornness. And so, too, will Claude earn his. But

Cather's technique is different for him, her proxy son. Claude will experience glory only in torture; his abundant vitality will always make itself felt in shuffling, in shame, in masochism.

This shame has a national character not only because its aspect of failure and disappointment — or, in Claude, the fear of failure and disappointment — forms a transhistorical link among the large-spirited "children of the moon" but also because shame motivates the transfer of modest, small-visioned young men from the prairies to the ancient frontiers of Europe, and to refashion that Europe into a more modern version of itself, thereby making those men the "new," the European, Americans. When Claude is in France he encounters a series of distinctly maternal French women, all of whom have been touched by male death during the war; in one scene, Claude tries to explain to his host, Mlle. Olive, his wish that he had come to France earlier in the war — that Americans had come to France earlier. Mlle. Olive exclaims that whereas the young French were raised to expect German invasion, American youths could not conceive of any specifically national danger: "Nothing could touch you," she says; "nothing!"

> Claude dropped his eyes. "Yes," he muttered, blushing, "shame could. It pretty nearly did. We are pretty late." He rose from his chair, as if he were going to fetch something. . . . But where was he to get it from? He shook his head. "I am afraid," he said mournfully, "there is nothing I can say to make you understand how far away it all seemed, how almost visionary. It didn't only seem miles away, it seemed centuries away."
>
> "But you do come, — so many, and from so far! It is the last miracle of this war. I was in Paris on the fourth day of July, when your Marines, just from Bellau Wood, marched for your national fête, and I said to myself as they came on, *'That is a new man!'* Such heads they had, so fine there, behind the ears. Such discipline and purpose." (315)

This small interview neatly encapsulates the thematics I wish to link in my sketch of the war-generated secret nationality that provides Claude with an ancestry: by the language of Claude's posture and speech, his lowered eyes, his muttering and inability to explain himself, his aimless motion around the room, his blushing, Cather eroticizes her young soldier. Through his vague sense of something happening that began centuries ago, and in Mlle.

Olive's racialization of the Marines, her interpolation of their public display of national celebration and discipline into a bodily index for the new age, Cather casts over shuffling Claude the carapace that most generously accommodates that shame and gives it the shape its erotic charge, however delicious, cannot give itself. Claude is, as the woman remarks a moment later, "a man of destiny." Adolescent shame, with its unavoidable hint of incipient flowering, is the transfer point between the two genealogies Claude haunts: the men of destiny and the children of the moon.

This floating cross-ancestry means for Claude a melancholic nationality, an adoptive French past made possible only through the deaths of other young men—and separation from American women. Cather offers as a parallel to Claude's story a brief episode in which one American soldier recovers from a trauma unable to remember the women in his life. An army doctor explains to Claude:

> "Oh, yes! He's a star patient here, a psychopathic case. . . . He was shot in the neck at Cantigny, where he lost his arm. The wound healed, but his memory is affected; some nerve cut, I suppose, that connects with that part of his brain. . . . The queer thing is, it's his recollection of women that is most affected. He can remember his father, but not his mother; doesn't know if he has sisters or not,—can remember seeing girls about the house, but thinks they may have been cousins. His photographs and belongings were lost when he was hurt, all except a bunch of letters he had in his pocket. They are from a girl he's engaged to, and he declares he can't remember her at all; doesn't know what she looks like or anything about her, and can't remember getting engaged. . . . He deserted soon after he was sent to this hospital, ran away. He was found on a farm out in the country here, where the sons had been killed and the people had sort of adopted him. He'd quit his uniform and was wearing the clothes of one of the dead sons. . . . They call him 'the lost American' here." (272–73)

When the doctor reiterates amazedly that the soldier cannot remember his wife-to-be, Claude smiles and replies, "Maybe he's fortunate in that."

Just as her unexpected link to the "ancient people" prevents Thea from marrying in *The Song of the Lark,* the trauma of this soldier's wound provides him with a new family, without the danger of an impending marriage—

without women altogether, except for a benign French mother. Wrapping him in the garments of a "dead son," Cather returns to the farm life where her young men all begin—but transposed, this time, into a different, a "lost" America, where the vastness of the "loss" will mask his particular relief and safety: "Maybe he's fortunate in that."

This shockingly convenient elimination of women makes room for male-male romance.[7] Claude's closest companion at the front is David Gerhardt, a brilliant young violinist who forsook his musical career to fight in the trenches. David is everything Claude wishes he were: unafraid, decent, intellectual. When Claude first encounters David, he is instantly jealous of his quiet poise. "He seemed experienced," Claude thinks, "a finished product, rather than something on the way" (280). David speaks French and German with ease; he makes no remark when at camp the soldiers unknowingly play a recording of his on the record player. Gradually the two men come to spend all their time together; David remarks that he and Claude are the only two men in their company who have not gotten engaged to French girls (355). And shortly before his death, when the company is under heavy German assault and David has been sent across dangerous ground to get reinforcements, Claude bargains with the gods for David's life: "If They would see to it that David came back, They could take the price out of him. He would pay. Did They understand?" (364).

Claude's adoration of David is the apex of his masochism, not only because David is handsome and kind and worthy of Claude's affection, but because David, though American, is another kind of American, an American in the vein of Thea Kronborg—for whom the boundaries between Europe and the United States were readily to be traversed even before the war. He is sufficiently imbued with the history of art, of ideas, that it does not require a "roughneck's miracle" for him to participate in the moving of the geist. And the privilege of that U.S.-European position compels Claude to tortured admiration and love. Shortly before they return for the last time to the front, David takes Claude to visit some old French friends, the Fleurys, who remember David as the friend of their son René, killed in the war. The Fleury boy was a musician, and Mme. Fleury persuades David to accompany her on René's violin. As their music wafts out into the Fleury's garden, Claude listens.

He was torn between generous admiration, and bitter, bitter envy. What would it mean to be able to do anything as well as that, to have a hand capable of delicacy and precision and power? If he had been taught to do anything at all, he would not be sitting here tonight a wooden thing amongst living people. He felt that a man might have been made of him, but nobody had taken the trouble to do it; tongue-tied, foot-tied, hand-tied. If one were born into this world like a bear cub or a bull calf, one could only paw and upset things, break and destroy, all one's life. (338)

For Claude the difference between European America and prairie America is suffused by sexuality: it is the difference between bondage and flexibility, the flush of shame and the demure of accomplishment, between dull prairie marriages and cross-national, cross-generational, cross-familial passions too complex to name. Poor wooden Claude, unable to articulate to himself what he feels for David besides envy, is able only, in his moment of deep privacy, to offer his life in exchange for David's. If, as Cather writes in *Not Under Forty*, "the world broke in two in 1922 or thereabouts," then Claude, the lost American, with no grand past but only a vivid loyalty to a grand past that does not belong to him, is certainly among the "backward" who slipped into the inaccessible side of that divide.

Stubborn Primitive: The Professor's House

Reading *The Song of the Lark* and *One of Ours* shows us that adolescence is an excellent place for Cather to explore the relationship between affect and affiliation, not least because her young protagonists are so passionate in their search for genealogies. Thea's "savage" desire to "have some things" and Claude's "futile dream" of sacrificing himself for David and the war are both completely reflexive: Cather makes it seem that her characters' desire to fulfill themselves by identifying with a European or Indian past is absolutely necessary if the novels are to work as stories. But in reading parallel to those adolescent aspirations, I have focused more on *how* Cather creates affective genealogies than on their contexts or consequences. In a later novel, *The Professor's House* (1925), Cather's atavistic protagonist is a middle-aged man, whose desire to be Old World rather than New feels more a matter of stubbornness than aspiration.[8] Unlike Thea's proud pursuit of art, or Claude's embarrassed love of Europe, Godfrey St. Peter's loyalties are cranky and difficult; and they have led more than one critic to reject the novel because of the conservative politics his disposition implies. In this section, then, I address some of the political questions I have thus far left suspended—in particular, the politics of Cather's valorization of European and American Indian cultures and of her dismissal of heterosexual femininity as merely a matter of distasteful consumerism.

The Professor's House is the story of Godfrey St. Peter, a history professor who willfully resists the pressures of modern American capitalism and favors, instead, a nostalgia for French and Spanish culture. Although raised in a family of "American farmers," Professor St. Peter was moved by early studies in France to these affiliations, such as the French garden he has painstakingly cultivated for twenty years in resistant Michigan soil and his eight-volume series of books on the Spanish conquest of the Americas, whose scholarly authority merely confirms his features—he is "commonly said to look like a Spaniard" (4). The professor has built up an Old World haven for himself over the years—his house, his habits—and when professional success makes it possible for his family to move into a newer, more generously apportioned house, he resists. They can go but he will keep his upstairs study in the old house. There, in the company of old Augusta, the sewing woman who is likewise nationally contrary ("a German Catholic and very devout"), St. Peter whiles away the hours with the conquistadors (8).

Trilling identifies this resistance to the demands of the present with an "implied praise of devitalization." Indeed, for the professor, family duties and family dramas are lifeless: he muses that his family is "not his life at all, but a chain of events which had happened to him" (240); he wonders, regretting that his daughters are less entertaining now that they are grown, "Was there no other way but Medea's?" (107). And the wire-frame busts over which Augusta drapes dresses, busts he refers to as "my women," recall to him "disappointments" and "cruel biological necessities" (13).

St. Peter reserves his loyalty for Tom Outland, a former student who was killed in World War I. Tom was the great extramarital romance of the professor's life, a romance "of the imagination": by his undomesticated brilliance and his knockabout past in the wilds of the Southwest, Tom brought the professor "a kind of second youth" (234). In particular, Tom brought stories and artifacts from an ancient cliff-dwelling Indian tribe whose long-untouched city he encountered the summer before coming to Michigan, a tribe toward whom he feels a deep "filial piety" (227). This piety, which transmits to the professor, replaces or re-elaborates American nationality: through Tom, St. Peter can experience himself as connected to another history than the mundane domestic "chain of events" to which he feels he has been tethered.

The Professor's House climaxes with St. Peter preparing a preface for the upcoming publication of Tom's diary. The St. Peters are in France for the summer, and the professor is free to hide away in his old house, free to be haunted at last by the spirit of the dead boy. He contemplates his life from the vantage of that haunting:

> The man he was now, the personality his friends knew, had begun to grow strong during adolescence, during the years when he was always consciously or unconsciously conjugating the verb "to love"—in society and solitude, with people, with books. . . . When he met Lillian [his wife], it reached its maturity. From that time to this, existence had been a catching at handholds. One thing led to another and one development brought on another, and the design of his life had been the work of this secondary social man, the lover. It had been shaped by all the penalties and responsibilities of being and having been a lover. Because there was Lillian, there must be a salary. Because there was marriage, there were children. Because there were children, and fervour in the blood and brain, books were born as well as daughters. His histories, he was convinced, had no more to do with his original ego than his daughters had. . . .
>
> The Kansas boy who had come back to St. Peter this summer was not a scholar. He was a primitive. He was only interested in earth and woods and water. . . . He was not nearly so cultivated as Tom's cliff-dwellers must have been—and yet he was terribly wise. He seemed to be at the root of the matter; Desire under all desires, Truth under all truths. He seemed to know, among other things, that he was solitary and must always be so; he had never married, never been a father. (240–41)

These ruminations give compact voice to the novel's great argument, which is that heterosexual relations are merely economic, merely "cruel biological necessities"; and because they are also merely teleological ("One thing led to another"), those relations have no affinity to the timeless ideal, Desire. Heterosexuality is work—at once biological and economic—for "the secondary social man, the lover." Exhausted not only by "conjugating the verb 'to love,'" St. Peter is worn out by purchase: returning from Chicago, where his overenthusiastic daughter Rosamond has taken him shopping, he says to Lillian, "Let's omit the verb 'to buy' in all forms for a time" (134).

Implicitly, too, St. Peter's reverie over the pages of Tom's diary affiliates him, through Tom, with the "cliff-dwellers"—the Indians who link him, in turn, to Tom. He is "a primitive," like they were, and if he is not "so cultivated" as they, he is at least able to see, through their eyes, the spuriousness of his "secondary" family life and the sharper reality of his adolescence, in which he is like Tom, a simple "Kansas boy." In other words, the idea of an ancient, vanished culture becomes the ruse and condition of St. Peter's homosexual yearnings, a perfectly mystified counterpoint to the unrelenting economics his family represents to him.[9]

Masochism and Analogy: Race in Sapphira and the Slave Girl

The primitivism of such novels as *The Professor's House* and *The Song of the Lark* is the perfect foil for Cather's dissatisfaction with the choking atmosphere of life in the nuclear family, since the Indian cultures she counterposes to it are unspecific, un-named, and easily rendered as disappeared. The literary benefit of this strategy for Cather is that, through it, she is able to supply her characters with an interior life untamed by the routinization and mass-cultural clichés she despised and to touch on modes of feeling—pride, shame, stubbornness—that she clearly felt to be beyond the compass of the marriage plot or of the work of the "lady novelist"; but the literary cost of this strategy of primitivism is that Cather must isolate her characters in order to visit the primitive upon them: in the Michigan woods, in the Panther Canyon or the Cliff City, or even in Claude Wheeler's moonlit prison cell, St. Peter and Thea and Tom Outland and Claude all become their true selves alone, subtracted from the "secondary" social world—which is not in itself a bad thing, except that it leaves us wondering whether the transformations that take place in such isolation can last once these characters return to the "group life." Often Cather kills her characters or suspends the narrative before we can find out: Claude, Tom, and St. Peter are all whisked beyond the borders of the plotlines that have shaped them, and Thea is sublimed into a fairy-tale register of fame that precludes questions of her interior life (there is talk of "the stars" everywhere in *The Song of the Lark*).

I have been arguing that such strategies—Cather's close focus on male adolescence (or a fantasized return to it, or an imagined similarity to it) and attraction to the artisanal cultures of Southwest Indians—are ways of circumventing the marriage plot and of breaking away from a femininity that Cather understands to be rote, mechanical, fictionally dull. I have been arguing, in other words, that Cather is an interesting writer partly because of the acrobatics by which she avoids or dismisses what she does not want to write about. I have been calling these acrobatics the literary tracery of her lesbianism. In her last novel, however, Cather comes closer than ever before to an explicit declaration of herself as marked by political identity. The identity, though, is racial: *Sapphira and the Slave Girl* (1940) is a novel about the moral anguish of liberal white people in the age of black slavery. In the discussion that follows I sketch two things I think are important about this novel: the unprecedented way Cather writes about race without making recourse to primitivist fantasy, and the way race shifts from its usual role in Cather, as a retreat from pressures on sexuality, to an analogy for them.

Sapphira and the Slave Girl is the story of how Sapphira Colbert, a slave-owning white woman in rural Virginia, turns on her once-beloved slave Nancy, a young woman with "golden" skin, by trying to have a disreputable nephew rape her. Sapphira is an invalid, confined to a chair, and must rely on gossip, especially the gossip among her slaves, for information about the world. And when she hears her slave Lizzie insinuate that Nancy is sexually involved with Sapphira's husband, Henry, Sapphira sets about to destroy the girl's sexual virtue. Ultimately Sapphira's daughter Rachel, a woman with firm abolitionist feelings, helps Nancy escape to Canada. The novel concludes with an epilogue in which, twenty-five years later, Nancy is reunited with her mother, Sapphira's servant Till.

Toni Morrison has written the definitive account of the novel, demonstrating that Cather, although she "undertake[s] the dangerous journey" to depict the destructive effect of racism on white people, does so at the cost of her own novel, which strains believability and succumbs to a theatrical solipsism by which black suffering and redemption is staged for the white narrator, five years old, for whom Nancy and Till's reunion is delayed until she can watch (Morrison 28). Morrison, describing the novel's problems of plausibility, argues that Cather falls prey to two fallacies that warp the plot: first, Cather's notion that none of the other slaves at the Colberts' would protect or even sympathize with Nancy, who is sexually hounded by Sapphira's cousin Martin for weeks before Rachel Colbert arranges her escape; and second, that Nancy's rape could have any moral significance in the eyes of the white man, Henry Colbert, for whom Sapphira is staging it. Morrison specifically refers to this first fallacy, of Nancy's entire isolation from black sympathy, especially from her mother's sympathy, as the belief that black women are "natally dead"—"that slave women are not mothers" (21). Similarly, she argues that Cather gives Sapphira no real motive for "ruining" Nancy by having Martin rape her, since this implies an idea of feminine "virtue" that can only be "ruined" in white women, who are not owned (25).

Morrison does not ascribe the racism that mars the plot to Cather; she writes instead that Cather, fugitive from a literary language that demands black-white relations be rendered entirely in a power vacuum, as exotic fetish, "does not arrive safely" in literary free territory (28). What is interesting to Morrison is the attempt, amid racism, to outmaneuver it, even if the attempt fails. I take this as an exemplary antiracist literary reading, which manages to acknowledge that authors are not the entire creators of their imaginations and that the moral life of fiction lies in how authors may celebrate or mistrust what their imaginations bring them, not in what they imagine.

I also take Morrison's reading of Cather as a chance to understand the workings of an analogy Cather makes in *Sapphira and the Slave Girl* between homosexuality and African American racial identity—or, perhaps more precisely, an analogy between the injustices of slavery and marriage that fits into a career-long attempt of Cather's to understand her lesbianism while still contending with the demands of the marriage plot. This is to say that I see, when Morrison notices the implausibility of Sapphira's jealousy of Nancy, not only a white fabrication of a "virtue" for Nancy that has no corollary in slave society but also a signal instance of Cather's apathy toward the idea of heterosexual marriage as a narrative catalyst—signal because she actually tries to deploy it, with implausible results. It is true, then, not only that the irrelevance of Nancy's "virtue" has to be disguised by a vague notion of Henry Colbert's all-around liberalism but also that Sapphira's lack of sexual desire for her husband has to be disguised by the novel's elaborately sadistic plot. It is as if the "truly dramatic" relationships between men and women that Trilling found lacking in Cather's earlier novels crowd in on this last one, producing an excess of "heterosexual" plot devices—obsessive jealousy, a man's sexual harrassment of a woman, his attempted rape—whose proliferation does nothing to change Cather's deep lack of interest in them. If *Sapphira and the Slave Girl* "does not arrive safely" in a new literary world of antiracist imagination, it has been lured to the uneasy place where it does finally arrive as much by the imperatives of heterosexuality as by those of racism.

Cather imagines the Colbert's marriage in *Sapphira and the Slave Girl* along the same lines as marriages in her earlier novels, always avoided entirely, as with Thea Kronborg, or aborted by circumstance, as with Claude and Enid Wheeler, or stable but deeply alienated and "secondary," as with the St. Peters, or somehow gender role–inverted, as with Ántonia Shimerda in *My Ántonia* (where Ántonia takes control of the family farm before marrying). In *Sapphira*, Cather's last novel, the characterizations come quickly and easily: Henry Colbert is described as a little feminine—he is beardless and has long eyelashes that "would have been a charm in a woman" (780). Like Godfrey St. Peter, Henry is also faintly un-American: his English is spoken as he was taught, by English settlers, so that he has no Southern accent—which in backcountry Virginia, Cather tells us, "amounted almost to a foreign accent" (780). Sapphira, meanwhile, took over the family farm and its adjoining mill as a young woman, much like Ántonia Shimerda. When she chooses Henry Colbert for a husband—and it seems clear that she chooses him, not the other way around—there is no courting. Henry was a business associate of Sapphira's invalid father, and Sapphira, caring for him and for the farm, came to know Henry through business affairs (he had "never been so much as asked into the parlour") (791). And, of course, upon marriage they "[omit] the elaborate festivities which customarily followed upon a wedding" (793). Over the years they develop a domestic life that involves Sapphira's overseeing the farm and the slaves, while Henry works and sleeps in the front room at the mill. In one scene, where Sapphira wryly remarks that Henry "would always be very welcome company in the evenings," meaning to indicate her jealousy of Nancy, Henry replies: "Now don't put on with me, Sapphy. . . . You're the master here, and I'm the miller. And that's how I like it to be" (807).

All these details, along with the implausibilities that Morrison points out, make it very hard to accept the overt message of the novel, which is that it is about the intersection of racism with heterosexual jealousy. But the very queerness of the Colberts' marriage, whose terms Cather must champion as she has in her other novels, gets in the way of the project, just as she is hampered by her false assumptions about slave women. What emerges, instead, is an analogy between the punishment of black women and the punishment of masculine affect in girls.

In a chapter relating the history of the African slave Jezebel, the oldest slave on Sapphira's farm, Cather describes Jezebel's capture and transport to North America, including along the way a story about how Jezebel attacks one of her captors and manages to escape the punishment of death for it. She bites into the thumb of one of the ship's mates, Cather tells us, but she is merely flogged rather than being thrown overboard because the captain of the ship, above and beyond his economic interest in the slave, admires her for her pride, as well as her body. Like Cather, the skipper has "a kind of respect for a well-shaped creature" (830). Jezebel is proud and silent in the face of the flogging she receives.

The scene is significant for being the only description of the slave trade in Cather's work; but it is also significant to the shape of *Sapphira and the Slave Girl* because it is one of two flogging scenes in the novel—which, taken together, tell a miniature story about Cather's imagination of the relationship between race and sexuality. The other flogging scene takes place in the novel's present tense: its victim is young Casper Flight, a quiet, studious local boy, who is being framed by the bad Keyser brothers for stealing the communion set at Bethel Church. When Rachel, Sapphira's do-good daughter, hears about Casper's being dragged up into the woods by the Keysers, she and a friend dash to the scene:

> They had not gone far when they came upon the three Keysers and their captive. A young boy, perhaps fifteen or sixteen, was stripped naked to the waist and bound tight to a chestnut sapling. Three men

were lounging about the tree making fun of him. The brother called Buck had his sleeves rolled up and his shirt open, showing a thick fleece of red hair on his chest and forearms. He was laughing and cracking a lash of plaited cowhide thongs. The boy tied to the tree said not a word in answer to Buck's taunting questions. (849)

This scene takes place only about twenty pages after the description of Jezebel; the two scenes call out to each other as parallel instances of something: but what? *Sapphira and the Slave Girl* is structured episodically, and except for the main events of the novel, no one of the episodes is discernibly more significant than any of the others. The only obvious "commentary" Cather makes, through Rachel and Henry, is that slavery is wrong, however friendly the relations between master and slave, which suggests that other episodes, which largely deal with the goodness or badness of the Virginia characters in the Colberts' orbit, are to be read as extensions of or analogies to the novel's primary moral preoccupation: slaveowning white people's dilemma in the face of slavery. But how is Casper Flight like a slave?

I hope my reader, familiar now with the ways Cather treats adolescent boys, especially the "good" ones, will recognize what I see here: Casper is Tom Outland, he is Claude Wheeler, he is young Godfrey St. Peter. He is every young man Cather had admired, celebrated, and punished with death or dreams of suicide throughout her work. He is, in short, the literary projection onto a young man's body of the boy Cather wanted to be, the "Will" Cather she briefly signed herself as; he is the masculinity, expressed elsewhere in a "well-shaped" body and a love for other men, that Cather thinks must be beaten out of her. In this light, Jezebel's flogging is not only a singular attempt of Cather's to describe the suffering of a powerful black woman—Jezebel has a muscular body, too—but also a preview for, and analogy to, the suffering of the woman whose fervent desire was to be a boy. Cather's homosexuality, routed over and again in her work through male homoeroticism and male suffering, appears in *Sapphira and the Slave Girl* not only in the implausibility of the marriage between Henry and Sapphira but in the use of race to provide symbolic shape to what Cather never said directly in her fiction: female homosexuality, lived and understood as gender inversion, produces suffering that must be proudly defied, just as black women's suffering is proudly endured and defied.

This analogy is lifted easily out of the novel because the threads that hold it in are so loose: thinly plotted, never cumulative, *Sapphira and the Slave Girl* does offer us a way to understand why Cather could not see the ugliness of the narcissism on display at the end of the novel, where Till and Nancy's reunion is staged for the young Cather: she needs too much to write herself into the scene of suffering. Morrison, writing about Cather's inability to wrestle free of a racist social imagination in this novel, might find her argument further solidified here, where one reason for the novel's racial strain lies in Cather's imagination of her own body as like a boy's, which in turn is rendered like a black woman's.

For those of us reading Cather with an interest in the literary workings of her lesbianism, this tortured analogy is helpful because it offers a link between the literary language in which Cather wrote and some of the theoretical language in which she is currently being assessed. I hope, that is, that queer criticism can come to understand Cather not just as that abstract identity, "lesbian," but as a lesbian doing later generations the great service of having struggled to make art: I hope we can take an interest both in Cather's unconscious and in her conscious attempts to manipulate what her imagination brings her.[10] Neither a purely psychoanalytic reading nor a purely literary one can do what I would like reading Cather to do, which is to mobilize her writing politically, by claiming her as a lesbian forebear, and to recognize that Cather's art, and not just her unconscious, makes her worth claiming in the first place. She is not simply a writer who could not understand the racial and gender substitutions she was making when she wrote herself into her novels; she is also a writer for whom those substitutions are a piece of the work of passion. And it is her passion, which makes white women look like Indian boys or white boys look like black women, that takes wounded or invalid or "savage" bodies and makes them the center of a fiction, that continues to lure her readers, in and out of the academy.

Conclusion: Claiming Cather

In November 1995, as I was finishing an earlier version of this chapter, the *New Yorker* published an article by the critic Joan Acocella called "What Have the Academics Done to Willa Cather?" Actually, this chilling question was only the lead-in to the article, blazoned on the advertising flap the

New Yorker sometimes ships with; the article itself, once you turned to the appropriate page, was more mildly entitled, "Cather and the Academy."

Acocella's article is an interesting survey of Cather's critical fortunes over the last six decades, beginning with the story of her novels being lobbed back and forth across critical goodwill's divide by H. L. Mencken, Edmund Wilson, and Lionel Trilling in the early part of the century, following them through their dismal anonymity during the New Criticism, and concluding with a tour of Cather's reclamation at the hands of feminists and gay critics. It is these last who have "done something" to Cather; they have turned her into a lesbian and a feminist, and the project of Acocella's essay is to reclaim Cather from these critics, since Cather, for Acocella, is no feminist, and—interestingly—a lesbian only in her mind.

Acocella turns to "the lesbian argument" with a brief survey of Cather's biography, noting her lifelong attachment to Isabelle McClung and, later, to Edith Lewis, recalling Cather's heartbreak when McClung married a man and Lewis's devotion to Cather's work. "On the basis of the evidence," Acocella concludes, "I would say that Cather was homosexual in her feelings and celibate in her actions." This distinction, meaningless unless we understand sexuality as a cold, unmotivated string of acts with no relation to the personality of the actor, seems important and satisfying for Acocella, who uses it to dismiss sex altogether: "Many of the important women writers of the nineteenth century were celibate," she writes. "If Jane Austen and Emily Brontë managed without having sex, why not Cather?" (68).

It is important for Acocella to distinguish sex and feeling, because for her, what "the academics" have done to ruin Cather in calling her a lesbian is to drain her writing of its great feeling, its literary passion. But Cather's contribution to world literature, Acocella tells us, is exactly about feeling: "The only real life is in the imagination, in desire and memory" (62). This contradiction leaves Acocella, exiling and then elevating feeling in her reading of Cather, unable to understand the violence of Cather's writing, the despairing farm-country murders and suicides, whose "very clarity is baffling" (59). What Acocella is baffled by, and what I have been discussing, is Cather's ambivalent attachment to her characters, which manifests itself in admiration for suffering. Cather's "feelings," that is, her "desire and memory," are shaped by the need to master violence by incorporating it, to kill what she admires, and this is what is "baffling." This deep ambivalence, which also shapes the lesbian pulp fiction of the 1950s and 1960s, has an intimate relationship to homosexuality as a punished, disavowed sexual identity and is impossible to avoid in Cather. It should remind us that to claim Cather as a lesbian is itself as much a gesture of feeling and affiliation as it is some kind of abstractly "political" gesture.

A recent exchange on Cather between Eve Kosofsky Sedgwick and Judith Butler bears this out. The two theorists, both interested in claiming Cather as a lesbian forebear, differ on how to interpret Cather's career-long distaste for femininity, both in men and in women. Sedgwick, writing about Cather's 1905 short story, "Paul's Case," sees Cather coming to terms with the storytelling possibilities of the feminine not by including "strong women" or overtly lesbian narratives in her fiction but rather through a tentative, residually judgmental embrace of effeminate Paul. The clumsiness of this union mimics for Sedgwick the awkwardness of a historical shift in the symbolic relationship between homosexuality and sex:

> In what I am reading as Cather's move in "Paul's Case," the mannish lesbian author's coming together with the effeminate boy on the ground of a certain distinctive position of gender liminality is also a move toward a minority gay identity whose more effectual cleavage, whose more determining separatism, would be that of homo/hetero *sexual* choice rather than that of male/female gender. ("Across Genders" 172)

Sedgwick's interest in Cather, in other words, is that she represents the breathtaking, awkward moment in which two impossibly different identities begin to seem to have something in common. "We're both outsiders," Sedgwick's "mannish lesbian" uses her short story to say to the sissy. The union does not get much further than that—Cather does, after all, let Paul die at the end of the story—but that partial reach is exactly where Sedgwick feels tenderness toward Cather, who was not in a historical position to reach all the way. There is no full extension, either of mercy to the sissy or of open adoration between two women, because "a lesbian love did not in Willa Cather's time and culture become freely visible as itself" (175).

Butler takes issue with Sedgwick's suggestion that lesbianism might ever simply "be itself," in any "time and culture." She argues that the cross-identifications between lesbian and sissy, woman and man, that Sedgwick notes simply indicate how lesbian identification will always work. Writing about how, in *My Ántonia,* Cather passes the narration of Ántonia's story from an unnamed, ungendered "I" to a man, Jim Burden, Butler points to the pathos by which we find the lesbian in that disappearing "I," which has given itself over to the masculine narrator in an act at once concession and subterfuge:

> Within Cather's text, this sexuality never qualifies as a truth, radically distinct from heterosexuality. It is almost nowhere figured mimetically, but is to be read as an exchange in which sacrifice and appropriation converge, and where the name becomes the ambivalent site of this prohibited taking, this anguished giving away. (145)

This description of how a woman musters narrative authority by appearing to ground her story in a man's name could almost be a replay of the strategy Joan Rivière describes in "Womanliness as a Masquerade"—a curtsying abnegation that women of position or talent feel obliged to perform, in order not to seem to be claiming phallic privilege (145). But what makes Butler's description of Cather's storytelling technique in *My Ántonia* specifically lesbian is its affect: its "ambivalence" and "anguish"—the difficulty and awkwardness that surround Cather's attempts to move within spaces prohibited to femininity, much less a femininity aimed at admiring another woman. That painful affect becomes Butler's as well, in the conjuration of her repeated word, *"this . . . this"*— the oddness of Cather's cross-identification through a male narrator, the thrill and pain of it, become the thrill and pain of Butler's identification of Cather as an imperfect lesbian forebear.

This is what Butler shares with Sedgwick, then, despite differences in theoretical approach: a sense of the ambivalence and passion involved in clumsy, difficult cross-identifications. Sedgwick, trying to recuperate Cather's 1895 denunciation of Oscar Wilde by reading "Paul's Case" as a symbolic rapprochement with Wilde, refers to Cather as "a passionate young lesbian" ("Across Gender" 170), giving back to Cather the youth she so admired in her protagonists. Butler, meanwhile, gazing at what she calls the "fading horizon" of the lesbian narrator's brief appearance, refers to that narrator simply as "the passion of that nameless 'I'" (*Bodies That Matter* 147). Both Sedgwick, reading Cather's lesbianism into her reluctant embrace of an effeminate man, and Butler, reading it in Cather's nameless narrator's donation of authorship to a man, are identifying with Cather's ambivalence about femininity: where Cather mistrusted it as the sign of a merely consumerist relation to mass culture, Butler and Sedgwick mistrust it as the sign of a false, historically "pure" lesbianism. We will never discover Willa Cather as a woman-loving-woman. Butler does not think that any such lesbianism is possible, and Sedgwick implies that it might be now but certainly was not in Cather's time. But what is important here is the way both theorists come under Cather's sway—the way they find themselves trying to understand the historical possibilities for Cather's lesbianism because they care about her characters.

I suggest, then, that far from coldly manipulating Cather in the name of a purely political "lesbian agenda," as Joan Acocella might have it, contemporary queer theorists are struggling to use theoretical insights to bring them closer to what they love. This attempt at claiming, at bringing close, is also deeply political, of course: not everyone is going to want to hear that Cather's literary value is utterly related, at every level, to her being a lesbian. But the politics involved are not merely some kind of "special interest" politics, designed to tally one more lesbian on the new, post-modern roster of achievement in Western civilization. These politics are bigger hearted: they are an attempt to understand, through an identification with an ancestor, how history works, what it looks like, what possibilities it has offered in the past, and what those possibilities suggest about our ineffable present tense. In this case, "history" looks like Godfrey St. Peter's dream, where what matters is what is never known or said: not "the chain of events which had happened to him" but "his life." This life, "nowhere figured mimetically," is important as individual psychic experience and as history, as the buried location of the past that, by virtue both if its unsayability and its stubborn persistence—by virtue of its secrecy—survives into the present as historical seed. "As silent as a mirror is believed, / Realities plunge in silence by," wrote Hart Crane, and this is what he shares with Cather: an acute sense that what is not said is what posterity most needs to know.

In the early part of the century, then, a literary attraction to scenes of silence and unfulfillable longing—the secret desire to conquer the world, like Thea, or to be a young primitive, like the professor, or to be elevated, like Claude, into modernity when modernity is imploding—this attraction to impossible desire is a supple sign for queerness. Now, at the end of the century, queerness, with its academic theories of incomplete identity and its urban politics of endless sign-manipulation is a supple sign for the unfulfillable longings of late modernity. It is very queer, if queerness is an experience of constant inarticulate frustration about core life experience, to live now. This reversal of what explains what, from modernity explaining queerness to queerness explaining modernity, should remind us that history, if it withholds the secret of vastness from the body, nonetheless endows it with legibility from some angles, among them a certain affiliative retrospect. It should remind us that queer histories are exemplary, at the end of the twentieth century, in their drive to explain what kinship never quite explains: what kind of body does it take to survive into posterity? This question will preoccupy the next generation of lesbians and gay men, more self-identified than Cather, in whose mid-century literary and image production we will find attempts to make history explain lesbian and gay bodies—attempts that likewise revert under our latter-day scrutiny to the other project, the project of making lesbian and gay bodies illuminate history.

chapter three

THE SECRET PUBLIC

OF PHYSIQUE

CULTURE

Reading them both, you get the sense that Willa Cather would have enjoyed the muscle magazines of the 1950s. They share a rich admiration for the beauty of young men; and the aggressive wholesomeness of the physique magazines might very well have appealed to Cather, if she could have swallowed her distaste for the hair gel ads and pictures of fur-lined jock straps on the back page. Certainly Cather's hostility to mass culture places her leagues from the world of the muscle magazines, which in fact inaugurate the mass distribution of homoerotic images of male bodies in the United States; but what Cather could not have predicted (and what I wonder whether the muscle editors recognized) was the migration of some of her central concerns from modernist New York to the ramshackle, make-a-quick-buck-then-lose-it scene of California muscle culture a generation later. The reasons for this migration—which I sketch momentarily—are complex. What links Cather and the muscle culture today is their shared understanding of homosexuality through the lens of an abiding philosophical idealism. Cather's homosexuality is all about feelings that link her characters to an inaccessible ancestry and a dreamy, self-actualized future; for the muscle magazines, homosexuality is bound up in visions of easygoing sociability among young men. One way of thinking about the continuity between the novelist and the beefcake photos would be to say that the photos inherit a high-cultural sincerity about sexuality-as-beauty that has since made both forms painfully susceptible to our latter-day irony. Another would be to say that the muscle magazines burst open Cather's closet—but not so much by making explicit what she had displaced as by making explicit the pleasures of displacement.

A glance within the pages of physique publications confirms their central place in the history of gay male print culture: along with poolside posers and flexing young Marines, magazines such as *Grecian Guild Pictorial* and *Physique Pictorial* included elaborate political editorials, letters columns, pen pal clubs for readers, and even a system of mail-order "membership" that puffed up purchase of the magazines with the aura of participation in a "movement." Compared with their print contemporaries, the newsletters of the homophile movement (*ONE* and the *Mattachine Review*), the muscle magazines are striking not only in the factor of a hundred by which they outcirculated their "political" counterparts but also in the far more direct resemblance they bear to contemporary lesbian and gay publications. Because, unlike the homophile publications, which were largely accommodationist and focused on educating medical and psychological professionals about the "plight" of homosexuals, the physique magazines took for granted from the outset the normality of homosexuality, and—later— a link between a homosexual politics and a gay male body culture.

Thomas Waugh's 1996 history of gay male image-making, *Hard to Imagine,* has permanently changed the face of scholarship on physique culture. Waugh's landmark study emphatically confirms the importance of the physique magazines as predecessors to contemporary gay male print culture, especially pornography. The book is a landmark in the study of how gay men have represented one another's bodies since the birth of the photograph; it is a passionate and heroic work of scholarship. In a long chapter on physical culture, Waugh locates the beginnings of homoerotic body-photography in turn-of-the-century pictures of wrestlers and boxers printed by popular U.S. newspapers, the German Frei Körper Kultur movement, and Bernarr MacFadden's wildly successful *Physical Culture* magazine (177–214). Tracing those early developments through World War II and into what he calls "the Kinsey generation," Waugh cites the postwar displacement of young men from home and family, along with an economic prosperity driven by commodity consumption, as factors leading to the explosion of physique photography in magazine form. However the political economy of the United States at mid-century may have shaped it, he writes, "the exponential expansion of 'physique culture' constitutes the most significant gay cultural achievement during the formative quarter-century following World War II" (215). For Waugh, the networks of readers that the magazines found waiting after the war, and those they helped consolidate—made possible the mass self-identification as "gay" we now shorthand as "post-Stonewall."

Waugh's argument for the centrality of the muscle magazines to pre-Stonewall gay male culture is compelling, not least because it is so comprehensive. His interpretation of the magazine's sexual codes, though, is surprisingly punishing. He is disappointed that the scenes physique artists prefer to depict are heterosexual-but-homosocial spaces such as locker rooms and army barracks—"an iconography," as he puts it, "not of *our* distinctive ghetto space and our bodies, but of theirs" (228). "Theirs," here, means "straight men's"; his complaint is that the physique magazines are too closeted and even masochistically self-hating—sports, manual labor, military endeavor, all these are read by Waugh as a "valorization of non-gayness." "Gayness," in his reading, is not quite specified, although it seems to become visible for Waugh in the rare appearance of what seem to be romantic couples in the magazines (229).

Waugh sees the physique magazines as inadvertently political inasmuch as they created a mass audience for homoerotic images and helped foster a later, self-identified gay male print culture; when Waugh considers the magazines' iconography, however, he sees them as disappointingly pre-political, or perhaps as merely prehistory to Stonewall. My reading of the magazines follows a different course. I am interested in the function of the closet in physique culture because it seems, even years after the fact, to insist on the immiscibility of gay male sexuality and a male sociability that may or may not turn out be homophobic—a move that returns us, reading the magazines, to a prepolitical or protohistorical "moment" that does not simply lie in the chronological past but takes hold of gay male viewers nowadays, too, as a theory of homosexuality as what is *about to enter* the social body.

This theory is elaborated, especially in the *Physique Pictorial* of Bob Mizer, the Los Angeles photographer who founded the magazine, through the juxtaposition of physique photos with editorial "captions." The captions sometimes run to several paragraphs, which are often about censorship or police corruption or the role of the state in civil society. These diatribes have largely been dismissed by commentators, including Waugh, as simply the drag coefficient on honesty that the closet produces. The muscle editors ran such bravado statements alongside the photos, the argument runs, because the danger of being arrested on obscenity charges was so potent in 1955 that they could never advocate for what was really on their minds, the moral, sexual, and legal legitimation of male homosexuality. What seems more interesting about the rants that run alongside the photos, though, is the work they do in moving male homosexuality away from an inversion model, or even a perversion model: for many of the physique editors (especially Mizer) the project is to equate male homosexuality with sociability itself. The equation can be read as both anti-homophobic and closeted. The fun, friendly homosexual of physique culture—the regular guy who just wants to hang out with the guys and lift weights—is never quite a homosexual, it turns out, because the meanings of "homosexual" in the 1950s orbited too closely around ideas of morbid, narcissistic femininity in men. This closeting strategy worked very well, even preventing the U.S. Supreme Court from putting a stop to the distribution of the magazines through the mail.

There is an additional significance to the equation of male homosexuality with male sociability: to locate male homosexuality in the interstices of the social body, as Bob Mizer and some of his cohort did, is to pluralize homosexuality—to prevent it from being understood as a sexuality belonging to single persons. And this displacement of homosexuality from persons to forms of sociability (such as comparing muscles), while it sacrifices the pleasures of femininity and keeps gay sexuality in a perpetual closet, also politicizes it by preventing the isolation of the single homosexual.

Let me offer a few examples from the 1955 volume of *Physique Pictorial*. The first, from the summer issue, is a typical photo-caption pairing, in which the model is briefly described, and then used as an occasion for the editor's thoughts on a social issue (Figure 1). The "issue," usually, is censorship, framed in one way or another; but in this and the next example I draw on, the rhetoric runs a little farther afield. In this example, that means a speech about capital punishment. From the caption:

> ABOVE: GLEN HOWARD 18 5′10 1/2″ 180 lbs. waist 32. Chest 42 Neck 16. Football player at high school, avocation is deep-sea diving. At the time this photo made was attending College of Chiropractic. . . . Glen would prefer to become a doctor if he can eventually get the education for it. He likes people, wants to help them, and considers the saving of a human life perhaps one of the most wonderful things a man could do.
>
> This point of the sacredness of human life brings up an interesting question: Is society itself ever justified to murder?

The text continues with a long description of the injustices of the death penalty, particularly the race and class biases that lead to unequal prosecution, concluding that "only the poor and friendless man, perhaps with a court-appointed defense attorney, ends up in the execution chamber." Readers are encouraged to contact the American Friends, who are working against capital punishment.

And it all begins with Glen Howard's body—moving from his vital statistics to his biography, then on to the significance of his biography for a question about what is acceptable in the social body: "That state itself cannot be a murderer or it sets the cruel example." This movement from the muscular body to the social body, mediated by the details of biography, is easily understood as a maneuver of the closet, designed to distract censors from the photographic attention to the model's body—but that is too easy. Of course readers of the magazines were buying them to see biceps and athletic thighs—but to dismiss what frames the muscles again and again as a contentless "closeting strategy" is to lose sight of at least two impor-

Figure 1. "The friendless man"? *Physique Pictorial* (summer 1955). By permission of the Athletic Model Guild.

tant things. First, we would miss the pathos of the incidentals following the model, whose otherwise entire invisibility to history is captured in these few statistics and sentences, written telegraphically so as not to distract readers from delectating over his body. Second, we would miss the strong move to contextualize that body utopically, as part of a vision of a nonpunishing social fabric, without "cruel example" and buffering "the friendless man." These both, of course, relate to homosexuality, which is to say the advocacy of a noncruel mimesis can be read implicitly as a call for men not to become a homophobically punishing horde, and the similarly implicit call for "friendship" can be taken as a plea, YMCA-like, for the cultivation of less cruelly "exemplary" bonds among men. The tenuous connection between the discourse on the death penalty and the attractions of Glen Howard's physique is indeed a kind of closet. But it is also a real connection that links the muscleboy's body to a utopian vision of the social body and links a particular understanding of group life back to the homoerotic pleasures of the body. Glen Howard's physique, here untypically rendered in an innocent, boyish seated pose, rather than fully flexed and standing erect, renders this particular text-image combination especially gentle, although such postures are not requisite for utopian fantasizing in the world of *Physique Pictorial*; hard bodies can project a future too.

The fall 1955 issue offers a perfect example (Figure 2). Physique drawings, which emerged alongside physique photography, offered the editors of the muscle magazines a chance to portray young men in situations more elaborate (and often more populated) than photography allowed. Because drawings need no props or actors they are a perfect medium for the fantasy scenarios that Waugh, for one, takes as typical of a closeted "ghetto" culture. The picture by "Art-Bob," punningly titled "Caught Short," is a good example because of the improbability of the prank it depicts: three youngsters in a sports buggy, two in front and one hidden in the trunk, have been pulled over by a policeman for speeding. The two boys in front are shown wearing only the tiny shorts of the title and have the hypermuscular torsos, tiny waists, and tumescent bulges that are a hallmark of these drawings. The third prankster, tucked away in the trunk, is of uncertain sex: the muscled forearm extending from the rear of the car looks like a boy's, but its delicately arched finger, letting the air out of the policeman's tire, seems potentially a girl's. In any case there is a clockwise movement from the mas-

"CAUGHT SHORT" is the title of the Art-Bob drawing above. We trust that the mischief of these young prangsters will not be interpreted as encouragement for any delinquents at heart to show gross disrespect to vested authority. Not to say that such contempt is not sometimes well-earned. Greedy communities tolerating speed traps in isolated areas, corrupt and dishonest police willing to purjure themselves for the sake of convictions have made many good citizens regard their police force as an enemy. But it should be remembered they are our public servants requiring our understanding and cooperation. Organizations such as the American Civil Liberties Union carefully watch the activities of police groups least they exceed their function and develop into a Frankenstein Monster overwhelming their creator. In large cities it is particularly difficult for a police force to function free of corruption. Outmoded and unrealistic laws (many of purely religious origin, but certainly not enjoying the support of truly religious men) present problems of enforcement which if effectively pursued would require a ten-fold increase in personnell. Hence pay-offs, favortism, rotating arrests etc., are inevitable. When will we be willing to face reality?

The boys in this drawing had been guilty of speeding which is often wrongly credited with being a prime cause of accidents. Certainly an accident occurring at a high speed will be considerably more fatal than one at a slower speed, but on proper roads away from hazards, speed of itself has little significance in causing accidents, and most slow speed limits set up in such areas are done so to enrich the city's coffers and not with any consideration to making our highways safer. The real villains of almost every accident are thoughtlessness and/or SELFISHNESS---particularly lack of courtesy and consideration. Two solid objects cannot possibly occupy the same spot at the same time, and if every driver would be just as willing to "give in" to the other fellow and always give him the benefit of any doubt, the percentage of fatalities would drop sharply---Remember "Courtesy is contageous" and everytime you go out of your way to be extra friendly, the recipient feels compelled to pass on your warmth of feeling. Unfortunately the reverse is often true and a discourteous unfriendly act will trigger a mentally immature person to a revenge reaction. Shall we then generate chains of goodness-- or chains of evil? Page 17

Figure 2. "Courtesy is contagious." *Physique Pictorial* (fall 1955). By permission of the Athletic Model Guild.

culine to the feminine in the drawing, beginning with its upper right-hand corner, where the muscular, uniformed policeman begins the narrative at its most manly, down through the boys' bodies, still entirely hard, then to the ambiguous arm, then to a sketched-in woman's body, with bikini and beach ball, in the background of the upper left. The scene, in other words, spirals out so that the graphical energy of the man-to-man encounter, drawn in the most detail and with greatest attention to the curves of muscles, is grounded and closeted faintly but insistently by the presence of the woman in the background.

Meanwhile the closet is completed by the pretext of the scene itself. It is all-American, not queer; even if the uniformed cop, looming over the stripped-down boys, suggests the possibility that viewers can write themselves into the scene masochistically, as bottoms waiting to be punished, the grin on boy number one, and the puckish whistle of boy number two, supposedly keep things in the realm of adolescent fun. It is a delicate closet, one that falls apart in 1990s hands, because we see more than the artist can, now. We see that being "all-American" might involve both adolescent fun and a phantom masochism, for instance. In one reading, the progressive reading of gay history, the closet bursts open for us because we see what the artist cannot: the desire for punishment that lurks behind the pleasure of the prank.

It is this concealed truth of masochism that strikes some contemporary readers as lamentably unliberated. But this is why it is important to read the captions: the small diatribe printed alongside "Caught Short" is so oddly related to the drawing that it suggests another interpretation of the closet altogether. Here are the two paragraphs accompanying "Caught Short," presumably written by Bob Mizer:

> We trust that the mischief of these young pranksters will not be interpreted as encouragement for any delinquents at heart to show gross disrespect to vested authority. Not to say that such contempt is not sometimes well-earned. Greedy communities tolerating speed traps in isolated areas, corrupt and dishonest police willing to purjure [*sic*] themselves for the sake of convictions have made many good citizens regard their police force as an enemy. . . . In large cities it is particularly difficult for a police force to function free of corruption. . . .

The boys in this drawing had been guilty of speeding which is often wrongly credited with being a prime <u>cause</u> of accidents. Certainly an accident occurring at high speed will be considerably more fatal than one at a slower speed, but on proper roads away from hazards, speed of itself has little significance in causing accidents, and most slow speed limits set up in such areas are done so to enrich the city's coffers and not with any consideration to making our highways safer. The real villains in almost any accident are thoughtlessness and/or SELFISHNESS—particularly lack of courtesy and consideration. Two solid objects cannot possibly occupy the same spot at the same time, and if every driver would be just as willing to "give in" to the other fellow and always give him the benefit of any doubt, the percentage of fatalities would drop sharply—Remember "Courtesy is contagious" [*sic*] and everytime you go out of your way to be extra friendly, the recipient feels compelled to pass on your warmth of feeling. Unfortunately the reverse is often true and a discourteous unfriendly act will trigger a mentally immature person to a revenge reaction. Shall we then generate chains of goodness—or chains of evil?

The easiest way to read this magnificent passage is as camp, in which there is one interpretive key: for speeding, read gay sex. This reading makes phrases like "give in to the other fellow" and "go out of your way to be extra friendly" worth a knowing chuckle, because we understand that the Cold War–era closet keeps the rhetoric less direct, less clever than we are. Thinking of the Cold War, in fact, we may be moved to take up a slightly more "serious" reading, the historicizing reading that interprets the particular valences of this closet according to what languages and material relations it is caught up in, what it cannot extricate itself from. We might supply "history" in this instance by attention to the way contemporary vocabulary from reflex psychology takes hold here: for instance, the way one act "triggers" another. We would certainly read in the description of police corruption a protest against the raids of photo studios that plagued physique photographers in the fifties and sixties, and, expanding our compass a bit, we might even seek the origins of the editors' displacement of sex onto driving in the massive expansion of the U.S. highway system at mid-century—an illuminating linkage by which our interpretation could move to situate homosexuality more squarely in the story of national ideologies of liberty and personal realization made so vividly manifest by the joint explosion of highways and suburbs in this period. These are relations worth pursuing, but I want to propose another way of reading this passage that is not unfriendly either to camp knowing or to historicizing contextualization but that differs from those other two readings by interpreting the magazine's closeted rhetoric as theory in its own right—here, as a theory of homosexuality in the social body, rather than in persons.

The text alongside "Caught Short," in fact, prefigures a major document of gay theory: Guy Hocquenghem's 1972 discussion of "anti-homosexual paranoia" in *Homosexual Desire*. In a brief chapter, Hocquenghem describes the arc by which Freud's description of unacknowledged homosexuality as the cause of paranoia is reversed by psychiatrists and becomes, over the course of four decades, a rote insistence that homosexuality is just a bad response to paranoia (56–61). Hocquenghem, incited by this reversal, insists on Freud's original interpretation: paranoiacs do not suffer because of their homosexual yearnings but because those yearnings are repressed. Furthermore—and this is where he begins to sound like the editors of *Physique Pictorial*—Hocquenghem pushes Freud's formulation into the realm of politics.

> Society's discourse on homosexuality (which is internalized by the homosexual himself) is the fruit of the paranoia through which a dominant sexual mode, the family's reproductive heterosexuality, manifests its anxiety at the suppressed but constantly recurring sexual modes. The discourse of medical men, judges, journalists and educators is a permanent effort to repress the homosexual libido. (56)

I think Hocquenghem's direct attack on men of power for repressing homosexuality carries no inherent theoretical advantage over the way *Physique Pictorial* denounces police corruption in order to open a path to celebrating homosexuality through the metaphor of speeding. Hocquenghem's formulation benefits by being more obviously global: it is part of an overarching critique of capitalism. But Hocquenghem's global critique of capital, which is that it phallicizes and objectifies pleasure at the expense of anal delight, thereby shutting off the social body from the free circulation of pleasure, rings oddly true to the question *Physique Pictorial*'s editors pose, in their "ghetto" idiom: "Shall we then generate chains of goodness—or chains of evil?" Both passages, that is, clearly refuse the idea that either social discord (in this case, homophobia) or sexuality is located inside persons and bluntly displace the problem onto the social bond itself.[1] For Hocquenghem, this means "homosexual desire exists only in the group" (112). For *Physique Pictorial* it means, "Remember 'Courtesy is contageous.'"

What I mean to suggest in these opening examples is that the physique magazines encourage us to interpret the bodies in their pages as standing in for the many bodies of their readers—a move that, as I show, is suspected but never quite provable to censors and yearned for but never quite confirmed by those readers. This is the "secret" in the "secret public" of physique culture: that the single body might represent desires that are, in fact, more elusive and more collective than single bodies. I hope to show that this relationship of replacement and exchange between the individual gay male body and its collective audience has historical interest for contemporary queer critics.

This chapter is organized into four parts, each of which takes on different questions about gay bodies and gay history that the physique magazines have raised. The first part examines the confusion, in the broad context of mid-century sports publishing, about who was reading the muscle magazines and whether that readership could be assumed to have some kind of collective agency. The second part compares ideas about physical embodiment in the muscle magazine and in the discourse of 1950s sexology in an attempt to understand the relative roles of gender, object-choice, and the print marketplace in making a gay male body. The third part takes a look at the rhetoric of affiliation and collectivity that saturates the magazines and describes some of the ways that such rhetoric ends up locating gay men in a specifically body-based version of history. The fourth section relates that notion of history as "in the body" to the way gay men in the 1990s tried to incorporate the muscle magazines into their idea of a gay "heritage."

Muscle and the Secret Public

The flowering of the physique magazines in the 1950s is part of a history of visual culture, physical culture, media technologies, and market capitalism that extends, in the United States, at least to the late nineteenth century, when the male figure is first mass distributed in postcards and newspaper illustrations (Waugh 180). These intertwined histories come together in the form of a physique magazine in 1901, when Bernarr Macfadden began publication of *Physical Culture,* the granddaddy of muscle magazines. Macfadden published *Physical Culture,* in one form or another, until the early 1950s; but its heyday was the first twenty years of the century, when it enjoyed a circulation of 250,000. The magazine was not gay in any sense, at least not in its production; but it clearly prefigures the later gay magazines with its combination of evangelistic editorializing, letters columns, and provocative photography. Macfadden's own zeal about muscle building, too, is a striking precedent to the enthusiastic movement rhetoric I examine later in this chapter. Both of his unauthorized biographers stress the sheer sincerity of his belief that better bodies could make a better America and find evidence for that sincerity exactly in the wild variety of his schemes, which ran from opening health-food restaurants in Manhattan to founding "Physical Culture City" outside of Outcalt, New Jersey, in 1905 (Ernst 44). Finally, Macfadden's battles against obscenity charges mark him as the gay muscle magazines' most obvious predecessor: Macfadden faced prosecution periodically throughout his publishing career and was arrested in October 1905 by Anthony Comstock, who was trying to block Macfadden from staging his "Monster Physical Culture Exhibition" in Madison Square Garden. Macfadden took his case to the courts, lost twice, and finally managed in 1909 to win a pardon from President William Howard Taft, who thereby spared him the two years of hard labor his original conviction demanded (43–44, 49).

Macfadden's magazine format, his movement-style zeal, and his trouble with the law all call to mind the travails of the gay muscle magazines fifty years later, and no doubt his precedent became a model, unconscious or conscious, for the closeted righteousness that seems just barely to have kept gay physique publishers out of jail. But the similarities end there: Macfadden's biography, scandals included, is the story of Progressive Era entrepreneurial frenzy, of Macfadden's trying to "incorporate" physical culture — to use Allen Trachtenberg's term — to link physical culture to a stable economic base. For Macfadden, the production of healthy bodies fed directly into the production and consumption of urban pleasures such as the restaurant or of counter-urban remedies such as the retreat and spa. This is a necessarily public endeavor—we might call it the "mogul model" of physique culture—and becomes the model for later heterosexual physique empires, especially those of the interwar and World War II years. Physical culture businessmen from Macfadden on, from Bob Hoffman (whose *Strength and Health* magazine was the major outlet for physique photography during the 1930s and 1940s) to Charles Atlas, made use of the male body to support other economic endeavors: for Hoffman, a booming dumbbell and barbell business and for Atlas, a mail-order exercise instruction service.

Another way of saying this is that the physique moguls were not using representations of men's bodies to sell more representations of men's bodies and were therefore both less vulnerable to federal prosecution on obscenity charges and less invested in developing a visual culture of secrecy and coding to protect themselves. But the gay physique magazines, because they served as catalogs for a mail-order traffic in erotic images, never enjoyed that security. The earlier history of physique photography, then, is an appropriate context in which to place the gay muscle magazines, on the grounds of both continuity and contrast; but the other setting through which to understand them is the history of U.S. lesbian and gay struggle.

Much has been written about the immediate prehistory of the Stonewall riots as a dark time for lesbian and gay political hopes: John D'Emilio, for one, has made it clear that the homophile organizations of the 1950s and early 1960s were largely hemmed in by the prevailing languages of psychology and criminology, which all but universally construed homosexuality as a pathology, and by the constant threat of police raids, which were a regular feature of bar culture and which incipient political groups such as the Mattachine Society and the Daughters of Bilitis dreaded almost continuously. D'Emilio also points out, however, that the early 1960s were a time of increased public curiosity about homosexual culture, particularly in mass print media. Whereas a conservative Hollywood film code prevented all but a very few movies from representing any gay lives onscreen, a flurry of articles in the *New York Times* and the *Washington Post* as well as in *Time* and *Life* all gave Americans a glimpse of the "gay world."[2]

What I would like to focus on here is the inability of the producers of these print materials to account for who was reading them: in particular, I am interested in the carapace of secrecy that mass circulation provided gay readers, who might make of it something very different from their heterosexual counterparts. This secrecy inherent in mass publication applied to the muscle magazines as well as to the pieces in national news outlets. As D'Emilio puts it:

> Each novel, each physique magazine, each news report communicated to gay readers that their situation was widely shared. Homophile publications such as *The Ladder* and *ONE* offered the same message, but they reached too few people to carry much social significance. Popular novels and mass circulation weeklies, on the other hand, had audiences numbering in the millions. Regardless of their point of view, fictional renditions and journalistic accounts of lesbians and gay men filled in the outlines of a common predicament. (*Sexual Politics* 147)

And, elsewhere:

> Even the most vituperative articles. . . . served as resources for homosexuals and lesbians in search of a subculture. They frequently pinpointed the location of bars, cruising areas, and residential concentration of gays, as well as evaluations of which cities offered the most hospitable environment for homosexual men and women. (139)

In other words, in a time of highly pressurized secrecy, print media offered gay men and lesbians the opportunity to begin to identify as part of a group—to imagine themselves in parallel with other, invisible homosexuals and to identify with them through the portrayals made available through sanctioned outlets. From the outside, though, a persistent uncertainty hung around the idea of a collective gay readership: do homosexuals constitute a group? If so, is it identifiable to the outsider?

With the physique publications, there were other uncertainties as well, not least of which was the question whether there was a body type identifiable as gay or an enthusiasm for male bodies that was gay. As a fitness consumer culture began to spread through television commercials and comic-book advertisements, it prompted concern that perhaps in the midst of the craze Americans were encouraging a body cult that was as much about men desiring men's bodies as it was about an unspecified "public" wanting to get in shape. Was physical culture the perfect hiding place for homosexuals?

A 1959 *Sports Illustrated* article titled "For Love of Muscle" brought the question to the vast readership of sports enthusiasts. The piece focuses on the mysteries of the relationship between the happy capitalist fitness craze, which had made Charles Atlas and Vic Tanny wealthy men, and the "lunatic fringe" of muscle culture, where pumping up was seen to be related to all sorts of unsavory behaviors. That "fringe," for the purposes of journalism, had a specific location—Santa Monica's "Muscle Beach"—and it was the site of the most sordid conjunction of muscle and perversity. Stephen Birmingham, the *Sports Illustrated* writer, describes the fall of Muscle Beach from a sportive, family-oriented gathering place for fitness to a seedy haven for "beach bums," young men with nothing to do but lift weights and associate with one another, building to the suggestion that the murder of an eight-year-old boy by a "crazed pervert" under a pier adjacent to the weightlifting area was linked to the local muscle culture: "Although [the killer] himself was no weight lifter, he was considered quite typical of the group who composed Muscle Beach's camp followers" (62). The panicked public attention to Muscle Beach that followed the crime led to several arrests for lesser offenses, including "lewd vagrancy"—the one charge actually directed at some of the bodybuilders—and finally to the shutdown of Muscle Beach itself. The hint from *Sports Illustrated* (and it was only a hint, given the absence of anything like evidence) was that bodybuilding, in its California variant, could lead to both homosexuality and murder.

The social problem such commentators perceived in muscle culture, and the muscle magazines that encouraged it, was this: it was all but impossible to distinguish the good, wholesome body enthusiasts from the crazed perverts. The failure to make this distinction plagued heterosexuals in 1950s muscledom, not least Charles Atlas, who when questioned by *Sports Illustrated* about the homosexuals in his midst, "reddened beyond his usual healthful ruddiness and said, 'Some of those people—why, why, they're not *normal!*'" This exclamation was followed up in the "For Love of Muscle" piece by a crisper pronouncement from Atlas's business partner, who said, "We wish to have absolutely no connection drawn between Charles Atlas, Limited, and the publishers of the male physical culture magazines. . . . Charlie Atlas has done too much good for his country to worry about people like that" (64).

Unfortunately for Atlas, the connection was already there, and *Sports Illustrated* knew it, however sympathetic the slant of its piece. Consider this fey parenthesis: "It is hard to know how much admiration for one's elbow is, as it were, helpful, and how much is, shall we say, overly time-consuming or morbid. From a dispassionate interest in pectoral muscles and calf measurements, it is only the briefest possible hop to a kind of abject body worship. . . . There is no limit to how far this sort of thing can be carried" (62). Atlas and the other capitalist muscle kings must resign themselves, in other words, to the inevitable proliferation of more than one kind of attention to the body, to the fact of there being only "the briefest possible hop" between the heterosexual muscle-building of family and nation and the body culture of homosexuals—who by virtue of their closeness to the root of bodybuilding can never be separated out from that larger culture, never quite identified.

The physique magazines posed this problem in the simplest terms: how to know who bought them? Whereas the shutting down of Muscle Beach gave moralists the momentary satisfaction of dispelling perverts ("They were all so nice and concentrated there," one vice squad officer remarked), the magazines were untraceable to their purchasers because they were sold from newsstands and not by subscription. *Sports Illustrated* frets over this dilemma:

> There is, for example, the curious and ambiguous case of the many "little magazines" whose contents are devoted to photographs of the male physique, lightly clad. Certain of these publications, which are pocket size and sell for up to 50c apiece, are so-called "one-shots." A magazine, in other words, may appear only once devoted to male body culture; when a magazine next appears it will be devoted to another subject, in another guise entirely, with another title. Others, however, manage to publish regular monthly or quarterly issues. In nearly every case their contents are supplied by photographic studios which specialize in the male physique, and all the magazines, they keep saying, operate under principles that are almost embarrassingly respectable. When accused, as some of them have been, of catering only to homosexuals, they act shocked; editorially they protest that they are eminently "cultural," devoted to "esthetic appreciation of the male physique," no naughtier than *The Atlantic Monthly.* . . .
>
> Wholesome or not, the following facts seem clear: a number of the gentlemen who appear as "models" in these magazines are former

Muscle Beachers; the circulation of all the magazines (each one sells between 10 and 20,000 copies) is considered by the newsdealers to overlap—one audience, in other words, is supporting them all; a number of the publications carry West Coast addresses, though not all. Beyond this, it is anyone's guess—and there have been several—what the editors are trying to accomplish. (63)

It becomes clear, then, that the mysteries of publication—not knowing who produced these fleeting but widely available print materials or who consumed them or with what desires and objectives—fed a heterosexual paranoia about a gay "audience" with solidity and purpose that, ironically, was not even close to existing yet. The publications of the incipient homophile movement, primarily *ONE*, the *Mattachine Review*, and the *Ladder*, had circulations of a few hundred to a few thousand and because they were explicitly lesbian and gay faced severe limitations in newsstand distribution (D'Emilio, *Sexual Politics* 110). The much more widely circulating physique magazines, on the other hand, could not claim the ties among readers that the homophile publications could; but they suggested the possibility of such ties, and—more frightening—the possibility that those ties might be as extensive as the print marketplace itself. Hence the fear that the editors of the muscle magazines were trying to "accomplish" something, as if there were a Gay Physique Agenda.

From a certain vantage, this fear seems justified: the post–World War II years witnessed a major flowering of gay male visual and literary culture, even if the politics were not yet keeping pace with them. Some high-cultural forms, like the coolly glamorous nude photography of George Platt Lynes, Paul Cadmus, and Minor White, were buffered from the difficulties of federal prosecution and police raids, while others, such as the writing of the Beats, occupied the center of a mid-century struggle over propriety and obscenity—especially, in the case of Allen Ginsberg's *Howl*, whether frank representations of male homosexuality could legally be considered obscene. Indeed, the publication of both Ginsberg's poems and the physique magazines led to prosecution. It was not their content alone, however, but also their wide distribution that landed them in court. Unlike the photography of Platt Lynes and Cadmus or the homoerotic art films of the period (especially the films of Kenneth Anger), Beat literature and physique photography were widely and anonymously consumed—a fact that raised the specter, for government censors, of a vast, unlocatable audience with uncertain motives.

With physique magazines, the mystery of their consumption prompted several anxious questions—about the difference between a bodybuilder's body and a gay man's, between "cultural" and pornographic representations of male bodies, between an audience and a movement—all of which wound into a single knot in 1962, when the U.S. Supreme Court heard arguments in the case known as *Manual Enterprises vs. Day*. The case, along with the Court's 1957 decision in *ONE, Inc. vs. Oleson,* firmly established the constitutionality of distributing materials dealing with homosexuality through the mail.[3] But while the homophile publication's successful argument before the Court centered on the idea that homosexuality was a "fundamental human problem" that demanded "every legal latitude" to be solved, the physique publications argued their case by asserting that it was impossible to specify the audience reading them and therefore impossible to determine how the images in them might be taken up and acted upon—or, indeed, whether images in magazines could be said to lead to any specific sexual preferences at all.

Manual Enterprises vs. Day was argued against the backdrop of the Court's 1957 definition of obscenity in *Roth vs. United States:* "whether to the average person, applying contemporary standards, the dominant theme of the material taken as a whole appeals to prurient interest." D'Emilio points out that this standard differed from the Court's earlier approach to obscenity in two ways: it shifted emphasis away from particular passages in texts to their overall cast, and it established the idea of the "average person" as the reader or interpreter of potentially obscene material (*Sexual Politics* 132). The definition of obscenity that had been in place for decades before *Roth* had singled out readers whose "prurient interest" might be aroused by the particulars of a text—that is, if a novel were preoccupied with foot fetishes, then the simple fact that it would arouse foot fetishists was grounds for labeling it obscene. After *Roth,* however, the question became: is a novel about foot fetishes likely to arouse the general population to perverse activity? That the answer to this question was an obvious no is born out by the fact that under this new definition of obscenity, the Court declined to label any materials obscene that it viewed between 1967 and 1972, a period in which very explicit pornography was brought before the bench (134).

Manual Enterprises, then, fell out quite simply: counsel for the Postmaster's office argued that the muscle magazines were specifically aimed at homosexuals; the magazines' attorney argued that they were not. In particular, the attorney for Manual Enterprises insisted that the magazines were addressed to bodybuilders and that if there were homosexuals among them, the pictures in the magazines would not of themselves lead to any "unlawful actions" (Friedman 136). The attorney for the Postmaster, faced with this assertion, could only respond that the "poses, costumes, props, and arrangements" of the muscle photos were "significant" to homosexuals —although he did not specify how—and that the magazines had to be for homosexuals because too many of the models had "undistinguished physiques" for them to be of use to bodybuilders (108). Such arguments, it seems, left the justices unmoved.

In a sense, *Manual Enterprises* was won on the strength of the closet: the Postmaster could prove neither that homosexuals were purchasing the muscle magazines, because they were sold to newsstands and not to individual subscribers, nor that homosexuals would be aroused by pictures of scantily clad men, because no one was sure just what homosexuals *did* find exciting. As the attorney for the magazines put it: "Well this was my argument, and it appears in the record, that there are so many myriad different things that would appeal to homosexuals, that you could not possibly have any sort of photographic magazine without it appealing to some different phase of homosexuals" (137). The Supreme Court confirmed what Charles Atlas feared: in a market culture saturated with representations of every conceivable object, and in which the act of purchase was completely anonymous, it was impossible to tell a bodybuilder from a homosexual. Although this determination may seem surprising, given our contemporary sense of the early sixties as the very pinnacle of pink-baiting paranoia, it makes sense when we realize that the Court's decision to throw up its hands in the face of the fuzzy boundaries of homosexuality was exactly a resignation born of another paranoia: in the eyes of the justices, homosexuals might get turned on by *anything*. To attempt to locate them was finally outside juridical bounds. That was a matter for other experts.

Sexology, Homosexual Morphology, and Mass Publication

The tension at work in the Supreme Court's deliberation about the muscle magazines—are male homosexuals identifiable as people, an "audience," or are they just members of the "general public" who sometimes commit homosexual acts?—this tension had its corollary in the burgeoning discipline of sexology. The publication in 1948 of Alfred Kinsey's *Sexual Behavior in the Human Male* suggested so wide a prevalence of postadolescent homosexual activity among American men as almost to jeopardize the label "homosexual" itself, since, suddenly, it seemed that anyone might engage in homosexual acts, given how many already had. George Henry's *Sex Variants: A Study of Homosexual Patterns,* meanwhile, although a miniscule study by comparison, created enough interest in its proposition that homosexuals might be identified by physical traits that it survived three editions from 1941 to 1955, each aimed at a wider audience than its precursor.

Kinsey's great polemic, which remains to this day closely associated with ideas about homosexuality, was that sexuality is best understood in terms of acts. He was loath to attach sexual identities to people on the basis of those acts—or, rather, he blithely attached sexual identities to people on the basis of sexual practice in order to empty those identities of their ideological content. In other words, if a heterosexually identified man reported to Kinsey that he had allowed another man to fellate him but insisted that because he did not reciprocate he was not homosexual, Kinsey's response was: any contact between men is homosexual, however the more "masculine" of the participants may feel about the encounter. He similarly dismissed the claim made by some of the gay men in his study that one was only "really" homosexual after a certain amount of sexual experience. If you are a man, then while you are sucking another man's dick, or fucking him, ran the argument, you are, *statistically,* gay (Kinsey, Pomeroy, and Martin 623).

Kinsey's attempt at absolute empiricism was mirrored by George Henry's, although Henry worked from a very different set of assumptions about homosexuality. Most important, while Kinsey pointed out the prevalence of homosexual activity within what had previously been considered the "general population," Henry studied only self-identified homosexuals and was much less interested in the sexual acts they engaged in than in the personality types they represented. Where Kinsey's empiricism was behaviorist—the type of contact determined everything else in his study—Henry's was expressivist. He deeply believed that homosexual personality types, however seemingly subjective, could be read on the bodies of homosexuals, and he set about parsing and cataloging homosexual bodies with the aim of proving, empirically, the existence of distinct homosexual morphologies.

Henry's research, with its elaborate charts and graphs describing homosexual hands and feet and cranial thickness, seems spurious today; but his drive to locate homosexuality on the bodies of lesbians and gay men actually participates in the same sexological ideology that motivated Kinsey's study: the attachment of homosexuality to a biologized model of male/female gender. Jennifer Terry describes the ways in which Henry's research group, the Committee for the Study of Sex Variants, assumed at the outset that homosexuality was the psychological condition of being cross-gendered: "Scientists assumed that the male homosexual was always effeminate, and that the lesbian was always to some extent mannish" (318). What we now consider "object-choice" was of almost no concern to Henry, who Terry points out "never warned parents to look specifically for same-sex sexual activities" when cautioning against the development of homosexuality in children but urged instead "that parents not only accept but encourage the gender characteristics appropriate to the anatomical sex of their child" (336). The appropriate function of gender, for Henry, was to mimic and repeat biological sex. Hence his insistence that signs of homosexuality could be found on the bodies of gay men and lesbians: if homosexuals were the victims of a gender dysfunction and the role of gender (as masculinity or femininity) was to reproduce genital sex on the rest of the body, then the behavioral traits attached to homosexuality would always manifest themselves physically, as the failure of the match between gender and anatomical sex. Hence, too, the program of parental advice the committee used to make its research appear relevant: if homosexual gender inversion was so ingrained as to be morphological, then Henry could plead for tolerance for adult homosexuals, for whom the attempt to alter their ways could only be a cruelty, while seeming to offer the childhood prophylactic of aggressive gender-training—as if the gender identity and body type of a gay man or lesbian did not develop until adolescence.

Kinsey's understanding of the relationship between homosexuality and biology was much more sophisticated than Henry's. As Paul Robinson has shown, Kinsey rejected both the prevailing biological (i.e., endocrinological or hormonal) and psychoanalytic (Oedipal) explanations for homosexuality, maintaining with an "uncompromising naturalism" that "the ability to respond to homosexual stimuli was a universal human, indeed a universal biological, capacity" (56, 72). And since Kinsey had found such a wide prevalence of homosexual experience among his subjects, his act-based definition of sexuality led to the conclusion that there could be no discrete type, "the homosexual." His "naturalism," in other words, reduced sexuality to sexual contact, ostensibly in the name of "clearer," more "scientific" thinking—but it also served the politically progressive end of depathologizing homosexuality. As Robinson puts it: "If there was no such thing as a homosexual, it clearly made no sense to speak of that nonexistent entity as effeminate, temperamental, or artistically gifted. No effort was made, in either the *Male* or *Female* volume, to test whether there might be a correlation between such character traits and the inclination to perform homosexual acts" (69).

In this sense, Kinsey was at odds with Henry: while the researchers of "sex variance" were determined to trace homosexual personalities back to their gendered bodies so as to detect it earlier and steer would-be homosexual children off to heterosexuality, Kinsey tried to expunge personality from the definition of sexuality altogether, so that persons might feel less obliged to identify their sexual habits with their existence in the world. To achieve that liberation, however, Kinsey abstracted homosexuality into gender: the only significant question regarding male homosexuality was whether an act had occurred, and the only way to ask that question was, was your partner a man, yes or no? Homosexuality in the Kinseyan model, then, was rescued from stigmatization only by virtue of being collapsed into the larger category of possible masculine sexual practices. Kinsey's empiricism was closer to a "social" definition of homosexuality than Henry's, we might say, because it required two people to exist—but it is a long way from this empiricism to Hocquenghem's assertion that "homosexual desire only exists in the group" (112). The social bond in a political sense is not under consideration in Kinsey, merely the act of sexual contact. For Kinsey, biological sex remained the defining category of all sexual activity, just as in Henry's research: if for Henry being a male homosexual made you a woman, for Kinsey it depended on your being a man.

From within these biologizing schemes, then, the question whether homosexuals were an identifiable physical or psychological type remained unanswerable, both Henry's yes and Kinsey's no collapsing under the weight of their own procedures. Terry points out that the morphological variety of Henry's own subjects made it impossible for him, finally, to maintain any correlation between sexuality and body type (338). Paul Robinson, for his part, shows that Kinsey was unable to speak of homosexuality purely in terms of acts and resorted to received ideas about gay male "personality" in order to explain gay male sexual habits (70–71). Both empiricisms, the one that would quantify the relationship between the psyche and the body and the one that would obliterate it, failed to offer an explanation for the mystery of the vast but elusive presence of homosexuals in America.[4]

The muscle magazines, however, had no trouble offering instruction on how to find a gay man without compromising this secrecy: the answer was to make yourself look like one. Several of the magazines included among their photographs and drawings of muscular young men instructions for drawing or taking photographs of muscular young men, with the not-so-implicit promise that depicting their bodies might lead to the refinement of the depictor's body. The spring 1955 issue of *Physique Pictorial* says as much:

> Creating a fine physique drawing can be a very aesthetically satisfying experience, and will give you an even greater appreciation of your own body and physical training. . . . Draw a picture of the physique you want to attain. Don't worry about the crudity of your first efforts. Remember you crawled, faltered, and stumbled quite a bit before you finally walked. Indeed, art work is considerably more complex than walking, but you will be surprised at how quickly you can respond. Your own physique will take on a new meaning as you study the anatomical relation of one muscle to another. (28)

This enthusiastic, condescending passage gets at the heart of the relationship between the readers and the publishers of the physique magazines— or, at least, it gets at the heart of how the publishers envisioned it. The idea is to encourage a participatory way of viewing the images in the magazines:

specifically, to encourage readers to think of themselves as students of body-building, who can benefit from the advice and merchandise the publishers are offering. Another enticement, in a 1952 *Grecian Guild Pictorial*, offers slides for sale to potential physique "artists" who need training in order to join the physique-drawing community:

> Just as a language can be learned by speaking it (even though the student is ignorant of its gramatical [*sic*] construction, etc.) so can fundamental figure drawing be learned by the simple expedient of drawing on top of a projected image. . . . However, projected slide drawing is not limited to amateur artists alone. Many seasoned professionals take advantage of the procedure when faced with a particularly perplexing problem. (6)

The pedagogical tone of these two sales pitches is, I think, one of the many closeting strategies the publishers used to guard against the Postmasters and police. In their constant attempt to mock up a relationship to their readers that was not identifiable as traffic in gay male desire, many of them settled on the pretense that physique photography and art were fields of expertise whose secrets required publication to initiate new recruits. This para-homosexuality not only closeted its primary motives, though; it also integrated gay men's desires for contact with other men (or images of them, at first) into the field of advertising and mail-order sales. The materials required for "projected slide drawing," for instance—the projectors and slides—were available through the *Grecian Guild*'s main supplier of photos, the Athletic Model Guild, for five to ten dollars. In this sense, the sales pitch *was* the closet, not only as a market rhetoric displacing a sexual one, but as a delineation of the place for sexual contact through the purchase of objects, whether "Deluxe Tarzan Posing Straps" or packets of slides for the "Collector on a Budget" (7).

The closeting functions of pedagogical language and advertising chatter should not, however, obscure the fact that a generation of gay male bodies was shaped, literally, by the physique publications, which not only established a physique ideal but encouraged those who were able to pursue its materialization at home, in gyms, on Muscle Beach. That is, despite Kinsey's insistence that there was no one trait that made a person identifiable as "a homosexual" and despite the winning argument before the

Supreme Court in *Manual Enterprises* that there was no way to identify readers of the muscle magazines on the basis of their sexuality, *Physique Pictorial, Grecian Guild Pictorial,* and their like were indeed helping consolidate a distinct male homosexual identity that linked body culture and consumer culture in exactly the way they are linked today. The simultaneous appearance and shadowing of that identity in the social symbolic system of 1950s America is not so much a mystery of the relation between materiality and ideality in writing, as Lee Edelman would have it, as it is a tension inherent in the mass distribution of images. No one gay man could be linked to a photo of a body in a magazine because too many others, not necessarily gay, could be presumed also to view the same image—a mass simultaneity that confounds both the private preciousness and the public vulnerability in the idea of individual personhood but that consolidates nonetheless a sense of "identity" through participation in that simultaneity.[5] The morphologizing promise of the muscle magazines, then, was the doorway to a fascinating readerly and consumer system, a proto-print public sphere, in which acts of purchase and identification together encouraged the initial development of a gay male community.

Race, Tribe, Guild, and Market: Affiliations in Physique Culture

Academic work on physique culture has to face the question of what kind of collective the magazines encouraged exactly. What are the bonds that reading makes? Recent work in lesbian and gay studies provides a frame for thinking about the formation of a gay male community through print media. Some of this work specifically focuses on the ways physique photography has dallied with ideologies of whiteness, using race privilege as a cover or legitimator for homosexuality. In this section I take up the ideas in that work and develop an argument of my own about the relationship of race and racism to ideas of affiliation that the muscle magazines first fashioned and that still shape the contemporary language of our collectivity.

For Tracy Morgan, the photographs in physique publications reflect the state of racism in the culture around them. Morgan, a historian, is interested in the muscle magazines of 1955–60 because, in their almost completely exclusive focus on white men's bodies, they provide early evidence of the exclusion of black gay men from emerging white gay culture. As one of the first forums for a gay male visual culture, she argues, the magazines had an important effect in determining what a gay man should look like and set a racist precedent in gay print media that remains (we can easily infer) to be overturned. Describing the historical significance of the muscle publications to the gay wing of the lesbian and gay liberation movement, Morgan writes:

> They functioned, in the final analysis, yes, to build community. But, the terms upon which this idea of community was built accommodated forms of discrimination and depersonalization that, in the end, would turn in on themselves. Seeking normativity, physique publications reinforced codes of shame. Summoning forth white skin privilege as a salve and a smoke screen in a quest for respectability, physique magazines were part of a larger phenomenon that often sought individual, privatized solutions to group problems. (123)

Morgan points to telling indications of this link between emphasizing whiteness and confining identifications to the private sphere. Most important to her argument is that white men in the muscle magazines were most often photographed alone, and with classical "Greek" props when there were props at all. For black and Latin men, meanwhile, an array of racially coded props—chains, straw hats—was more the norm; and on one occasion, at least, she finds a photograph of a black bodybuilder with a woman labeled his "wife"—a heterosexualizing gesture not to be found, it seems, in photos of white bodybuilders (119–20). The isolation of white men into solo, "classical" frames, then, has a twofold effect on them: it monumentalizes them, Greek-ifies them—a closeting gesture—but also keeps open the possibility of a one-to-one erotic relationship between the reader of the magazine and the man in the photo. There may be no other men in the photos to suggest mutual homoerotic relationships, that is, but neither are there any women. By contrast, men of color are for Morgan tethered to reductive historical symbols, or to a wife, both of which imply that they are not available for white male sexual delectation.

The limitation on Morgan's essay is that she views racism as primarily a matter of exclusion and secondarily of appropriation. She distinguishes between physique magazines with Greek pretensions and those oriented toward bodybuilding only to remark that the latter included more men of color in their pages in the late 1950s, which she judges politically significant by itself. Elsewhere she points out that certain versions of 1950s masculinity, like the roguish Beat persona, owed their rejection of Cold War, suburban, suit-and-tie manhood to the style and culture of urban black men. But again, this observation is left unincorporated into a theory of what racism is, what its effects are, beyond its empirical presence (114–18).

In other words, Morgan does not have a dynamic idea of race and racism: races, which are defined by something loosely called "power," pre-exist racism, which then locks them into static dominator-oppressed relations. This immobile model leads Morgan to some startling remarks, as when she writes that "the all-but-complete erasure of black male homosexuality from American public consciousness is puzzling," her argument being that because homosexuality is a denigrated category in the United States, it should be more directly associated with black men, because they are denigrated too. We assume people "in power" are white, so why do we not assume that people who are not are black? The white face of homosexuality in U.S. print culture does not lead her to question this symmetrical theory of oppression, however; she simply refers to it as a "lapse in American racial logic" (109).

What Morgan seems to overlook about white racism is the medley of desires, envies, and fetishes that propels both its exclusionary and its appropriative practices and that brings race into existence as it proceeds. This simple point, that races exist only in relation to one another, is important if we hope to study the history of gay culture, because it is rife with cross-racial identifications and mimicries that shaped gay whiteness, gay blackness, and white gay racism in the twentieth century. To overlook this is to formalize racism into an ontological political category, something that "belongs" to a metaphysical concept called "whiteness." And—theory aside—to overlook the role of desires in the formation of race also reduces the physique magazines to empirical evidence for a thesis dazzlingly easy to prove: the predominance of white bodies in their pages suggests a racist exclusion of non-white men.[6]

Indeed, Morgan's own impressive research gives us a window onto how black men may have consumed the mostly white images in the physique magazines. In an unpublished paper on the black photographer and writer Glenn Carrington, Morgan notes that his papers from the 1940s and 1950s include photographs of his own, featuring young black men wrestling or posing affectionately with each other, as well as photos culled from the mail-order systems run by *Physique Pictorial* and its fellow publications. This simple juxtaposition suggests a great deal about the inextricability of white and black gay male sexual infrastructures, even in the face of their obvious differences (the small scale and narrower compass of Carrington's production, for instance, compared to the network of studios that contributed to white physical culture). Historical work on Jean Toomer, author of *Cane* and a correspondent of Hart Crane's, suggests a similar complexity of cross-racial identification as early as the 1920s. Where Morgan notes that Carrington was a social activist with leftist sympathies that ran from the International Workers of the World in the 1930s to the Black Panthers in the 1960s, historian Matthew Pratt Guterl beautifully describes Toomer's ambivalent relationship to the ideology of the New Negro, in particular his attempts to rewrite his biracial origins as a universal manhood that depended equally on the practice of literature and of Macfadden-style physical culture.[7]

I pause over this excellent work on men of color and physical culture to point out that, even given the difficulties of historical recovery, it is possible to see that the cross-racial identifications of white men with black culture are also operating in the other direction (which is not at all to say they are symmetrical or have the same valences but merely to say that "race" is not a category that pre-exists the production and consumption of images). Another source for such an argument is of course the magazines themselves. There are hints throughout the pages of the physique publications that readers wanted more than white muscle in their fantasies. The fall 1958 issue of *Physique Pictorial,* for instance, includes alongside a black muscleman the information that "so many readers have requested colored models that we have made up a special catalog" (30). This is interesting not only because of the quick glimpse it offers into the desires of the men—white? black?—reading the magazines for a change in editorial policy but because of the dodge a special "All Negro" catalog represents: why not just include more black men in the regular issues? The offer of a special black magazine suggests both an editorial ambivalence about mixing races in physique photography and a publishing strategy that attempts to reduce an attraction to black men's bodies to a fetish: a separate catalog, with only black men, marks off their bodies as more different, and undoubtedly more forbidden, than if they were included with their white counterparts. Whatever the aims of the editors of the magazines, however, my point is that readerly desires to see images of black musclemen outpaced what the publishers themselves were willing to provide.

This is not to say that the physique publishers had no understanding at all of racism or cross-racial desires. Consider this caption from the May 1964 issue of *Physique Pictorial,* attached to a photo spread of young Japanese musclemen:

AESTHETICS AND RACE PREJUDICE

"And how would you like one of those sickly-looking, pale-faced Caucasians marrying your pure-bred, dark-skinned beauty?"

Almost every race of people considers its own to be the zenith of perfection, sometimes to the unfortunate extreme that it is blinded to the beauty that may exist in others. At any rate, aesthetic taste is something that can never be effectively legislated (though basic human rights can and must come under the protection of the law).

Apparently most races at least secretly feel an admiration for one another. The Japanese has an operation to put bags under his eyes that he may look more occidental, while the Western woman plucks her eyebrows in order that she may have the thin clean line of the oriental. The Caucasian spends millions on sun-tanning lotions and hair curling preparations, while his Negro counterpart is buying bleaching cream and hair straighteners. The more we can admire in others, the richer our own lives become. (15–16)

The patched-together rhetoric of this passage is typical of defensive physique culture editorializing, linking as it does a strange and motley variety of approaches—satiric monologue, insider wisdom, sociological essay, pious maxim—but there is, in the mix, something coherent shaping the commentary: the closet. Construed as a system of "secret admiration," race takes the place of homosexuality in this argument against categorical "legislation": we sense the substitution in the odd, seemingly superfluous objection to racism as an injustice against "aesthetics." But in the third paragraph what we suspected was mere displacement and analogy takes on some literal punch: we are reminded that, indeed, race and racism, like homosexuality and homophobia, really *are,* sometimes, about submerged desires.

Two things are happening here. On one hand, as Morgan points out elsewhere, the writer of this passage is indeed using race as a closeting decoy. As long as "secret admiration" is discussed as a racial question, addressed to a father objecting to a mixed marriage or cited as an example of the vagaries of heterosexual women's beauty culture, then the appearance of non-white images in physique magazines will be read as heterosexual and the possibility of gay male desires attaching to non-white men will remain foreclosed. On the other hand, the writer convincingly suggests that racial divisions are heavily involved with sexuality, so that the person who is reading the passage for its gay content—translating, that is, remarks about the fluidity of racial aesthetic preferences into a manifesto on the legitimacy of male-male desire—even that reader cannot help but take the caption as an argument about race and racism too, however deflating its complacent last "enriching" sentence.

In other words, the use of non-white bodies as a decoy to distract government attention from white gay male desires deepens, at the same time, the historical analogy between blackness and male homosexuality as like forms of social difference. In this quirky Cold War rhetorical system, blackness is given heterosexual trappings even as it is compared to homosexuality. It is like homosexuality in the secrecy of its desires, as well as in the subjugation of the group it marks; but it is like heterosexuality in its connection to women, marriage, and paternal approval of the family line ("your purebred, dark-skinned beauty"). The two tones race strikes here—the closet blackness makes for white male homosexuality and the analogy to blackness gay men make—are an example of why the physique magazines can have an interest today for gay men curious about where substance lies in the idea of our "community." The muscle magazines used analogies to race, or tribal affiliation, at once to mask homosexuality and to give their readership a sense of historical heft; and in pursuing this strategy, they made it possible to see how homosexuality is and is not like racial identity—and how shared readership is and is not like either of them. These intermittently successful analogies are important to our understanding of gay and lesbian history because, for better or for worse, they have held: queer people in the United States still figure themselves as a "tribe," and virtual forms of communication (queer newspapers, the Internet) continue to form the basis for our sense of collective presence.

I do not want to study the effectiveness of the racial or tribal analogies in 1950s physique publications *instead* of focusing on the racist exclusions and fetishes we find there; but neither do I want to allow the fact of racism to obscure the role of race and cross-racial identifications in shaping muscle print culture's legacy to us: our simultaneity in print; our idea that we share communal bonds stretching beyond the local and the seen. To do so would be to shy away from the crucial task of understanding racism historically as well as morally, and to scant the real tribalization of U.S. lesbians and gay men in the second half of the twentieth century—however unsavory it may seem to us that that tribalization has come in large part through consumer choices, like purchasing images.

But I get somewhat ahead of myself. In what remains of this chapter I would like to look at some of the fantasies and metaphors of affiliation to be found in *Grecian Guild Pictorial* and *Physique Pictorial* and to think about the dynamic by which those fantasies and metaphors take on truth despite the awkwardness of their phrasing or the inappropriate nature of their grounds. I am eager, in closing, to point out that readership of the muscle magazines, consumption of their images and rhetoric, helps us understand more clearly the types of affiliation we normally call racial and sexual.

It is useful, as we turn to the question of readership as a form of affiliation, to remember a few of the conditions in which the gay physique magazines were being produced: not only the slow burgeoning of a homophile movement but also the much more dramatic explosion of their own publication, which reached by some reports fully 9 million copies a year in 1965 (Polak 9). This publishing boom, along with the proliferation of gyms and weightlifting and bodybuilding contests in the 1950s, made it possible for the editors of the muscle magazines to sell the idea that physical culture was becoming a social movement. Here, for instance, is a particularly enthusiastic exclamation accompanying some pictures of British and Brazilian muscleboys:

> As people of many nations discover the many interests they have in common they become more willing to put aside their differences. In weightlifting and bodybuilding contests, fine friendships have devel-

oped among the entrants from varied nations. Like music, these and other forms of sports are a "universal language" which draw all participants closer together. While we may not see it in our own time (though we can always hope for it), the time is surely coming when all men will be brothers, when hatred, selfishness, and bitterness will have almost vanished from the earth. And physical culture will play a part in this! (*Physique Pictorial* (spring 1955: 15)

This excitement, however childish, was always in the background during the heyday of the muscle magazines, and it can help us understand the relationship between the political movement for lesbian and gay liberation and the consumer movement toward physical fitness. We can see that although the homophile movement and the physical culture boom were contemporary, it was physical culture that suggested the possibility of a mass movement for gay liberation, on the basis of the vast circulation of the magazines alone. Another way of saying this would be that although the first articulations of a rhetoric for liberation emerged from the small and sophisticated circles of the Mattachine Society and the Daughters of Bilitis, it was sex that came to fuel the fire.

It is easy, reading the oblique and displaced language of the captions lacing muscle photos, to look down on the publishers for believing that anyone would actually be tricked into thinking that the magazines were about anything but sex. But we should remember that the closet was a pas de deux: the government knew, intuitively, that the muscle magazines were selling sexual images to gay men, even if they were never finally able to prove as much; and the publishers of the magazines knew that the government knew it, harassed as they were at every turn with threats of prosecution (Waugh 273–83). If *Manual Enterprises vs. Day* demonstrated that the government would never be able to establish who was reading muscle magazines, despite its being intuitively obvious, the sheer numbers of men purchasing them suggested to the publishers that something major was afoot. To get the flavor of the language in the magazines then, the vaunted descriptions of an imagined day when "all men will be brothers," and so on, we should realize that such language served two functions: first, indeed, to closet the magazines by pointing toward a higher purpose, but second—and crucially—to cast a net around the amorphous excitement of the discovery that the enthusiasm for male erotica was vast. There needed to be a name for what was being discovered—and why not call it a movement, if that would serve the happy second function of deflecting prosecution?

I make this detour because I have marveled more than once at the sheer silly elevation of the rhetoric of the piece I turn to now. George Quaintance was one of the first physique artists to be included in *Physique Pictorial* in the early 1950s, and his paintings can be found in almost any muscle magazine from that decade. In the spring 1956 issue of the *Grecian Guild Pictorial,* he "tells his own story" with a long personal essay about how he came to be "America's greatest physique artist." The essay, which is accompanied by photos of various Quaintance paintings of musclemen in the Wild West, makes rich the links I have been previewing here among physique culture, modes of affiliation, and the way the pressure of the closet encourages men to turn to vaunted language to describe them.

Quaintance's essay is built around responding to questions frequently asked (he says) by *Grecian Guild* readers; the first, his hilarious, heartbreaking response to which I will quote at some length, is "How did you come to be an artist?"

> I am not necessarily an advocate of reincarnation, but I do know that we are not born into this life new. We come here equipped with the experience and the memories of many lives we have lived before— with a background of knowledge that has nothing to do with our parents or our direct ancestry. I was born into a Virginia farm family. My ancestors were all farmers. There were no artists or talented people among them, yet I drew, painted and modeled in clay as early as I can remember. . . .
>
> That is why I do not believe in heredity. No one should, for as long as one believes that he is born of a certain family, a certain race, color, religion—into a certain locality, country, language, profession—he will be chained by this belief, and everyone he meets will place their stamp of finality upon his accepted fate. . . .
>
> Naturally I grew up in a dream world. Those high blue mountains [surrounding the family farm] were no barrier to my roving imagination. In that great, undisturbed silence I came to feel and know all the past great events and the many lives I was sure I was mixed up with

in some way through a thousand years of History. I read a great deal. Most of the events of history were not new to me. I knew I was there and saw them happen! (14–17)

We are not used to reading such idealistic language these days, except perhaps within the confines of the New Age. But just as thirty years from now we may be able to read the brutalities of the Reagan years into the idiom of crystals and self-actualization all the more clearly for its desperate escape, so here we can see—because of and not despite the reverie—a hint of the social conditions shaping the life patterns of gay men in mid-century. In particular, Quaintance's description of his childhood indicates the two acutest pressure points facing any queer child, at least in America, both to do with origins: what to make of one's family, or one's alienated place in it, and how one is related to the larger story of History, especially in the absence of an endorsing family narrative that would otherwise provide the small but soothing answer, "You come from us."

Instead of that enfolding background, then ("high blue mountains"), the queer child discovers a sense simultaneously of isolation and affiliation: a sense of having "nothing to do with . . . parents or . . . direct ancestry" but of being nonetheless "equipped" with "the experience and the memories of many lives." Perhaps this sense of exile and lineage, born of childish imagination and the early knowledge of a horrible secret, can help explain Quaintance's rejection of "heredity," under which rubric he includes family, race, and country. Because none of those categories suggests a welcome, the acute sense of having a place, of being in the world regardless, must come from somewhere else.

And so, History. Child, artist, little homosexual, or philosophical idealist—for whatever combination of these reasons, the gay boy turns to his notion of History not so much for narrative as for palette. And this thoughtlessly appropriative, escapist means of finding a place takes him to certain nodal points or mythologies, fantasy locales where questions of origin and participation find an easy answer—and that mask and legitimate love of men's bodies. Not least of these is a movie version of the Wild West, probably Quaintance's favorite setting for his paintings, and a motif that ran throughout the magazine art, unrivaled until Tom of Finland began turning gay men's imaginations to the backwoods and the police station. Included alongside Quaintance's *Grecian Guild Pictorial* essay are reproductions of paintings depicting shirtless wounded matadors, naked cowboys settling in for a night around the campfire, and naked Indians doing much the same. Indians and Mexicans, in particular, bring together Quaintance's sexual desires and his Historical closet. Here is the caption accompanying a small collection of paintings of Indians: "When Quaintance came to Arizona, he set out to find a perfect Indian model, conducting his search all over the state and in many different tribes. In EDUARDO he found the right type, combined with a lithe, plastic body that registers fine shape and line in any pose" (16). And, elsewhere: "ANGEL AVILA provided Quaintance with a distinct and dramatic type for the artist's outstanding group of Bullfight paintings. Avila is physically and temperamentally characteristic of the young Mexican Matador of today" (18). To be sure, the three white models included in this spread are also described as "types"; but their descriptions would not make sense if the non-white models had not first been used to establish the base line of what makes a "type": race and ethnicity. Those characteristics are, indeed, "objective" designations that only faintly disguise the more subjective categories to follow, that describe the white models ("young California giant," "Levi boy"). The Mexican and Indian models, meanwhile, drawn as they are from "many different tribes," are always being used to keep in place a small racializing, anthropological distance between physique art and pornography.

Race, then, did serve as a closet for physique art—but also as a gateway to the dream of affiliation. Quaintance, however we might grimace at his prose, was fantasizing in his passage through "a thousand years of History" a kind of history—a "type"—not only where men could delectate over each other's bodies but where such pleasures made sense; where they felt like part of some story, even one no more specific than a collection of "great events" (wars or white exploration of the West) linked by the absence of women and the possibility of nudity. Quaintance's vividly idealistic autobiography, then, clarifies both functions of race in physique culture: its service as a displacer of potentially "obscene" desires and as a projective, analogical model for nascent bonds among gay men. Those fantasies are most interesting when we place them in their wider setting—a burgeoning gay male print culture whose participatory spirit replays in the world of publication Quaintance's direct identification with "History."[8]

To reject "heredity" in favor of "History" is really to trade in one notion of history for another. Here Quaintance tries to replace the idea of history as determination, as fate, with another idea of History as individual actualization (freeing oneself from the "stamp of finality"). There is a contradiction built into this exchange, however, since the "heredity" Quaintance rejects is really historical ("My ancestors were all farmers") and not genetic. The choice he makes is not so much between history and heredity, then, as it is between history and History: between anonymity and being named, between being humbled and being actualized. And since this actualization is not something we can choose, Quaintance's description of its utopian possibilities, of being "mixed up" with "great events," feels more like delusion than a piece of recuperable heritage for those of us who come after him. To be fair, however, this is a genuinely difficult problem: how can we experience an identification with a "history" that seems to offer us no place? Is it possible to live without any fantasies at all of being a part of "great events"? [9] And what role do muscular bodies play in those events? In what remains of this chapter, I would like to suggest that the dilemma Quaintance faces has not left gay male culture, and that we can see it persisting in latter-day gay male discussions of the meanings and the worth of the muscle magazines, as an enthusiasm about uncovering in the physique magazines a gay male "heritage."

Conclusion: What Gay Men Have Made of Physique Culture

One of the "great events" that followed on the age of Quaintance and the other physique artists was the transformation of gay male print culture between the mid-1950s and the 1970s. Within a very short time, actually, magazines and newspapers directed at a self-consciously lesbian and gay audience displaced the physique publications as the primary means in print culture for queer people—gay men, certainly—to experience a connection to one another. Rodger Streitmatter cites a tenfold increase in the total circulation of lesbian and gay publications between 1965 and 1969, as well as a burgeoning of queer print culture in the aftermath of the Stonewall riots so rapid and so grassroots (he argues) that it remains largely unstudied (84, 117). Meanwhile, too, censorship codes and public mores had shifted so much by the late 1960s that physique publications were having to vie for readership with the first real pornography magazines, which in general offered much more explicit material than the editors of the muscle pictorials felt comfortable printing — perhaps because they still had fresh memories of the government threats and jail sentences of only a decade before.

In a sense, then, the bottom dropped out from beneath the muscle magazines in the 1970s: lesbian and gay print culture differentiated itself into porn, national magazines such as the *Advocate,* and city and regional newspapers. The 1980s brought a wide variety of thinly closeted "workout" magazines to newsstands — a stepping-stone to homosexuality for a whole new generation of gay men — but those later magazines never encouraged fantasies of the fitness movement becoming a social force or implied that reading their pages was to participate in anything beyond the building of one's own body. The most enlivening thing about the older physique magazines — their hybrid nature, their tension between movement and closet — no longer made sense in a highly specified market. To be sure, *Physique Pictorial* outlasted its competitors and survived until 1990; but by the 1980s the magazine had become more of a catalog for wrestling and bondage videos than a free-standing publication. Strangely enough, these later video-catalog volumes of *Physique Pictorial* place much less emphasis on the physiques of the models than they did in the 1950s and 1960s — what is important, later, seems to be their youth, and on their willingness to participate in the fantasy scenarios the videos demanded. It is difficult to say how much this change in body culture is the result of editor Bob Mizer's changing tastes over the years, and how much is the result of the differentiation of the marketplace. Perhaps young men with stellar physiques went to younger, better capitalized porn studios, where in the 1980s a "hard body" aesthetic was being developed that would far outpace even the early muscle magazines in championing gay male physical perfection.

If the muscular bodies of gay men migrated in the 1980s to porn studios higher-tech than Bob Mizer's, on one hand, and into the closet of the fitness magazines, on the other, the 1990s saw the mid-century physique aesthetic resurface as part of a gay "heritage," both in academic books like Waugh's *Hard to Imagine* and in a number of coffee-table books, postcards, video collections, and — in 1999 — a feature-length film.[10] In 1997 the German publisher Taschen republished virtually the entire run of *Physique Pictorial.* Taschen also brought out, in 1995, a physique picture book by F. Valentine Hooven called *Beefcake: The Muscle Magazines of America, 1950–1970,* which features scores of photos from *Grecian Guild Pictorial, Physique Pictorial, Vim,* and *Tomorrow's Man* and a smattering from other, smaller magazines. It is Hooven's aim to resuscitate an appreciation for the muscle photography of the 1950s, both as a source of erotic thrill and as a turning point in U.S. gay history. Indeed, he sees the two as closely related. Here he discusses the significance of Bob Mizer's founding *Physique Pictorial:*

> Photographs of men in the near-nude were common in the health and body-building magazines, but readers were constantly reminded that those men were there to inspire ideals of health—mental and moral as well as physical—and not for anyone's mere enjoyment. (45)

> What *Physique Pictorial* did was to strip away all that obfustication. A glance through the magazine made it instantly clear that it celebrated the male body with a directness that had not been seen since the collapse of the Roman Empire. (50)

> A miniscule magazine featuring a bunch of guys with their clothes off but not completely naked might not seem like much of a revolution in the history of sex. But to the men who bought them, they were definitely something new and daring. It took courage to purchase one of those little magazines in 1955. . . .

> But the creators of the magazines were the truly courageous ones. When they stopped pretending that those handsome boys were being photographed naked for any other reason than that they looked good that way, they were doing much more than just defying the conventional conceit that "Physical appearance is irrelevant in real men." . . . In other words, what Mizer and the others did was all but unthinkable for that day and age—they came out. (53)

> For much of the fifties, those little physique magazines were not just an aspect of gay culture; they virtually *were* gay culture. Not bad for a bunch of guys in baggy little posing pouches! (74)

This is both sexual history and history sexualized: the posing straps *and* the magazines are "little." The boys in the muscle magazines may just "look good," that is, but after their obscurity in the 1970s and 1980s, their erotic charge is also historical: they represent a collective, symbolic adolescence, before AIDS, before identity politics and its corresponding political polarization of the U.S. into pro- and antigay belief. Furthermore, in Hooven's story of courage and coming out, the editors of the muscle publications become our ancestors ("They virtually *were* gay culture"), rewriting adolescence as a historical style to which we can return when we consume images of a gay male past, rather than as a lost bodily state we must all give up one day.

The sexual appeal of rewriting adolescence as historical style is very clear to the men who are recycling physique culture. Consider the box copy accompanying Campfire Video's 1993 release "AMG: The Fantasy Factory." The Athletic Model Guild in Los Angeles, or AMG, was also run by Bob Mizer, whose huge photo and film studio is the main source from which contemporary publishers are drawing 1950s materials. Along with the stills it supplied to the various physique publications, AMG sold 8-millimeter short films to their readers, mostly posing sequences and lightly storyboarded tales of young musclemen's wrestling antics (making Mizer, incidentally, one of the forefathers of the very video porn that would make him look so obsolete twenty-five years later, despite his own flirtation with the medium). While Hooven's *Beefcake* lays an emphasis on the courage it took readers and producers of muscle photos to "come out," the makers of Campfire Videos repackage physique films to gay men by playing up the sexiness of their displacements and indirection.

> Remember the good old days, when erotica was still fun?
>
> Join us for an hour and relive the days before erotica became so hard, sweaty and impersonal. Sit back, relax, and enjoy the AMG stable of actors romping, rassling, and obviously enjoying the thrill of "gettin' nekkid" and making movies for your entertainment. See Jim Paris, Monte Hansen, Ed Fury, Joe Dellesandro and many, many more of yesterday's favorite stars. Visit with top AMG model Joe Leitel thirty years later, as he recalls the early days of AMG. Campfire's own Steve Malis hosts this nostalgic look back at the erotica of a kinder, gentler era. ("AMG")

Of course many, if not most, of the men watching the AMG videos cannot remember "the good old days," because they were not born yet when the "good old days" were happening. But the video makers are not asking a literal question; they know that even if consumers were not alive when the AMG films were made, they can still "remember" the muscleboys of the 1950s because there is another narrative of development encoded on the bodies onscreen, which begins in adolescence and—well, it begins in adolescence, and the viewers supply the adulthood. As with Hooven's essay for the *Beefcake* book, the AMG copy replaces an earlier historical moment with modes of sexual "earliness"—foreplay, adolescence, wrestling and spanking instead of sex. I suggest that the effect of such a displacement is not merely to "closet" the homosexuality of these scenes but also to highlight the earliness of any sexuality understood so clearly as plural: if it is everywhere, according to the muscle magazines, it is also always about to begin. Interpreters of gay male sexuality, whether they are reading Hart Crane or muscle magazines, tend to identify such eroticized forms of "earliness" developmentally: as Crane's nostalgia for a prelinguistic union with the universe or as muscle culture's eagerness to avoid censorship and the feminizing stigma of a fully exposed homosexuality. But, as with Crane, the earliness of the sexuality in the physique pictorials is not just a closet, it is a sketch of interstices, of the perpetual becoming-historical of gay male sexuality. I think this is interesting for us at the turn of the century because this "becoming-historical" model, in Crane as in physique culture, does not depend on a developmental story of moving "from pathology to politics" (to return to Jonathan Dollimore's phrase) whose sense of progress pays the price of privatizing homosexuality: once it belonged to individual inverts, this story goes; now it belongs to individual liberal subjects. The silly utopias of muscle culture (as well as the complex utopias of Crane) can serve, if we let them, as sketches for the movements of a sexuality that, because it is never isolable in persons, is also open to a hopeful earliness *in* history, not before it; an earliness available to people other than the young and to groups other than those who officially participate in "the movement." Which is not to say that, if the physique magazines suggest a route away from pathology by pluralizing, rather than by liberally individuating, an adolescent homosexuality, there are not benefits to age. In the next chapter I will suggest quite otherwise.

chapter four

THE AMBIVALENCE

OF LESBIAN PULP

FICTION

Like the physique magazines, the lesbian pulp novels of the 1950s and 1960s have enjoyed a resuscitation as tokens of a pre-Stonewall queer "heritage." Latter-day commentators celebrate the courage it took for women to purchase explicitly lesbian pulp novels in the days before the lesbian and gay liberation movement and note the crucial role they played in forming community among women. And some contemporary women celebrate the content as well as the consumption of the novels, reading courage and defiance into their melodramatic, convoluted plots, much as their gay male counterparts have understood the wrestling and the costumes of the muscle photos as part of a brave coming-out.

The remaining similarity between the muscle magazines and the lesbian pulps, though, is also a key difference. Both forms write history as the history of a queer body; but the type of body that stands in for the collective is much different in the pulps and differently interpreted. Whereas the muscle magazines celebrate adolescent boys' physiques as an ideal type of manhood, the pulps most often understand lesbian bodies in terms of a discourse of gender inversion—in which to be a lesbian is to be a man in a woman's body. And unlike the muscle magazines, the pulps crucially include the bodies of older women in their field of description.

This last distinction, between a youthful body and an aging one, implies another difference between the muscle magazines and the lesbian pulps, the difference between image and narrative. It is possible, in a novel or in a series of novels, to depict bodies as changing over time, whereas a photograph is obviously limited to depicting an instant of the body's life. The muscle magazines do sometimes showcase, through a sequence of photographs, the development of a young boy's muscles as he matures from, say, sixteen to twenty-five; but the key difference is that the writers of the pulp novels—and especially Ann Bannon, the novelist on whom I spend the second half of this chapter—are interested in the narrative meanings of aging as well as the quanta of youthful development.

Another way of explaining this difference between narrative and image would be to say that the pulp novels are as invested in the experiences of lesbians as the physique magazines are in the bodies of gay men. This is not to say that there is not a close focus in the pulps on lesbian bodies—I plan to show that such a focus is the key to understanding the novels' latter-day reception—but simply that the narrative form of the novels guarantees that lesbian bodies will always be rendered experientially as well as morphologically. In Bannon's fiction the link between experience and gender-inverted embodiment is so perpetually close that it is possible to read her novels as having something like body-plots that encode, preview, and reread the novels' narrative plots.

The differences in content and style between the pulps and the physique magazines are augmented by differences in the dynamics of consumption and historical claiming that have come to specify each form. Both the muscle magazines and the pulps are outgrowths of the advances in cheap printing and distribution brought on by World War II—specifically, in the case of the pulps, because inexpensive mini-novels were originally thought up as an easily shippable way to entertain GIs abroad—and both forms, there-fore, are subsections of a national mass public. And this status of mass-distributed subcultural specificity gives both the pulps and the physiques a shadow relation to mass readership that in one sense, at least, takes the shape of the closet: if the gay muscle magazines were only elusively different from Macfadden's *Physical Culture* or Bob Hoffman's *Strength and Health,* the lesbian-plotted pulps written by women existed in a larger subgenre of lesbian pulp written by men, which in turn was part of an avalanche of racy mass-circulated subgenres.[1] But where the muscle magazines were a "fan-tasy factory," churning out Greek and Roman and Wild West scenarios as part of their closet, the pulps were distinctly uncloseted in their depiction of lesbian romance—especially in the novels written by women, which slightly softened the punishing plot lines of the novels written by men. The two closets surrounding the muscle magazines and the lesbian novels were not identical, then. Whereas the Supreme Court decided it was impossible to know who was reading *Physique Pictorial,* censors and other moral watch-dogs seemed to assume that lesbian pulp novels were being read by men.

This essentially patriarchal difference in mid-century closets—"we can never presume to know what men might desire of each other, but we can always be certain that women's desires are designed to be consumed by men"—this difference is met by a gender difference in late-century queer nostalgias. That is, where contemporary gay men most often celebrate the muscle magazines as "innocent" erotica, their lesbian counterparts read the pulps through the lens of feminism, whose history since the 1960s entails a specifically political focus on the pulps, so that issues of social class, butch-femme role playing, and self-esteem, for example, are always present in one form or another when commentators discuss the novels. These social and political issues are filtered, at least in Ann Bannon's stories (which form the basis of most discussions), through the anguish of her protagonists at being misembodied, or gender-inverted, so that another difference between the pulp novels and the physique magazines lies in the affect of their latter-day consumption. Put simply, contemporary lesbians are ambivalent about the legacy of the pulps in a way that repeats the ambivalence of their fictional forebears about being lesbians in the first place. This ambivalence, in turn, raises questions about how to consume the novels today: wistfully, ironically, defiantly? These are genre questions, and I hope to show that they are entwined with the bodies of the lesbians, both fictional and real, who form the culture of the pulp novel.

Thirty years after the demise of the genre, lesbian pulp fiction seems both funny and sad. This ambivalence is perhaps the result of a split-level reading of the pulps, which takes the covers as funny and the stories as sad. While collectors and documentary makers bring grins to audiences with reproductions of the cover art, journalists and reviewers step tenderly through the pain they find in every novel. A 1993 exhibit on the pulp novels at the Lesbian Herstory Archives in Brooklyn, New York, was called "Queer Covers" and focused readers' attention on the camp value of the outsides of the books but also confirmed that what lay between the covers was deadly serious—indeed, a "survival literature," in the words of the archives' founder Joan Nestle. I don't hope so much to trouble this ambivalence in this chapter, as to develop an analysis of the pulps that accommodates both feelings, because I think both feelings (camp pleasure and intense sadness) are crucial to the project of trying to understand why the novels interest contemporary readers, why they are becoming "heritage." To that end, the covers of the novels are a good place to start, because the amusement they offer is bound up with our contemporary sense of what history has passed between their moment and ours.

The camp appeal of most pulp novel covers begins with their attempts to shock and titillate potential readers, attempts that from the vantage of thirty years seem utterly simple and innocent, not least because of the sheer enthusiasm for their own sales strategies. Sheldon Lord's 1960 *21 Gay Street*, for instance, offers two nearly bare-breasted women, a submissive blonde and a towering brunette, in overemphatic poses—hips swiveled to the breaking point, eyes cast impossibly far to one side—while below them an entirely capitalized blurb alliteratively describes the neighborhood: "GREENWICH VILLAGE, WHERE ANGELS AND ADDICTS, LOVERS AND LESBIANS, BOHEMIANS AND BAWDS LIVE AND LOVE."

This is the frontal pitch, deliriously carried away with itself. The brunette reappears on the back cover, hips still painfully aslant, to preside over the copy, which, in the more intimate lowercase, hints at how the action will develop: "Joyce didn't know herself. She was alone and very lonely. She had to make friends with someone, anyone. Maybe she could become friends with the two girls, Jean and Terri. She would do anything if they would just talk to her, anything at all." Joyce's desperation hints at the athleticism of porn: "she would do anything, . . . anything at all"—and, by gum, she probably can. What gives this convention its particular spin is the set of possibilities Greenwich Village suggests. After World War II the Village, already a bohemian mecca for four decades, became a destination for thousands of young people, many of them gay and lesbian, whom the war had permanently detached from their families. These young people were hungry for something less stifling than rural life or the quietude of suburbs and by dint of sheer geographic concentration gave homosexuality a new descriptive feature: location. Lesbian pulp fiction takes advantage of this development in many ways, not only in its conventional choice of the Village as a colorful setting, but also in its manipulation of urban loneliness and desperation into something like sexual openness, which can then be punned into a location: 21 Gay Street. Other novels double this geographizing pun with the language of the "third sex": every Village address seems to suggest queer occupancy, from *The Girls in 3-B* to *The Third Street* ("the street where no questions were asked—the street where few men were ever seen"). Roommates abound on these covers; every ingenue seems to be folding or unfolding her clothes under the watchful and lascivious eye of a more experienced tenant.

The city was not the only setting for the pulps: publishing houses tried to tantalize readers with the threat and promise of lesbians in the suburbs, too. In *The Third Lust,* "the well-cared-for women in their well-tended homes had time on their hands—time to pursue the new community pastime . . . lesbianism!" Just as the new concentration of young, poor, single women in places like the Village suggested sexual frontiers, so did the new concentration of suburban women, physically separated from the centers of accumulation where their husbands worked, suggest a delicious underside to the official vision of man and wife together by the hearth after five o'clock. But the primary focus of the novels, on their covers as well as in their plots, was on the city, which in its mighty capacity to generate random encounters was still hands down the preferred location of sexual possibility. The cover of Sloan Britton's 1963 *The Delicate Vice*—"men had hurt her, so she embraced what she thought was a safer kind of love"—shows two women lurking in the tightly circumscribed halo of a streetlight, while behind them like the exact fulfillment of their encounter glows the awning of the "Transients' Hotel." And in the notion of the "transient" lies the most compelling titillation—the woman who could go anywhere is also the woman who might do anything.

More amusing than any of the delirious cover paintings is the accompanying text, whose declarations and insinuations are by now utterly exposed as outsider's talk, the squarest talk of all. The voice initiating readers into the mysteries of life in the Village is of course a male voice—women are always an objectified "they"—and its homophobic capitalization of lesbian sexuality into a force of evil (*The Mesh:* "A Novel of Hidden Evil") now reads precisely as obliviousness to what was *really* going on in the Village: women were having sex with each other. By telling the story only through lurid conventions, the producers of cover copy for the pulps have left contemporary lesbians with a complex legacy in which commentators struggle over how to incorporate the pulps' melodrama and cliché into lesbian literary history.

I turn at the end of this chapter to some of the ways that lesbians are enjoying and reinterpreting pulp novels today, but first I would like to examine some of the ways commentators have taken up the storylines as distinct from their covers—how the novels were seen, and are still seen, divided between a melodramatic overemphasis on suffering and self-destruction and an unexpected or inadvertent realism. This division is written as a mystery of historical tension and change, so that the pulps are read as both realist and melodramatic, politically subversive and literarily embarrassing, with one term or the other coming to triumph as their true nature depending on how the reader interprets the progressive story of pre- to post-Stonewall liberation.

People writing about lesbian pulp fiction are compelled to remark on the unstable nature of the genre; in particular they notice that changing historical conditions have altered it retroactively, so that their attempts at genre classification are also attempts to tell the story of the rise of the lesbian and gay liberation movement. Such commentaries function, furthermore, as arguments about what lesbians (sometimes gay men) should *feel* about the early development of the movement—what they should feel, in short, about the history of suffering and resistance that led to the Stonewall riots in 1969. Since these contemporary writers are trying to understand lesbian history in tandem with the fluctuations of a literary genre, the emotional conventions of that genre become part of the larger story of where the movement has gone and what it has produced. In what follows, then, I try to show that, taken together, literary classification and the project of looking back at the movement generate an essentially affective—perhaps a melodramatic—notion of history.

Retrospection and Genre

Lesbian pulp novels emerged in the 1950s as part of what Lee Server calls a "brief but gloriously subversive" boom in American paperback publishing, in which hack writers of all stripes turned out tales of sex and violence in huge quantity, falling into a variety of subgenres—teen drug abuse, white slavery, murder mysteries—of which "lesbian lust" was among the most successful. Server points out that Vin Packer's 1952 novel *Spring Fire,* for instance, was reported to have been the first paperback to outsell Erskine Caldwell's *God's Little Acre,* reaching several million copies (51).

What Server implies is "subversive" about the era of pulp publishing, although he never specifies, is that pulp fiction opened the door to unregulated consumption of literary materials, out of reach—briefly, indeed—of censors but readily available to readers. The pulps were sold at newsstands, usually for about twenty-five cents apiece, and their cheapness and extra-literary distribution suggest to most commentators that they were a working-class form. The luridness of the pulps is seen as nonbourgeois, and they are taken implicitly to be thumbing a nose at traditional literature, not least by virtue of their vast sales. This conclusion seems true enough, but there is another "subversiveness" embedded in the lesbian pulps: unlike their true-crime and white-slavery counterparts, they helped form a network of readers who were beginning to experiment with forming alternative communities. Roberta Yusba, a long-time collector of lesbian fiction, describes their production and reception:

> The vast majority of these lesbian novels were written by men, designed to fulfill straight men's fantasies. . . . But perhaps 40 or 50 lesbian novels were written by women, and were also good enough to become underground classics. Dog-eared copies of books by Ann

Bannon, Valerie Taylor, Artemis Smith and Paula Christian were passed among friends in lesbian communities. The pulps also reached isolated, small-town lesbians who could read them and see that they were not the only lesbians in the world. (30)

Elsewhere, in the introduction to the 1993 exhibit of the pulps at the Lesbian Herstory Archives in Brooklyn, the books are given a more specific emotional backdrop.

> The act of taking one of these books off the drugstore rack and paying for it at the counter was a frightening and difficult move for most women. This was especially true during the atmosphere of the McCarthy trials. . . .
>
> Although tame by today's standards of lesbian literature and erotica, these volumes were so threatening then that women hid them, burnt them and threw them out. At the same time . . . they helped form many a fledgling lesbian's idea of what life might be for her. And perhaps, miraculously for that time and environment, happy endings could be found in mainstream media. ("Queer Covers: Lesbian Survival Literature")

Again, we should pause here to remark on the difference in the nature of the closet surrounding the purchases of pulp novels by women and muscle magazines by men: latter-day commentators point out the courage it took to purchase such materials; but the ruse of the closet that kept the physique magazines barely legal in the early 1960s does not apply to women, who when they purchased pulp novels had no alibi, however flimsy, akin to the "fitness alibi" Thomas Waugh describes as available to men. There is not, in the gay male sense, a secret public, imagined as mass perversion of bodybuilding—there is simply the exposure guaranteed in being a woman purchasing novels designed for men. The lesbian rhetoric of print-public networking, of community real and imagined, produces instead a vision of a "fledgling" public, whose secrecy lay more in its subsistence-level consumption of scarce resources—like "happy endings"—than in an imagined endlessness of male desire.

These "happy endings" were so rare because the prevailing language for homosexuality in the 1950s was a toxic mix of the psychopathological and the criminal: hence their appeal to the publishers of other subgenres focusing on the "dark side" of American life. Most commentators make an argument that the lesbian pulps were somehow both limited and unimpeded by this default language. Yusba writes: "Those women who came across good lesbian pulp found welcome relief. The characters were at least real people in real situations, not clinical case histories from some psychiatrist's files. In the context of repression, many pulps were pro-sex, pro-bars, and pro-lesbian!" (30–31). She adds, however: "Psychiatric notions of lesbianism being caused by rape, trauma, or demented or sexually abusive parents find their way into most lesbian pulps. Even the best of pulp authors were unable to keep from using them" (43).

What begins to emerge in reading these accounts is a sense of deep ambivalence about this "survival literature" and the conditions it imposed on its readers, the tax, in a sense, it leveled for the right to read about lesbians at all. John D'Emilio writes that lesbian activist Sally Gearhart threw her lesbian pulps out the window of her car because she was "embarrassed to possess them" and quotes an interview with Kate Millett in which Millett describes the pulps as "books about grotesques" that she kept as long as she did—eventually burning them—only because "they were the only books where one woman kissed another" (135–36). The pulps were written within rigid genre conventions, not least the demand for *un*-happy endings: Vin Packer, the author of the best-selling *Spring Fire,* reports that her editors at Fawcett Gold Medal insisted that the novel's protagonist "go crazy" at the end to prevent the Post Office from seizing the book on obscenity grounds (Server 52).

The imperative of the publishing industry to punish its lesbian characters was never uniformly enforced, however, and lesbians honed in quickly on the less sadistic novels, developing an apparatus of literary assessment, a seeking-out of the "best of pulp authors" who put "real people in real situations." At the center of this burgeoning criticism was Barbara Grier, pseudonymously known as Gene Damon, who wrote assessments of the output of lesbian fiction for the *Ladder,* an early and important lesbian newsletter, throughout the fifties. Grier's remarks about the novels are fascinating for her commitment to evaluating them on literary terms, even as she factors in the limitations the genre of "problem fiction" imposed on the novels. Writing as Damon in a 1966 retrospective, Grier touches on the appeal of the low-cultural end of the spectrum: "The good lesbian paperbacks served a definite purpose by satisfying vicariously the need for 'happy endings' which are so often lacking in more literate treatments of the subject. They also provided generally youthful, theoretically romantic figures and contemporary settings. To some extent they were responsible for better public relations with the public" (4).

Grier's evaluation is quite a bit cooler than those of Yusba and the Herstory Archives, void of the poetics of "survival literature," the "dog-eared" paperback, and the "fledgling lesbian." She is interested in the novels specifically as low-cultural phenomena and takes note of the advantages of the milieu. Pulp novels are designed to produce satisfaction in readers, and since that satisfaction in the case of lesbian pulps is to be derived from "happy endings," from the rare delight of finding one's identifications with a text undestroyed, the pulps manage what "literate treatments" cannot: they garner a wide audience; they enter into the field of "public relations." Grier was, after all, writing for the *Ladder,* a newsletter whose purpose was decidedly to encourage lesbians to wear an acceptable public face, and the popularity of the paperbacks seems to have suggested to her a possibly populist route to greater understanding of lesbians. Her investment in the novels, then, is divided between evaluating their content and articulating their social efficacy.

One might say that unlike Yusba or Joan Nestle, Grier is as interested in cataloging the novels as in reading them (she was trained as a librarian). She wants to shape a canon of good lesbian pulp fiction, and her concerns are therefore hybrid between the pleasures of identifying with the stories and evaluating them for something like literary worth. To be fair, the two types of analysis are not entirely separate: in the course of her retrospective, as Grier carefully elaborates a checklist of qualities that distinguish "good" pulps from worthless ones, we begin to see that the checklist is organized around the knowledge that, for lesbians, to consume the novels is to identify with their narratives, probably intensely. She elevates, accordingly, those stories with special characteristics: limited sex and violence, a believably happy ending, psychological insight into the characters, and decent writing. But Grier also recognizes audience loyalty as a significant feature of a novel's standing, however unliterary a criterion that may be for canonical status. In the passage that follows, Grier tries to understand the fallen fortunes of the novelist Artemis Smith by comparing her to other, less accomplished writers in the pulp industry:

> Another debut of 1959 was author Artemis Smith with *Odd Girl,* Beacon. This was an unusually good book, and Miss Smith followed it a little later that same year with *The Third Sex,* also published by Beacon. These were so good, that her third and last book to date was a dreadful disappointment. Unlike other authors who go on to greater heights, Miss Smith never topped her first two books. After the third, she simply stopped writing. This was sad because she wrote very well, better than Bannon or Salem or Christian and nearly as well as Valerie Taylor. Once again it was a matter of gimic. Bannon has an all-star cast full of familiar figures who go from book to book. Salem can make the peanut gallery weep. Christian plots very well and Taylor writes on a par with Gale Wilhelm. Somehow Artemis fell short. (6–7)

What interests me here is the acuteness with which Grier is able to separate her own sense of literary worth, based primarily on "good writing," from what makes a lesbian classic. Most striking is Grier's remark that other writers' success "was a matter of gimic"—a distinctly nonliterary route to popularity but one that is unignorable because "gimic" is the way to reach an audience. Bannon's "all-star cast" and Christian's well-made plots entice the same "peanut gallery" that bursts into tears reading Salem's love scenes, and it is the peanut gallery, in the end, that determines what will be canonized. These are "public relations," too: if the sheer volume of the pulps made it possible for straight America to understand lesbians more clearly, or at least to conceive of their existence, that volume also made it possible for a lesbian readership to choose from among representations and to elevate some of them through the power of purchase. "Customer relations," perhaps—customer relations distilled into a canon whose roster is charged with a collective, but personal, nostalgia. Noting that with the easing of censorship the lesbian pulps have become outmoded by the mid-1960s, Grier writes: "The era began in 1950 and ended in 1965. Hopefully, in many memories, some names will remain bright for years to come: Valerie Taylor, Ann Bannon, Paula Christian, and one or two others. But for now; Ave Atque Vale!" (15).

As it turns out, the author whose name has remained the "brightest" in the canon of lesbian pulp is Ann Bannon, whose five-book series of Greenwich Village escapades is now firmly ensconced as the premier fictional representation of lesbian life in the 1950s and 1960s. There is something uncertain in the small but growing bibliography of writing on Bannon, though: how should we read the novels thirty or forty years later? The changes in lesbian and gay political and sexual culture in that short time have been immense, and aside from acknowledging their value as "survival literature"— as a record of what was in danger of going unrecorded—it remains an open question just how to attach value to the books. And critics want to: Nestle's designation, while it highlights the intense writer-audience relationship that the lesbian pulps created, does not account for why younger readers, who came out after Stonewall, are still so interested in Bannon's novels.

The essays written on Bannon since 1980 begin to answer this question, and I consider three of them in this chapter: one in the gay press, one in a mass-circulation weekly, and one in an academic journal. All three writers share an affection for Bannon's novels, and all three claim that, essentially, the novels have changed genre since their original publication. They argue, in other words, that readership influences genre identity, not least because books like Bannon's can be claimed for different purposes in the 1980s and 1990s than in the 1950s and 1960s. In what follows I try to establish some links between critical retrospection and genre identity, in order to argue that what is at stake in interpreting and reinterpreting pulp fiction is the charging of movement history with something like "real," contemporary, affect.

In a 1980 essay called "Sad Stories: A Reflection on the Fiction of Ann Bannon," Andrea Loewenstein describes her friends as ashamed of the lesbian pulps, or disdainful of them, because the characters are so clichéd, or because they are so often abusive or alcoholic or otherwise unable to live happy lives. Loewenstein makes a bid, however, for claiming Bannon's novels as an emotionally realist form whose message of pain and self-destruction must be included in the story of lesbian and gay political struggle if it is to continue to grow. For Loewenstein, resistance to Bannon's novels suggests repression—or, perhaps more precisely, traumatic disavowal—and she argues that if the quality of pulp writing is middling by definition, it nonetheless has literary worth because of the identificatory reckonings it sponsors: reading pulp novels can help you recognize and manage your pain.

Loewenstein sees her argument about the quality of pulp writing as class-based. She assumes, along with most commentators, that the readership of the pulps in the 1950s and 1960s was working class; she further assumes that pulp writing itself is somehow the product of the class background of the writer. This assumption leads her to a consideration of the nature of the cliché, and of its function for latter-day readers of pulp fiction. In high literary writing, she argues, strategic use of clichés can create a critical consciousness about language in the minds of readers; not so in the world of the pulps. Comparing Bannon's novels to *The Death of a Salesman,* she writes:

> When Willie Loman swears that anyone "well-liked will climb to the top rung of the ladder of success," or that every "real man knows how to use tools," [Arthur] Miller is showing us how the false promises of the American dream have pervaded even the everyday language of the "little man." But when Ann Bannon's butch tells her lover-to-be, "You'll never find love with a capital 'L' if you're gay," Bannon is *not* trying to show us how society has caused self-hatred in gays. She is directly reflecting her (and her culture's) ideas. The language of cliché, while it is rarely the exact language of our speech, may reflect even *more* closely than a more realistic rendition of speech, the mores and assumptions of our culture. The writer of the pulp, whose language is less original or transcendent, is thus, in his or her choice of language, acting as a mirror, in the way a more sophisticated writer could not do if she tried. (8)

In this fascinating argument, clichés and writerly limitations produce a historical truth inaccessible to high art, the truth of the ideological imprinting of people. That imprinting includes Ann Bannon as well as her characters: Loewenstein, in depicting Bannon as a "mirror" for "her culture," gives her no credit for ideological resistance or subtlety. Indeed, Loewenstein equates the writing of cliché with the most ideologically passive social position, neither elite nor lumpen, simply susceptible: what she calls the "often stultifying mainstream" (8).

Why, then, read the novels? For Loewenstein, the answer is that it is therapeutic. In the passage that follows she links the absence of historical consciousness to the immobilizing grip of shame.

> A friend who has come out only quite recently found the books boring and badly written, and I found myself responding with some anger. Another friend who has been out 10 years longer than I have was both more angered by them and more upset than I, which leads me to the perhaps natural, since much of our past is so bitter, tendency of our (gay and lesbian) movement to pretend away even our most recent history. . . . Roles? *They don't exist.* Jealous rages? *We don't do that anymore.* . . . Then, when we get jealous, or find ourselves playing a male or female role . . . we give ourselves neither patience nor understanding. Instead, we hate ourselves even more. We are bad lesbians/gays. We have failed. (8)

It is costly to refuse to read the pulps, then, or to read them merely as past-perfect accounts of transcended behaviors, because those reading practices repress a continuity of past and present that Loewenstein clearly experiences as both deeply personal and intrinsic to collective action. The pressure on the slash in the sentence, "We are bad lesbians/gays," the pressure on it not to be clinical and to be inclusive instead is heartbreaking and nearly comic— much like the pulps themselves.

Indeed, by the close of her essay, the pressure to elucidate this affect leads Loewenstein to reclassify the pulps in the name of movement continuity. Comparing Bannon's bleak stories with those of other novelists, she puts the word *pulp* in quotation marks, as if to protect the books from critical assault: "It is important for us, as readers, to remember that other lesbian writers were drawing different conclusions from the same . . . life evidence. But it is also important to understand and to bear witness to the kind of pain which is behind the clichéd writing in these "pulp" novels. This pain and self hatred is not our only past. But it is a part of it" (12). What began as a denunciation of the social position from which she imagines Bannon wrote the novels has resolved into a tenderness that implies a specific outcome of historical consciousness in the lesbian and gay ("lesbians/gays") movement: forgiveness and claiming, an emotional formation that trumps, in Loewenstein's analysis, the ideological divide between "mirror"-like, reflective beliefs about lesbians, and critical, class-conscious awareness of the limitations of cliché.

Loewenstein wrote her essay for a movement newspaper, Boston's *Gay Community News,* and that context accounts in part for her sense of the urgency of rereading novels like Bannon's: she is addressing her cohorts. In the *Village Voice,* however, writing about the pulps takes a different tone. The mixed gay and straight readership of the *Voice,* as well as its far wider circulation, lead Jeff Weinstein, in his 1983 article "In Praise of Pulp: Bannon's Lusty Lesbians," to take up Bannon's novels as an example of the radical potential of lowbrow culture for all of us, lesbian or not. Where Loewenstein valorizes Bannon's novels negatively for the lesson their limitations may teach later lesbian readers, Weinstein revels in the "cultural" freedoms he imagines Bannon seized, weaving the story of lesbian and gay liberation into the fabric of culture wars in general: "during the 1950's, when little or nothing honest about gay male and lesbian lives was available culturally, how could a truth teller grab a niche? Others had learned the lesson: not through high culture. So Bannon stormed the low" (8). Weinstein praises Bannon for choosing to write "potboilers" because they "aren't subject to systematic cultural censorship," adding that other, more literary treatments of lesbians in the 1950s "lack the protective subterfuge of genre conventions" (8).

Weinstein's use of the word *culture* serves two functions: it satisfies the need for a term that certifies Bannon's novels as literature, without sounding academic, and it has meanings for a broad constituency that may or may not be lesbian. Where Loewenstein's concern with "the past" speaks primarily to movement readers who know roughly what "past" is being referred to, Weinstein's focus on "culture" keeps the question of lesbian and gay politics available to the nongay readers of the *Voice,* who can be presumed to take an interest in any movement struggle if its politics can be seen to affect some sort of "big picture." *Culture* is the catchword of the left-progressive feature writer's pitch.

There is, however, nothing cynical about Weinstein's piece — simply that an awareness of his audience leads him to think carefully about what interests him in the pulps: the unexpected turns the genre takes in Bannon's hands. He comes close to Loewenstein's analysis of Bannon's language, taking note of its conventionality. But where Loewenstein focuses on that conventionality as the result of clichés, Weinstein sees it as a product of melodramatic exaggerations:

> Potboilers use simple exaggeration to accomplish their tasks, but when Bannon exploits melodramatic conventions something unusual happens: they become realistic. The only explanation I have is that her lesbian and gay characters are influenced by the melodramatic conventions of the culture that excludes them. . . . I can't say that melodrama-as-life is realistic pre-Stonewall *behavior,* though camp with its selective exaggerations has for years been used by gay people as a mode of self-definition and self-defense. I can say that melodrama does throw its arms around the arenas of daily '50s gay struggle: not the courts or battlefields, but the dormitories, the apartments, and bars. No high-cultural language existed to play out "lesbian heartbreak" so truthfully. Through melodrama, Bannon has backed into a kind of gay realism of her time. (9)

Weinstein begins this paragraph sounding like Loewenstein: Bannon's characters are realist in their melodramatic behavior because 1950s queer culture *was* melodramatic—they are a "mirror." But Weinstein takes this analysis in a slightly different direction: he recognizes that, in literature at least, there is more than one "culture" a writer might reflect, even if her writing is conventional. And Bannon, he suggests, wisely gravitated to "the dormitories, the apartments, and bars" because they were the places where melodrama might be realistic after all. Implicitly, that is, a lesbian melodrama of "the courts" or "the battlefields" would not have been realist in the 1950s and 1960s (as it is today: witness Barbra Streisand's court-and-battlefield lesbian melodrama about navy colonel Grethe Cammemeyer, ousted from the military because of her homosexuality) because those other contexts had not yet been politicized by "daily struggle" for a lesbian identity.[2]

In other words, for Weinstein, Bannon's characters—college girls and Village loiterers—are realist reflections of a messed-up culture not because Bannon is a bad writer whose badness is the least common denominator of historical truth; instead, her characters are perversely accurate reflections of a melodramatic culture because of her subcultural choices. She chose the right setting, Weinstein says, and the rightness of that choice—to "storm the low" end of culture by taking a look at the pizza-delivery dykes and elevator operator lesbians in the Village, and not its bohemians or its artists—is more important to him than the quality of her writing. Indeed, when Weinstein does touch on the limitations of Bannon's prose, calling it "wooden" with overexplanations of characters' motives, he is quick to argue that Bannon's padded prose is a function of her desire to "protect" her characters from too-raw representation, as if she is "afraid to exhibit her people without herself as buffer" (9).

Simply put, Weinstein gives Bannon more credit than Loewenstein does. One reason for this may be that Weinstein's article in the *Voice* was written when Naiad Press began reprinting Bannon's novels in 1983. That republication, which postdates Loewenstein's essay, decisively moved Bannon's novels from underground, word-of-mouth distribution to a commercial plateau of accessibility. This new accessibility has implications for the books' canonical relation to the lesbian and gay movement, as well as for the genre status of the books, and Weinstein picks up on them:

> Are reprinted potboilers still potboilers? Naiad's jacket notes call these novels "lesbian classics," and whatever their initial genre strategy, they have become something other than train-station propaganda. Passage of time, and liberating action—for which Bannon may have planted some of the seeds—have pushed *Odd Girl Out* and the others into history, gay and lesbian history. These stories were brave, original, and sly. They still are. Readers will recognize the ghost of the old potboiler, but the books have won another life. (9)

If, for Loewenstein, Bannon's novels must be wrenched from behind denial to be claimed queer history, for Weinstein the novels are actors in a liberation struggle whose victory has been the swerving of history into alignment with their claim for the interest of lesbian lives. In his version of the story, the genre of Bannon's fiction has shifted not because of a shared pain but because of shared victories. Indeed, we might say that in highlighting victories over traumas, Weinstein himself makes a genre choice about how to experience retrospection, a choice between genres as modes of pathos.

Suzanna Danuta Walters, in her 1989 essay "As Her Hand Crept Slowly Up Her Thigh: Ann Bannon and the Politics of Pulp" also reclaims Bannon, but unlike either Loewenstein or Weinstein, she does so by emphasizing the sexiness of her novels—which were, after all, devoured by readers looking for exactly that, sex between women. Walters is writing about the pulps for an academic audience—her essay appeared in *Social Text*—but she is also concerned that the language of literary criticism not eviscerate the genre, which she fears may be "rendered abstract and safe" by theory. She focuses, therefore, on the "radical sensuousness" of Bannon's novels, seeing in her characters' sex lives a way to ensure that the books not be too easily categorized according to formalist principles (83). Sex, for Walters, outpaces literary form; she sees form as more a product of academic analysis than of writerly traditions or imperatives.

Walters is, however, very concerned with the category of genre, because like her counterparts she understands that the mobility of Bannon's novels through genre categories has something to do with who has been reading them. Right away, she distinguishes the sex-saturated pulps from pornography—but not on the basis of content. "The Bannon pulps not only distinguished themselves [from porn] through their female *authorship* but through their female *audience* as well; an audience that was reading as much for the pleasure of self-confirmation as it was for the pleasure of the text" (84). Audience, then, and particular types of audience identification, make it possible for the pulps to escape being merely pornography, especially the pornography of "voyeuristic titillation" produced by men reading lesbian texts.

This idea of pornography as that which excludes self-confirmation in favor of "the pleasure of the text" flies in the face of the *Roth*-based test of obscenity the Supreme Court applied to the muscle magazines in the same era: according to that test, it was exactly self-confirmation that marked texts as pornographic. If foot-fetishists and gay men could become themselves reading certain kind of materials, then those materials were obscene because the selves excited by them were "prurient." Walters sees self-confirmation as liberating, however, which necessarily puts in parentheses all the copiously described agonies of Bannon's characters and prevents us from recognizing that, if gay male materials escaped censors by virtue of subtlety—we might say by the pleasure of the text—then lesbian materials escaped them by virtue of self-inflicted punishment, the price for the "self-confirming," uncloseted storylines.

Walters' argument in favor of the pulps as "self-confirming" is stronger when she describes the ambiguous class position the pulps occupied in mid-century lesbian life. "On the one hand," she writes,

> we had the appearance of new organizations such as the Mattachine Society and the Daughters of Bilitis [DOB] which ostensibly attempted the assimilation of gay women into the mainstream culture by attacking stereotypical and "negative" images of lesbians. Yet these organizations often found themselves at odds with the "other" lesbians—the bar dykes, often working class women whose affectional preference included engagement in "butch/fem" interactions. Butch/fem lesbians were seen by much of the leadership of DOB as helping to perpetuate negative stereotypes about lesbians. (85)

Despite the fact that pulps novels like Bannon's described "interactions" largely understandable in the terms of butch/femme gender style and bar culture, Walters adds, the pulps were a primary source of information about lesbians in the 1950s and 1960s, and so "could not be ignored" by groups like the Daughters of Bilitis. Far from seeing them as "perpetuating negative stereotypes about lesbians," Walters reads the sexuality in Bannon's novels as offering a positive model for lesbian agency: "The presence of an active and directed sexuality in these books both explodes the genre as well as redirects the content from the more overt determinism to a more complex mixture of determinism, choice, and sexual politics" (90). The "determinism" to which Walters refers is the idea that lesbians are helplessly, ineluctibly lesbians; by her focus on sexual activity and not on, say, personality, Walters seeks to highlight the aspect of defiant choice in lesbian identity.

Unfortunately, merely to highlight sex as a locus of historical agency for lesbians is not enough for Walters, who is determined to read that sex as *authentic* as well as subversive: "For these novels not only speak to us of lived history, but carry on a dialogue with high culture critics everywhere who would rather pore over Woolf one more time than dirty their hands with pop-cult smut" (90). This interpretation is paired with an assessment of her own practice as a critic:

> Have I now rescued Bannon from the clutches of the smut-brokers and safely delivered her to the (co-op) doorsteps of the friendly neigh-

borhood Literary Critic? I hope not, for it is precisely in Bannon's smuttiness and pulp sensibility that the subversiveness is located. . . .

Read these books, then, as cultural history, as political intervention, as sign-system. But read them as smut too. At the same time. And see what happens. (99)

The disagreement I have with Walters is not with her celebration of "smut," per se, but rather with the role she wants to give it, of "real" politics, in which sex is always "self-confirming" and self-confirmation is always subversive ("everywhere"). Much is lost in such a reading, as even a quick glance back at Andrea Loewenstein's memorialization of mid-century lesbian pain suggests. One wishes, reading these accounts, for a perspective on lesbian pulp that factors in both pain and sexual agency, both realism and melodrama, both the materiality of lesbians' bodies and the textuality of their fantasies, without insisting that one or another element of such pairs is the real part, that takes the idea of lesbian authenticity as a problem of oppression and not a solution to it. Luckily, the pulps themselves oblige.

Body-Plots: Gender and Narrative in Ann Bannon

What is it about Bannon's novels that has sparked and sustained such a variety of identifications? I hope to show in what follows that the powerful emotional pull of her fiction has not only to do with seriality or sexual autonomy or pain but also with the travails of Bannon's characters as they try to understand the relationship between their bodies and their desires. In particular, I believe Bannon's understanding of lesbian sexuality as gender-inverted is what makes the novels compelling to contemporary readers. All Bannon's protagonists are depicted as beautifully misembodied, women in boy-men's bodies or boys in women's bodies; and the anguish of this misembodied position is the emotional crux for all five of Bannon's novels, as well as the place where she foregrounds the question of what an authentic lesbian is. I also suggest that Bannon's critics, trying to understand historical and genre change by locating the origins of the lesbian and gay liberation movement somewhere in her writing, reproduce this inversion model, along with its concern with reality and authenticity, unwittingly transferring it from the characters to the novels.

Although Bannon wrote *Beebo Brinker* last in her five-volume series, the book serves as a prologue to all later adventures (kind of like the Henry plays) and introduces Beebo as a seventeen-year-old ingenue, free of the layers of cynicism and loneliness that will so thoroughly mark her character in the other novels. From the start, Bannon depicts Beebo as a bodily freak, but a beautiful one, and emphatically links her body and comportment to her destiny or to her prospects for love. In this early scene, Bannon's gay male protagonist, Jack Mann, is watching the young Beebo, whom he has invited to stay in his Village apartment: "She was a strangely winning girl. Despite her size, her pink cheeks and firm-muscled limbs, she seemed to need caring for. At one moment she seemed wise and sad beyond her years, like a girl who has been forced to grow up in a hothouse hurry. At the next, she was a picture of rural naïveté that moved Jack; made him like her and want to help her" (15). Later, when Beebo is in anguish over the possibility that she might be gay, she brings up the boyishness of her body as evidence. Jack tries to reassure her—"Your body is boyish, but there's nothing *wrong* with it"—but she insists that she is an invert, or a mutant: "There's a boy inside it," she says of her body. "Long before I knew anything about sex I knew I wanted to be tall and strong and wear pants and ride horses and have a career . . . and never marry a man or learn to cook or raise babies. Never" (50). She tells Jack, finally, that she grew up thinking "all homosexual girls were three-quarters boy" and that "they were all doomed to love feminine girls who could never love them back" (51).

For the young Beebo, the experience of being misembodied is continuous with her sense of gender identity and with her sexuality: she has a boy's body, she wants to enjoy the life accorded to men, and she desires femininity in a partner. Later, in Bannon's stories of postadolescent lesbian life, Beebo will emerge as that magical character, the butch, who can accommodate this continuity without necessarily wanting to be a man; but at the outset, this dysphoria is Beebo's organizing experience. And for Bannon, this adolescent anguish of not having orchestrated sex and gender and embodiment is the source of emotional response to Beebo. It makes Jack, for instance, feel solicitous toward her. Indeed, her "rural naïveté," like the "3-B" of *The Girls in 3-B,* or the girls on "Third Street," becomes a spatial manifestation of her gender freakishness or gorgeousness that inspires sweetness in the gay man watching her, and sexual fascination in the women she meets: "You're not from around here, are you?"

This is a way of saying that bodies and sexual desires, for Bannon, are always and directly linked to other means of understanding a self, especially other means of certifying that self as normal or viable. Part of the project of Bannon's books, of course, is to present homosexuality as an acceptable identity—and, more than that, as an acceptable *life*. So when Bannon describes Beebo's young butch body, she is trying not only to get at the root of Beebo's desires but to get at the source of her specialness, the source of her claim to be treated with dignity.

This nexus of bodily, sexual, and personal claims is most vividly articulated in Bannon's novels by the villains, whom she uses concisely to voice the spectrum of objections to homosexuality as a life. In *Beebo Brinker,* that villain is Leo Bogardus, the husband and manager of Beebo's film-star girlfriend, Venus Bogardus. Through a chain of events too arcane to describe here in detail, Beebo ends up moving to Hollywood with Venus before a scheming former lover in New York notifies the press, sparking the possibility of a career-ruining scandal for Venus, who must then ask Beebo to leave. While Beebo is still trying to make a go of it with Venus in the shadows of Hollywood fame, however, she must contend with Leo, who is at once sexually jealous of Beebo and professionally concerned that his wife's lesbian dalliance will dry up his best source of income. It is out of Leo's mouth we hear the homophobia that is the obverse of the language of Beebo's anguish. In the following exchange, in which Leo accuses Beebo of threatening Venus's career, he dismisses Beebo by defending his prejudices with a stunning self-awareness:

> "Nothing is innocent," Leo said flatly. "Especially not a classy young butch on the make."
>
> "Damn it, Leo," she said. "I'm clean, I'm healthy, I've worked hard all my life. And so help me God, I'm not ashamed of being what I can't *help* being. That's the road to madness." Her cheeks were crimson.
>
> "Well said, Beebo," he acknowledged calmly. "You're right—but so am I. You might as well face up to the world's opinion. I speak for the ordinary prejudiced guy, too busy to learn tolerance, too uninformed to give a damn. We are in the majority. I admire your guts but not your

person. As for the intolerance, it's mostly emotional and illogical. I can't help it and neither can most men." (163)

When Leo says, "I speak for the ordinary prejudiced guy," he sounds as if he has stepped onto the creaky floorboards of an Everyman play; he is certainly voicing opinions that his own person does not hold because he is not a person: he is a type. On the other hand, if we try to take Leo's statements as the product of a person's thinking, he becomes a fascinating homophobe indeed, partly because he does not resort to the language of what is natural and godly in order to make his denunciation of Beebo. Instead, he defends the structure (not the origins) of his opinions: he is "too busy," "too uninformed." This self-characterization matches Beebo's perfectly in terms of its recourse to broad, rather than specific, explanations: if Leo is busy and uninformed, Beebo is "clean" and "healthy" and has "worked hard all [her] life."

What I am trying to establish here is that Bannon is focused less on the origins and more on the ongoing consequences of homosexuality, even as she roots it deeply in her characters' bodies. It is important, in other words, that Bannon tell us both things: Beebo has a boy's physique, and she has worked hard all her life. In this pairing, "I'm a person too" coincides eerily with "I'm in the wrong body"—which creates out of the question of embodiment a notion of homosexuality as daily, as an ongoing dilemma of dignity. This pairing keeps the pathos of Beebo's embodiment active at the level of the plot, not just within the confines of character description. And in the novels dealing with Beebo's adult love affairs—much darker novels— Bannon makes Beebo's body and gender the locus of terrible violence.

Women in the Shadows is the third of Bannon's series, and it is the story of Beebo's long, miserable breakup with her girlfriend, Laura. Reading this book is extremely painful: characters that retained hints of good humor in the two earlier books seem to have lost everything in their repertoires except cutting sarcasm, and most of them are bitterly, exuberantly alcoholic. Bannon depicts Beebo in particular as capable of murdering Laura out of jealousy, as capable of brutally assaulting her. Oddly, Beebo turns out to be the victim of the brutal assault in the novel: she is followed home by a gang of toughs, who rape her repeatedly and then murder Beebo and Laura's dog, Nix. This, at least, is what Beebo tells Laura. Later it is revealed that Beebo not only beat herself bloody but killed the dog too in an attempt to make Laura stay with her out of pity. This horrifying sequence is presaged by a monologue Beebo delivers to Nix, her eventual victim, about how Laura cannot love her because she is in the wrong body.

> "Come here, dog. Help me think of something. . . . I'd sell my soul to be an honest-to-god male. I could marry Laura! I could marry her. Give her my name. Give her kids . . . oh, wouldn't that be lovely? So lovely. . . .
>
> "But Nix," she went on, and her face fell, "she wouldn't have me. My baby is gay, like me. She wants a woman. Would God she wanted me. But a woman, all the same. She'd never take a man for a mate." (28)

Indeed, Laura makes an attempt to escape both Beebo and the vicissitudes of her own lesbianism by moving in with Jack Mann, Bannon's gay male protagonist. Jack, whom Bannon uses to mix dry wit and an outsider's perspective into her narratives, feels wrenched by his homosexuality despite his good humor: he is masculine and "normal" appearing and cannot reconcile himself to his desire for other men. So he persuades Laura to marry him, and they arrange to indulge their homosexual desires discreetly, on the side, while they mock up a marriage on the heterosexual model at home. This move permanently alienates Jack from Beebo, who had been a close friend when she first moved to the Village. After Laura moves, however, Bannon depicts Jack and Beebo as gender opposites—both queer but offering opposing choices for Laura.[3]

Women in the Shadows offers Laura a third erotic choice in the character of Tris, a seventeen-year-old dancer who claims to be Indian and from New Delhi but who, we discover, is actually a light-skinned African American and married to a man. Tris speaks in a clipped imitation of British-Indian English, scents herself with jasmine, and tells Laura nothing about her marriage, recounting instead her frustrated sexual attachments to the gay male dancers she befriends. She is, in other words, Bannon's figure for the "shadows" of the title, which seem to stand for indecision about self, uncertainty about fate—and, in Tris's case—confusion about race and sexuality all at once. And while Bannon generally avoids the topic of race in her novels, a brief exchange between Laura and Tris on vacation at the beach in Long Island reveals that, when Bannon does address racial identity, she places it in the same nexus of body and plot in which she places lesbian sexuality—indeed, she figures race as a kind of sexuality.⁴ Just before this passage, Tris, who has not yet revealed to Laura that she is black, has lashed out at Laura for admiring the color of her skin, calling her "a dirty hypocrite." A moment later, though, she softens.

> Tris said, "Did you ever notice, when we lie on the bed together, how we look?"
>
> Laura finished, "Yes, I noticed." She looked at Tris in surprise. It wasn't like her to mention such things. "Me so white and you so brown. It looks like poetry, Tris. Like music, if you could see music. And inside, we're just the other way around. Isn't it funny? I'm the one who's always on fire. And you're the iceberg." She laughed a little. "Maybe I can melt you," she said.
>
> "Better not. The brown comes off," Tris said cynically, but her strange thought excited Laura.
>
> "God, what a queer idea!" Laura said. "You'd have to touch me everywhere then, every corner of me, till we were both the same color. Then you'd be almost white and I'd be almost tan—and yet we'd be the same." (95)

This romantic understanding of paired racial identities as opposites that merge and average each other out is, in one form or another, a trope in much twentieth-century representation of lesbians.⁵ Of course this conciliatory "poetry" of racial difference is arguably a way of depoliticizing it, of whitening the black—it is true that Laura, in this fantasy, darkens in contact with Tris, but where Tris becomes "white," a specifically racial category, Laura merely becomes "tan." If the bodies of Laura and Tris are implicitly in the service of a discourse of "opposites" that formalizes the politics out of racial difference, though, they are also enmeshed in Bannon's poetics of gender inversion: Laura's and Tris's interiors are both "just the other way around" from their exteriors—Laura is hot-headed but pale, where Tris is sexually cool but physically glowing. Race, in other words, is not only formalized in the service of sexual aesthetics; it is also made a metaphor for the opposition between inside and outside that govern Bannon's sense of what a lesbian is. And this pair of interior-exterior oppositions, which merge in the more "poetic" racial opposition between the two women, previews the novel's plot through its characters' bodies: Laura and Tris will break up because of what we might call the "iceberg on fire" problem.

I should be clear that Bannon does not leave Laura unmarked by the trials of this discourse of inside-outside opposites. As a white woman, and as a femme able to pass for straight, Laura might seem able to evade anything but the lightest poetic touch of the language of matched pairs of genders and bodies. But Bannon shows Laura deeply scarred by the anguish of the vocabulary of gender inversion, in her relation both to her butch lover and to her own femme body. Indeed, Bannon brings Laura in for a characterological drubbing, giving her perhaps the cruelest lines in all five novels. Here, at the beginning of their relationship (portrayed in *I Am a Woman*), Laura mocks Beebo for working as an elevator operator, a job Beebo chose so she could wear pants to work: "'You're ridiculous,' she said. 'You're a little girl trying to be a little boy. And you run an elevator for the privilege. Grow up, Beebo. You'll never be a little boy. Or a big boy. You just haven't got what it takes. Not all the elevators in the world can make a boy of you. You can wear pants till you're blue in the face and it won't change what's underneath'" (175). "Internalized homophobia" hardly does justice to this vituperation, which violently literalizes and decontextualizes Beebo from exactly the features of her sexuality—her work, her clothes—that make her butchness three-dimensional and alive. By insisting on this terribly narrow story of gender inversion, by taking the elevators out of Beebo's sexuality, Laura returns them both to a brutal ground floor in which desire is always the desire for something real, instead of something living, and every demand is a demand for total validation, or for total destruction—in which there is no distinction between hatred and self-hatred. Bannon makes this clear at the end of *Women in the Shadows,* when Laura returns to Beebo and asks Beebo to kill her the way she killed Nix (165).

Laura lives with a dysphoria about her body that is at the root of her motivations just as much as Beebo's butch body is at the root of hers. Laura, who is as femme as Beebo is butch, also experiences a foundational disjunction between her body and her desires. In *Odd Girl Out,* the first novel of Bannon's series, Laura tries to come to terms with falling in love with her sorority sister, Beth Cullison (herself the protagonist of another novel, *Journey to a Woman*); but she cannot believe she is a lesbian, because she does not have a lesbian body. She looks at herself in the mirror:

She had breasts and full hips like other girls. She wore lipstick and curled her hair. Her brow, the crook in her arms, the fit of her legs — everything was feminine. She held her fists to her cheeks and stared out the window at the gathering night and begged God for an answer.

She thought that homosexual women were great strong creatures in slacks with brush cuts and deep voices; unhappy things, standouts in a crowd. She looked back at herself, hugging bosom as if to comfort herself, and she thought, "I don't want to be a boy. I don't want to be like them. I'm a *girl*. I *am* a girl. That's what I want to be. But if I'm a girl, why do I love a girl? What's wrong with me?" (64)

Where Beebo defends herself with the justification that she is "clean and healthy" and has worked hard all her life, Laura turns for consolation to the idea that she obliges all the visible signs of gender. She *is* a girl; and, furthermore, she *wants* to be a girl. The sheer pressure on young Laura at this moment reveals that declaration of wanting as taking place in the register of aspiration, however: Laura wants to be a girl not only because she is a girl but because she might not be one.

It is not Laura, though, whom Bannon endows with lesbian authenticity when she draws her series to a close—it is Beebo. *Journey to a Woman* is the story of Laura's old college flame, Beth Cullison, who leaves the man for whom, in *Odd Girl Out,* she left Laura and embarks on a quest to relocate her. The twist in the novel, of course, is that Laura and Beth's reunion does not strike any flames but leads Beth—eventually, complicatedly—into Beebo's arms. Beth's "journey" is, like Laura's and Beebo's, prefigured on her body—or, in Beth's case, in her sexual choices. She leaves her husband, Charlie, with their two children, and she pretends not to have any children at all when people in New York ask her about her past. Beth turns out to have a whole alternative past waiting for her in New York, however. Everyone in the Village, when they figure out who she is, exclaims, "Oh, you're . . . Beth!" Laura's lost love, it turns out, is public knowledge.

Between her flight from marriage and motherhood, on the one hand, and the prematerialized existence with which Village gossip endows her, on the other, Beth charts a course across the novel that recapitulates, compressed, the variations on life happiness Bannon imagines as possible for lesbians. Beth starts out wracked by the guilt of feeling "unnatural" for not wanting the care of her own children; then, scrambling to find Laura in New York, locates her only to realize that Laura, married to a gay man and raising a child of her own, is not the adoring college girl whom it was so easy to reject. Beth spirals into a month-long alcoholic stupor after this shock and finds herself in bed with Nina, a writer of "lesbian fiction," who, in a fascinating turn, seems to represent for Bannon an overanalytic hopelessness about lesbian life ("She's a shrewd girl," says Beebo, "and she's made quite a success of this writing bit. But she has to analyze everybody") (140). The novel climaxes with Beth being held in her hotel room at gunpoint by Vega, a closeted and self-hating model instructor with whom Beth had an affair in California before she left Charlie. Vega, in a despair of jealousy and loneliness, kills herself instead of Beth and leaves her, exhausted and disoriented, to be picked up by Beebo.

I rehearse the manic plot of this novel because it represents Bannon's attempt to tie up the loose ends from the earlier novels, and because the way Bannon goes about bringing the five-book story to a close is to place the butch, timeworn but reliable, at the end of what is certainly, by page 223, the long and winding road. In other words, all Beth's other sexual options are gradually eliminated by the end of the novel by virtue of their untenability in the long term: her husband, Charlie, stands for an impossible heterosexual cover life; the older, wiser Laura, who rejects Beth, represents the impossibility of sustaining a lesbian identity that always returns to the moment of self-discovery; Nina, writing her novels practically at the same time she lives them, figures in literary production the cynicism and opportunism of Village life, since she is always seeking new lovers for new "material"; and Vega, whose murderous violence is written on her body as scars from an unsuccessful surgery, stands for the kind of self-hatred that plagued Laura and Beebo in the middle two novels. Not so much a narrativization of her own body, then, as a vantage from which to view everyone else's, Beth becomes for Bannon an Everylesbian who must walk—"journey"—her way through the other novels until she arrives at Beebo's doorstep, where Beebo, by forty, can embody her lesbian self as a lesbian *life*.

Beth, having survived two days of questioning in jail after Vega's suicide, is conveniently homeless at the start of chapter twenty-three. She goes to Laura and Jack's apartment, where, reconciled, she and Laura rehash their emotions pulp-therapy style ("The less we say to each other, the happier we are together") (217). When Beebo joins them—she had rescued Beth from her drunken meanderings before the standoff with Vega—Beth begins to recognize her attraction to Beebo: "She felt a slow, lovely enchantment going through her at the sight of Beebo; just the sight of her tired, handsome face pleased her oddly in a new and special way" (222). Beebo, "tired and handsome," begins to take on a post-violent butchness that recuperates what Laura so violently took away in the earlier novels: the work of a life. While years before, Laura mocked Beebo for working in an elevator, for Beth and Beebo the elevator down from Laura's apartment, which they take together, becomes a place for confession and trust.

> "It's funny," Beth said. "I was coming up in this elevator a couple of hours ago and wondering how I'd feel when I went down again. Scared and ashamed, or just glad it was all over."
>
> "Which is it?" Beebo said, leaning against the wall of the elevator and looking at her.
>
> "Neither," Beth admitted, smiling.
>
> "What, then?"
>
> "I guess it's closest to . . . a sort of happiness," she confessed shyly. "Or hopefulness, maybe." (222)

This emotion, which Bannon finally pushes past ellipsis and into speech, is what Bannon has been leading her readers to for four novels: the relief of finding, in butchness, something strong and vital. She does not alter her always implicit rendering of Beebo as cross-gendered—even here, at the last moment, she has Beebo tell Beth, "For the love of women, I've made a fool of myself, just like most of the men I know"—but now, at the last, she augments that rendition of butchness-as-maleness with something different: "looking into Beebo's fine, worn face [Beth] felt a solid reassurance. Beebo's eyes promised shelter, they promised love. . . . Beebo's strong hands held her shoulders. 'I understand, baby,' she said softly. 'I understand'" (223). It is solidity—in Beebo's face, in her eyes, in her hands—that Beth responds to and solidity that Bannon offers as the implied definition of the difference between butchness and maleness. Maleness, signified by wearing pants, is simply an index of conformity to laws of gender; but butchness, signified by wearing pants to work in, wearing pants for years, is too layered, too cumulative, to be simplified into a yes-no, male-or-not tabulation.[6] And the promise of the butch is that she "understands"—she has been there too, the places of denigration, of gender misery—in a way a man could not. It is as if Bannon, over the course of four novels, has so worn out the explanatory possibilities of her inversion model of gender, has so thoroughly tested which disastrous relationships it can produce that she arrives exhausted and almost by mistake (a little like Beebo herself) at an experiental understanding of lesbian sexuality in which there is actually room to live. There, in the confessional-elevator, Bannon has brought her lesbians home.

Conclusion: The Pleasures of Forbidden Love

If the Beebo Brinker novels offer readers, at the end of their narrative arc, another way to understand lesbian sexuality, it might be said that in doing so they outpace their latter-day reviewers. All three of the writers discussing Bannon whom I address earlier in this chapter—Andrea Loewenstein, Jeff Weinstein, and Suzanna Danuta Walters—remain in the same gravitational field in their characterizations of Bannon's genre mobility across time. What I mean is that these commentators all interpret the pulps as possessing a genre doubleness or inversion by which they seem to be one kind of writing but turn out to be another. For Loewenstein, this means describing the pulps as blind cliché on the outside but with an anguished realist interior that becomes visible only with erosion on their language (the "pain which is behind the clichéd writing"). Similarly, for Weinstein, the pulps look melodramatic on the outside ("melodrama [throws] its arms around the arenas of daily '50s gay struggle"), but their melodrama is merely a vehicle by which Bannon has "backed into a kind of gay realism of her time." And Walters grudgingly acknowledges that the novels look like "cultural history" and "sign-system" on the outside but affirms that they are "smut" down deep, so that the best way to read them is two ways at once.

This bifocal reading practice is the formal response to the ambivalence that puts quotation marks around the word and the genre "pulp," preserving its soft interior with an armor of historical distance—or, in some cases, softening the accrued hardness of its age with a warm readerly identification that brings it into the present tense, as memorial, as subversive action, as smut. Such ambivalence is a kind of historiographical theory that repeats, in retrospect, the technique of plot Bannon so consistently employed in her writing, which was to propel characters into confrontation with their divided selves. But where Bannon's latter-day reviewers fall short of Bannon herself is in hunting primarily for their realism—by separating what they seem to be (pulp) from what they really are ("pulp"). Bannon, at least in her key descriptions of Beebo, manages to extricate herself from a concern with what is "real" about Beebo and to focus instead on her allure—which is the result both of her depicted experience and of the artifice that goes into making her part of what Barbara Grier calls Bannon's "all-star cast." The bifocal readings of Bannon that result from seeing the novels as genre inverted, then, are admirable in one sense because they are layered readings. But they are layered at the price of relegating to the past the aspect of fantasy that gives Beebo such strong hands. Realism and fantasy are assigned one place each in these readings, either by ascribing to the past a realism that can be eroticized as a present-tense fantasy or by unveiling a contemporary realism that miraculously overcomes its earlier fantasy-clouded melodrama.

There is a fine counter-example to this mode of interpreting the pulps, however. Aerlyn Weissman and Lynne Fernie's 1992 documentary *Forbidden Love* frames interviews with Canadian lesbians who were young in the 1950s with a mocked-up pulp romance, so that between documentary passages we are treated to short episodes in the seduction of a wide-eyed femme ingenue, which culminates, at the end of the film's present tense, with the femme and her butch lover turning to the camera in defiance of any judgment a cold, harsh world might dare to pass on them. Cutting between the interviews and the pulp romance, I suggest, allows Weissman and Fernie delightfully to short-circuit the split between a melodramatic, clichéd past and a realist present and to reveal the lesbian past *and* present as a pas de deux between fantasized roles and the experiences that criss-cross them. The result is a kind of pleasure-in-history that celebrates the past as a terrain for the intermixing, and not the categorical separation, of both memorial and play—which is one way of saying such pleasure celebrates, as well, the intermixing of the past and the present.

Two features of *Forbidden Love* help Weissman and Fernie achieve this effect: first, their shifting among types of footage during the same voice-over, from old photographs of the interviewees to National Film Board propaganda to panning shots of lesbian pulp novel covers and so on, and second, the moments in the interviews when it becomes clear that the women being interviewed were themselves bemused by the conventions of lesbian culture that contemporary viewers tend to respond to laughingly, not least the primacy of butch-femme roles in bar culture. Both these features of the film suggest the intermixing of fantasy with historical experience *and* historical retrospection because of the way the pulp covers are turned into a present-tense and not merely a past fantasy by their serialized rejuvenation in the film and because of the savvy recognition of the women being interviewed that certain kinds of fantasy—especially butch-femme role-playing—were crucial to structuring their present tense back in the 1950s. This intermixing creates a pleasing sense of historical continuity in lesbian life between past and present and between experience and imagination.

Forbidden Love opens in its past tense, with a young heterosexual couple in a farm truck, racing along country roads to get to the train station. To viewers familiar with the conventions of pulp novels, it becomes clear within moments that the young man driving the truck is reluctantly taking his girl friend to say good-bye to her best girl friend, who is leaving town in a real hurry. At the station, "Meg" leaps out of the truck and runs to "Laura's" side, where Laura begs her to run away with her. Firmly but wistfully, Meg refuses, leaving Laura with a heart-shaped locket on a gold chain. We see Meg running into the arms of her waiting boy friend—and then a shot of Laura, hat tilted to one side, the steam of the train rising behind her as she is called on board, who lifts her hand to wave good-bye. And in the last second before the opening credits, the locket in her waving hand fires off a bright blue twinkle, like a star, whose flare is accompanied with a single high musical ding. Then a long shot, which establishes the signature technique of the film: the actress playing Laura is painted over and turned into a pulp novel heroine, over whom the words "Forbidden Love" appear in dime-store bold type, as Connie Francis begins to sing, "I was / Such a fool . . ."

Every audience I have ever watched this film with laughs in recognition when the locket flashes, and I think it would be reductive to say that we are laughing because we suddenly recognize the fictional register the flash signals as "just" fantasy; rather, it has always seemed to me that the laughter the locket's flash ignites is a recognition of the sweet *persistence* of melodramatic fantasy, a recognition that it can only work itself into larger narratives, that it will find its way onto the page or the screen by making use of whatever surface it can find—that it is irrepressible. I think we enjoy moments that signal a relief from the ideology of historical realism because they explain our own occluded vision, which is to say we understand that our biographies, especially our love biographies, are themselves overwritten by a retrospect that clings hopefully to bright surfaces. Such moments are especially pleasurable as a form of recognition when the fantasy they signal is complicitly subcultural—it can hurt to be a gay girl in love—and when it is enjoyed by a large audience.

Viewers of *Forbidden Love* are not the only ones alert to such pleasures. The producers and interviewees are also clearly aware that lesbian history, whether understood as a struggle with the outside world or as an erotic journey within lesbian culture, remains vital in the present because it has never really finished itself; it never produced "real," completed lesbians so much as lesbians who lived back then. The women of the past moved "in the shadows," as it were, between reality registers: between homophobic fantasies of lesbian life and the lived experience of it or between lesbian role-playing and a wry awareness of its limitations. The first interview is exemplary in this regard. Reva Hutkin, of Victoria, British Columbia, talks to the camera about being married in the late 1940s at age twenty-one but being deeply involved with a woman friend who eventually began passing along lesbian fiction to her. Finally the friend tells Hutkin that she is "like . . . that," meaning like the women in the novels. Hutkin recounts with amusement her initial panic ("Oh no! Not like *that*, whatever 'that' was") and then describes leaving her husband to live with this friend as a lover.

Hutkins's story turns to a description of going with her lover to Greenwich Village "to find the lesbians," since, as she puts it, "At one point we thought, well, all the lesbians obviously live in New York in Greenwich Village, at least the books said that's where they all lived, so we decided we had to go and find The Lesbians!" She describes putting on her "best butch clothing" and asking taxi drivers in New York where to look but says, "I don't know . . . we never found them," musing that perhaps The Lesbians were elsewhere, or that she and her girlfriend simply did not recognize them, since "they weren't wearing butch and femme things!"

Perhaps the best example of the dangerous and playful intangibility of "real" lesbian identity comes from Weissman and Fernie's interview with a woman named Lois M. Stuart, who describes being perpetually harrassed by men outside women's bars and deciding, one night, to put up with it no more. Recalling a confrontation with a group of threatening men on the sidewalk, she says: "I just pulled my jacket back and put my hand in my pocket, you know, and said something stupid like, 'I'm wearing a knife and I know how to use it.' Which is utterly ridiculous, I know how to peel potatoes, but that's about it. However, it worked!"

The lesbians of the past were not real, then, in the sense that they never superceded fantasies of what a lesbian was, thereby arriving at some untainted lesbian identity that might then map onto a later literary realism. This does not mean they did not exist as lesbians; it means their lesbianism was as vital, risky, and compellingly incomplete as any contemporary lesbian identity. Weissman and Fernie pay tribute to this continuity of fantasy and experience, and past and present, in the closing sequence to *Forbidden Love,* in which the fictional Laura ecstatically consummates her seduction by Mitch, the butch who has picked her up in a bar. They turn the next morning to the rituals of postcoital familiarity: Mitch brings Laura coffee in bed; they make a private joke about coffee being "her favorite" (which is what Laura said of the drink Mitch bought her the night before, kicking off their romance). And as they laugh they turn to face the camera, indicating an awareness of the melodramatic voice-over that has just filled the air, saying, "Laura thought she would be caught in the hideous trap of warped desires—instead she found her wildest dreams had come true. Now she knew what she was for sure: a Lesbian!"

I end with this voice-over, of whose arrival Mitch and Laura have been uncannily aware throughout the film, turning from their seduction obligingly to face the audience as they become painted over into pulp novel covers. This final voice-over counter-inflects the word *lesbian* with all the melodramatic glee that its mid-century speakers could never have dreamed, exclaiming it, capitalizing it exactly as the homophobic pulp novel covers did but reversing its affect. It also becomes a horizonal point for Mitch and Laura, who, having been frozen out of their conversation with each other, must now face us and withdraw into art, two lesbian angels of history, whose receding silence in the face of our scrutiny is not allowed to deaden just yet, not while the word Walter Benjamin might have called messianic, the impossibly inflected word, hovers in the air. The voice of the past speaks a word unknowable to the past in this closing sequence and reminds us by our inarticulate laughter (the moment is funny) that the bodies of these women, rejuvenated by documentary and fiction alike, have aged as we will age, not realistically, but melodramatically, in anguish and delight, into history.

CONTEXTS AND

AFTERLIVES

This book began as an attempt to understand how certain kinds of strong emotion could make some early- and mid-twentieth-century lesbian and gay writers "feel historical" despite a daily problem of feeling pathological. One answer my materials suggested was that these writers invested significant emotion in representing homosexuality as a secret relation to others, rather than a gendered inversion of self. This theoretical leap is not as easy as it might sound in retrospect; it demanded great imaginative energy, and sometimes patently counterfactual fantasizing, to produce different and more sociable theories of homosexuality than the ones offered by medical science and religious custom. It is also true that these theories are never entirely free of the inversion model they struggle to disown and, further, that the types of relationship elaborated in such theories are often hidden relationships, or even stranded ones, which is why I find the metaphor of "foundling" imagination appropriate for artists as different as Hart Crane, Willa Cather, Ann Bannon, and Bob Mizer.

The production of these foundling dreams in word and image is not the whole story, though. A second answer to the question of how some emotions powerfully make lesbians and gay men feel connected to history seems to reside in their consumption, in the claiming of these artists by the lesbian and gay readers who have come after them. In each of my chapters I try to describe how post-Stonewall readers, though they may at first look like the living fulfillment of an earlier dream of queer community, are in fact more complexly drawn to texts like Crane's or Cather's or Bannon's or to image-text combinations like Mizer's. Part of this complexity, I think, lies in the way earlier dreams of fulfillment ambivalently highlight the historical, rather than the post-historical, condition of the present. The many ways contemporary queer readers and critics have invested pre-Stonewall writing and images with romance or nostalgia or distaste all point to the funny communicability of shadow-relations and secret emotions across time, as if they acquire heft only in the long term, where the difficulty of the problems they want to solve (like historical isolation and suffering) can emerge in their full intractability.

To be fair, it is not only self-identified gay men and lesbians with a sense of politics and history who are consuming foundling fantasies at the end of the century; nor do the fantasies being consumed necessarily date from forty or eighty years ago. Although it is hardly the dominant model of homosexuality in the United States today, the foundling allegory does have a contemporary life—especially for young people but also for those who live in, or move in and out of, the mysterious space of the closet. Richard Dyer points out the attractiveness of vampire literature to late-twentieth-century queer readers, for instance; and Ann Weinstone, in a delightful survey called "Science Fiction as a Young Person's First Queer Theory," suggests some of the myriad possibilities for constructing homosexuality out of the figures and stories of imaginative literature. In each of these examples, part of the friendliness of the genre to a homosexual fantasy life is the way sexuality can be "read into" its texts as an analogy—to, say, the romantic exile of being a "child of the night" or to the arcane technical apprenticeship of joining a Starfleet—rather than as a solitary pathology. Both genres, too, take advantage of the connection between adolescence and homosexuality as excessive modes of affective production to create readerships for whom sexuality can be in a happily suspended state of coming-to-be, not yet domesticated by the imperatives to full-time work or heterosexual reproduction.

The world of muscle culture, too, has managed to maintain a closet that sometimes seems habitable in terms akin to those of earlier days. While *Burn!* and *Men's Fitness* and *Men's Workout* make no claims to any "Grecian" brotherhood among their readers and offer no pictures of Wild West scenes and no liberationist editorials, they do still mask their homoeroticism by alibis that faintly imply a collective identity—if only the shared consumer demographic of hip, in-shape young guys who are in the know about the latest protein shakes and club music (who are, that is, not so much Greeks as Dudes). The particular reference points have changed, as have the relations of production, in gay male print culture; but there is still, clearly, collective desire for a homoerotic closet, either as a prelude to a "historical" gay identity or as a scene of prehistorical butch potential to which even the most fully self-identified gay men can return from time to time. It may be true that consuming such magazines "instead of" reading porn or reading a gay newspaper is an index of some lesser degree of gay enlightenment, although I doubt it. It seems more likely that today's muscle literature is a mass-distributed reminder of the first postulate of the physique closet: that male homosexuality is not a gender inversion but simply male sociability given a particular opportunity or scene.

We can also locate, along with mass-market fantasy and science fiction and closeted fitness magazines, contemporary "literary" foundling narratives. Some of them, like the coming-of-age stories of Jim Grimsley (*Dream Boy*) and Dorothy Allison (*Bastard Out of Carolina*), depict hardscrabble southern U.S. childhoods whose economic misery and family violence breed a passionate prepolitical sense of there being an "elsewhere" less murderous and more welcoming, of certain secret forms of difference left unnamed: queer readers of these stories are left to fill in what are, for their young protagonists, still blanks. Other narratives, like James Merrill's trio of long poems, *The Changing Light at Sandover*, depict elite, self-identified gay men constructing elaborate kinship networks out of a celestial hierarchy of dead friends, famous figures, spirit-guides, and cherubim, all of whom point chauvinistically to the superiority of queer soul. What links these otherwise class-disparate representations as latter-day foundling texts is not so much a struggle to rethink homosexuality away from the inversion model, since that cultural work is less urgent than it once was, as a struggle to articulate the disjuncture between nuclear family and individual sexuality to make it produce, not just an individual or even a couple, but an affiliative system friendly to homosexuality, even generative of it.

There is something utopian about this notion of homosexuality as affiliative; its overtones are possibly the most interesting thing to me about foundling homosexuality. It seems to me, in other words, that what the homophobic nineteenth-century ideology of homosexuality as "inversion" shares with the contemporary, anti-homophobic, U.S. ideology of homosexuality as membership in a "tribe" is the way both ideologies construe homosexuality as the property of individual persons. The limitations on this possessive understanding of homosexuality are only just becoming clear to us in the United States, where our sense of triumph at disassociating ourselves from notions of pathology has allowed us to be taken by surprise by the unexpected confusion, after the days of ACT UP and Queer Nation, over what such homosexual "persons" might be said to share or to desire. That there is no single queer leader or organization in the United States today is not a dire sign of political disarray. But it is indicative of the looming limitations of a queer politics based entirely on "our" issues: marriage, the military, protection from violence. Urvashi Vaid argues forcefully for a coalitional queer politics that includes a queer moral obligation to be part of a larger, "straight" world (34, 378); another, less humanist way of thinking about the problem of how sexuality and politics inform each other might be to say, let's think of sexuality as a mode of address, as a set of relations, lived and imagined, that are perpetually cast out ahead of our "real," present-tense personhood, as a kind of navigation, or proleptic sketch of historical futures. Foundling dreams, however "closeted" or politically dubious in literal terms, have much to teach us about this less possessive way of approaching sexuality—we might call its huddled temporalities, allergic to the present tense and couched in allegories of coming-of-age or aging or becoming historical, a mid-century example of what we now call "performativity"—if we are willing to torque the meaning of the word to include a sense of "performance" as the perpetual activity by which subjects act out what the social body might be, on their way to catching up with it, never quite knowing whether they have got it right.

I close with one more example. The youngest hero of James Baldwin's 1951 novel *Go Tell It on the Mountain* (there are several) is John Grimes, fourteen, son of a tyrannical, egotistical preacher and a timid, complaisant mother. The novel is organized around backward movements in time that flesh out the history of the relationships among the adults in John's life. But his coming-of-age—particularly his dawning awareness of both his homosexuality and the political significance of his black identity—is the novel's present tense. John's upbringing is strictly Baptist, but his sense of his sexuality and his racial identity keep pointing him toward the secular world; and this tension between his membership in the community of "the saints" and his curiosity about the world beyond the church gives an acute suspense to his dreams of what it might be like to be an adult outside his family. Indeed, it is one of Baldwin's great successes in *Go Tell It on the Mountain* to filter so many of John's perceptions through a Baptist vernacular—a technique that allows us to recognize John as "naive," since he has not yet adopted a knowing, secular irony about the world, but that also quietly and insistently sheds light for us on a religious significance to scenes a "knowing" audience might mistake for secular.

Indeed, the climax of Baldwin's novel is one of the most intense moments of foundling imagination from this period, partly because the African American religious culture Baldwin is describing allows him to make manifest a messianic undercurrent at work in so much foundling idealism. *Go Tell It on the Mountain* culminates with John on the "threshing-floor" of his father's church, experiencing—or perhaps staging—a public religious ecstasy that seems finally to insure, rather than forbid, John's movement into the secular world. His father, the preacher, clearly does not believe that John has been "saved"; but Elisha, John's best friend at church, and the boy John is secretly, silently in love with, takes John's ecstasy at face value: John is now truly his "little brother." Indeed, we can construct an implicit narrative by which the new intimacy between John and Elisha that John's passion facilitates in fact gives the fatal signal of John's homosexuality to his father, who sternly watches Elisha call John through his throes: "rise up, rise up, Brother Johnny, and talk about the Lord's deliverance" (205).

A few scholars have commented on the quiet ways the black church has sometimes made a home for its gay male members in the twentieth century (Chauncey; Garber; Harper); but at the end of this scene, John seems ready to forgo the communal possibilities his baptism may have created. Instead of suggesting that John will be able to reconcile an adult homosexuality with a life in his church, Baldwin has John turn to his beloved Elisha and wish him a strange prospective farewell: "'Elisha,' he said, 'no matter what happens to me, where I go, what folks say about me, no matter what *any*body says, you remember—please remember—I was saved. I was *there*" (220).

You might say that this book is an attempt to describe the historical force of the affect that italicizes the word *there* as Baldwin does in this scene. For John, this moment signals the possibility that his public display of religious ecstasy rather than committing him to his family and his church can operate as a message in a bottle to his beloved, a sign that will turn out to have been some historical "other" place from which the unspeakability of his love can gain audition. For us, trained a little in hearing the call of homosexuality in analogies to secret, impossible affiliations, this promissory union between communities lived and imagined can sound like a particularly historical kind of afterlife, in which the *"there"* of having been saved also houses the "there" in which being saved commits the young saint to the adventure of the secular world. I want to highlight the significance of that "there" in lesbian and gay imaginations, since unlike the story of the invert or the "member of the tribe," it lies squarely in the future-anterior of historical uncertainty—of *historical* uncertainty—with all the camp sincerity and unwitting dignity the phrase implies. So, imitating those italics, I'll leave you here.

Introduction: The Invert, the Foundling, and the "Member of the Tribe"

1   By focusing on these three terms—*invert, foundling, ethnic*—I do not mean to suggest that the only idiom available for describing gay male and lesbian identities in the early part of the twentieth century was a sexological one, imposed from without. Historians of lesbian and gay culture have described a vast array of early-twentieth-century queer identities whose terms were generated by queer subcultures themselves. George Chauncey alone reports on a vast array of identities encompassed by the "bachelor subculture" of 1910s and 1920s New York, which included working-class sailors living in tenements or in the YMCA as well as single businessmen living in apartment hotels. He also describes male-male relationships based on feminine-masculine gender roles, such as the sex feminine "fairies" would offer for sale to masculine sailors, the entertainment

provided by "pansies" in Prohibition-era speakeasies, and—outside the city, in prisons and in hobo culture—a set of relationships between "wolves" and "punks," older and younger men, the erotics of whose couplings were based in part on the youth of the "punk." Lillian Faderman offers a similarly comprehensive study of late-nineteenth- and early-twentieth-century subcultural "lesbian" identities formed in very different class contexts and institutional settings, from the "romantic friendships" of middle-class Victorian women to the solidarity of working-class prostitutes of the same era, from the erotic relationships between young women at women's colleges in the 1900s to women like "Harry Gorman," who passed as a man for years while working on the New York Central Railway, and, in the 1920s, from the defiant sexual bravado of African American women blues singers in Harlem to bohemian women like Edna St. Vincent Millay, experimenting with bisexuality in Greenwich Village. All of these identities, formed in specific subcultural settings, suggest and intersect with the more abstract formulations of gender identity that the inversion model uses to describe them. My focus here is on the literary and mass-cultural abstractions that depend on and rework these historical specifics.

2   See Adam; Chauncey; D'Emilio, *Sexual Politics;* D'Emilio and Freedman; Faderman; Kennedy and Davis.

3   Will Roscoe in particular has written a series of thoughtful essays on the historiographical and political stakes in contemporary white and Indian claiming of berdache identity, notably "Was We'Wha a Homosexual?" in which he points out that the berdache identity is itself "always-already a hybrid, a creative product of complex interactions over an extended period of contact [between whites and Indians]" (218).

4   This ambiance is rooted in social and historical practices: in its fully articulate, post-Stonewall form, the ethnicity model of U.S. homosexuality is dependent on a specifically national system of mass consumption in order to survive. Observers both inside and outside the academy have remarked on the centrality of a national consumer culture to contemporary ethnic formulations of queer identity, notably Dennis Altman in his *Homosexualization of America* (1982), and John D'Emilio, in "Capitalism and Gay Identity" (1983). In a 1993 essay called "Queer Nationality," Lauren Berlant and Elizabeth Freeman celebrate the way this link between national markets and a queer sense of peoplehood was played out in the early 1990s activism of Queer Nation. Focusing primarily on the nation as a symbolic location for the activity of "consuming nationality," Berlant and Freeman argue that Queer Nation, whose actions included traveling in large, visibly queer groups to suburban shopping malls, "makes consumer pleasure central to the transformation of public culture, thus linking the utopian promises of the commodity with those of the nation" (208).

Elsewhere, in a much less optimistic rendering of this same correlation, Daniel Harris writes,

> As homosexuals are courted by Fortune 500 companies, we will be granted the respectability we were once denied and experience a gradual social rehabilitation. This improvement in our public image will in turn mitigate the oppressive conditions in which we live and thus undermine the whole purpose of the gay sensibility. It is only a matter of time before our distinctive characteristics as a minority begin to dissolve as they are rendered superfluous by our new sense of pride as an elite sector of the consumeristic society that is absorbing us into a featureless mainstream market. (38)

Despite obvious differences in their beliefs about the role of mass consumption in contemporary queer culture, both Harris and Berlant and Freeman are trying to maintain a link between the experience of sexuality and the experience of public collectivity: Harris in a valedictory call that queer people remember the gritty, local defiance of earlier, less visible subcultural practices such as camp, diva worship, and leather; and Berlant and Freeman in a celebratory exhortation to consume queerly, to develop a "discursive field" with which to fight "a hot war of words about sex and America" (225). As most ethnicities are, then, queer ethnicity is depicted as both endangered and vital, as both the lost and the burgeoning source of a tribal culture. For historical and political accounts of the prevalence of this tension in the formation of nationalism and ethnic identity, see Anderson; Balibar and Wallerstein; Hobsbawm; and Hobsbawm and Ranger.

5 See Adam, Duyvendak, and Krouwel; Berlant and Freeman; Harris; Harper, McClintock, Muñoz, and Rosen.

6 Arjun Appadurai, in his anthropology of affiliation in global culture, which focuses primarily on Indian diaspora, suggests that queer modes of affiliation, like the "queer nationalism" Berlant and Freeman describe, may be exemplary in the way it foregrounds the element of "postnationality" in late-twentieth-century life: "The queer nation may be only the first of a series of new patriotisms, in which others could be the retired, the unemployed, and the disabled, as well as scientists, women, and Hispanics" (176). While I am very interested in Appadurai's attempt to restore a critical edge to discussions of late or postmodern nationality by filtering the category of the nation through the aspirations of sub-, trans-, or intranational groups, I am somewhat hesitant to follow his path exactly, since it seems to involve heavy dependence on a shared consumer profile. As he puts it, "There is growing evidence that the consumption of the mass media throughout the world often provokes resistance, irony, selectivity, and, in general, *agency*" (7). But the agency he goes on to describe, the agency

of local cultures consuming mass culture in idiosyncratic ways, is very hard to distinguish from the "agency" of simply changing the channel on the TV. I agree that there is something exemplary about "queer nations" old and new, specifically their tone of longing and aspiration; but I do not think that to do justice to those longings we have to take them entirely on their own terms. Their subjectivity, while radically illuminating for a historiography of desire, is not the same as—or is only the first step toward—a political practice based on affects like longing.

7   It is further true that among my materials, only Bannon's novels describe something like subcultural life; and even Bannon was not writing from within the village but from the suburbs, basing her accounts of the Village on infrequent visits. This distance from subcultural milieux also distinguishes the longing in foundling texts from those other U.S. queer texts of the period, such as the writings of Allen Ginsberg and William Burroughs, or the films of Kenneth Anger, or the art of Andy Warhol, all of whom worked at the center of self-conscious artistic and subcultural movements that they helped to create (the Beat movement, underground cinema, Pop art). Not to say there is no element of longing in, say, Burroughs or Ginsberg: they both write achingly about the desire to touch or love men who will not love back. But their very frankness about that desire presumes a minimally present, self-identifying audience that even Bannon was not sure she had.

8   See Batten; Pazicky.

9   It is clear that queer culture has never left the inversion model behind. On one hand, gay men and lesbians still consume it when they read about scientific research on homosexuality, which is designed to account, once again, for the origins of individual homosexuals, mostly by isolating hormonal factors, like testosterone levels, that correlate sexuality to gender identity. In this contemporary scientific version of the inversion model, disseminated to gay communities through writers like the gay scientist Simon LeVay, to be a homosexual is to be hormonally akin to the "opposite" sex (Mondimore 97–157). On the other hand, there is a movement among some queer academics in the humanities to get "back to sex"—to prevent the study of gay and lesbian history from emphasizing historical "community" so exclusively that public conversations about homosexuality lose track of the radical political potential of specifically gay or lesbian sex—a specificity grounded in ideas of homosexuality as inversion. Leo Bersani, for one, has argued that the auroral bliss of anal sex between men, as well as of masochism in male-male sadomasochistic play, not only feminizes the receptive or masochistic sexual partner but "makes the subject unfindable as an object of discipline" (99). Teresa DeLauretis, meanwhile, has sought to outmaneuver psychoanalytic renderings of lesbian sexuality that, she argues,

desexualize lesbians by finding the origins of lesbianism in an oceanic maternal love or in a castrated wish for male sexuality in the form of a penis (literally) or phallus (symbolically). DeLauretis claims fetishism as the best place to launch a theory of lesbian sexual agency, arguing that fetishism can operate as a blithe disavowal of castration and allows women to desire each other's perversity, circulated in the form of specifically lesbian objects and fantasies—not least the signifiers of the "mannish lesbian" (251). For DeLauretis, the fetish allows lesbians symbolic access to a desiring masculinity in much the way that masochistic jouissance allows Bersani's gay man access to a feminine passivity. Both theories seek to restore a specifically sexual identity to gay men and lesbians in danger of desexualization through identity politics; and both resexualize their subjects through a nuanced insistence that what makes gay men and lesbians different from their straight counterparts is a traffic in cross-gendered sexual experience.

10 Thanks to Carolyn Dinshaw for bringing this essay to my attention.

11 In this regard—my interest in the value of close reading as part of a queer theoretical practice that is neither purely "theoretical" nor properly "historical"— I see myself following on a more recent essay of Biddy Martin's, "Sexualities without Genders and Other Queer Utopias," in which Martin suggests that the major theoretical narratives of what makes homosexuality specific have gone too far in the direction of making it extraordinary, gone too far in the direction of privileging a presumed fluidity of sexuality (we may have many love objects) over a presumed fixity of gender (we each have only one). Martin, in other words, is interested in a queer critical practice that honors the struggle of sissies and tomboys but also the struggles of those who appear to conform to gender norms but who feel just as anguished by the incompatibility between their sanctioned corporeal styles and their unspeakable object-choices. Although Sedgwick is Martin's main object of criticism in this piece, the nod Sedgwick makes in the direction of the sissy and the tomboy links the two pieces in their valorization of the experience of gender as the place where the lost details in Foucault's grand récit history of sexuality can be recuperated. "Gender is both more and less than we make it," Martin writes, meaning that it is neither "merely" fixed nor a fixity so central to our thinking that its deconstruction "would take apart personhood itself." She concludes by calling for "close readings" that foreground the contingency of gender without equating it with the very principle of contingency (94). Along with minority and universality, then, which are the terms Sedgwick uses to describe the two poles between which discourses of homosexuality must navigate, we might add, following Martin, "exceptionalism" and "ordinariness," and the affects that attend each of them, as experiences currently out of conversation with each other in descriptions of queer existence (45–70).

1. Hart Crane's History

1 Another reading of this attempt, more deconstructive than my own, is to be found in Lee Edelman's fine 1987 study *Transmemberment of Song*. Although he wrote the book before explicitly pursuing a gay textualist literary criticism, it nonetheless previews Yingling's work in its careful attention to the figural and allegorical resources Crane drew on in order to traffic between, in Edelman's terms, "memory" and "forgetting" (272–73)—or something like the border between the unsayable and the sayable in the imagining of time, sensation, and history, in mine.

2 Unless otherwise noted, all quotations from Hart Crane's poetry are from *The Complete Poems of Hart Crane,* ed. Marc Simon (New York: Liveright, 1986).

3 The poem is collected as "Reply" in Brom Weber's *Complete Poems and Selected Letters and Prose of Hart Crane,* published in 1966; Marc Simon's 1989 *Complete Poems of Hart Crane,* widely considered definitive, lists the poem by its first line, since Crane himself never gave the poem a title.

2. Feeling and Affiliation in Willa Cather

1 Indeed, the dynamic of Cather's relationship to the Menuhin children suggests a great deal about how she related the intimate sphere of family to the vista of the nation. Cather's biographers have pointed out that she encouraged the Menuhin children to persist in the cultivation of their prodigious musical talents, which she admired fiercely. There is a distinct sense, in Hermione Lee's account, for example, that the Menuhins represented exactly the American Europeanness that she, as a born American, envied but could never quite claim. On the same subject James Woodress writes, Cather was concerned to Americanize the children: not by teaching them to play baseball or to listen to records but by holding reading circles in which she familiarized the children with Shakespeare and other English literary classics. In a sense, the Menuhin children offered Cather a chance, late in life, to replay in ideal terms a vision of family and America that she was absolutely denied in her own prairie upbringing: an American family made more American by cultivating a set of European loyalties, and more familial by encouraging individual artistic achievement. This type of family, "layered" indeed over Cather's nuclear family, accommodates a nostalgic retreat from the "vulgarities" of mass culture and the demands of the market —demands that Cather perceived to be intimately related to the propagation of heterosexuality. Lee, meanwhile, writes that the Menuhin children "turned [Cather's] mind again to the double inheritance of American artists," and that "doubleness—America and Europe, youth and age, music and writing—came

back to her again as a subject for late work" (335). James Woodress (454) and Phyllis C. Robinson (266) describe Cather's leading of the Menuhin children through Shakespeare's plays, an endeavor Robinson describes as motivated by Cather's concern that the Menuhin children, with their world travels, were not learning English well enough.

2   For a survey of the ways in which Cather de-emphasizes the importance of heterosexual union in her novels, see Rosowski, "Willa Cather's Subverted Endings."

3   My sense of the types of sodality that attracted Cather might place her in Leslie Fielder's genealogy of American novelists who depict sublimated homosexuality as a way to get around themes of "impotence" and historical purpose-lessness. But Fielder's melodramatic distaste for his own thesis about the role of homosexuality in American literature makes it impossible for him to read homosexuality as having anything other than a "narcissistic" and regressive function (348). I show in a later discussion that the valorizations of adolescence Cather enjoys shy away from "adulthood" because "adulthood" has specific and punishing heterosexual meanings for her.

4   The definitive account of Cather's relationship to femininity as a social and a literary category remains Sharon O'Brien's *Willa Cather: The Emerging Voice.* Her determination to claim Cather as a feminist ancestor does, however, occa-sionally obscure the ways in which Cather was not only ambivalent about roles assigned women but dismissive, in her novels, of the women assigned them.

5   There is perhaps something particularly at stake for women writers in distin-guishing themselves as artists from the rest of the population: if the distinc-tion is absolute, then its privileges may trump the limitations placed on them as women. Louise Bogan, another woman who struggled with the competing demands of femininity and art, put it this way in her poem "Several Voices Out of a Cloud."

> Come, drunks and drug-takers; come, perverts unnerved!
> Receive the laurel, given, though late, on merit; to whom
>   And wherever deserved.
>
> Parochial punks, trimmers, nice people, joiners true-blue,
> Get the hell out of the way of the laurel. It is deathless
>   And it isn't for you. (*The Blue Estuaries* 133)

Bogan wrote admiringly of Cather in a 1931 *New Yorker* piece called "American-Classic"; she concludes in that essay that Cather, unlike so many other writers of her generation, "has made herself complete mistress of her talent"—a figure of mastery no doubt precious to Bogan in her own art as well.

6   Writing on *My Ántonia,* Katrina Irving argues that ethnicity in Cather's novel "displaces" homosexuality. Certainly the two are closely entwined, and the former is expressible in ways the latter was not—but I am interested in the effectivity of that "displacement"—not on its prevention of homosexuality from expressing itself as sexuality but on the lasting effect it has on how homosexuality gets modeled and understood from generation to generation. Homosexuality is not ethnicity; but neither, in Cather, is it merely hiding behind ethnicity.

7   Maureen Ryan writes about the split between men and women in *One of Ours,* arguing that although Claude is separated from women, he becomes feminized himself.

8   Morton D. Zabel provides a judicious assessment of the limitations Cather's nostalgia placed on her fiction, the "didacticism and inflexibility" that it hardened into as she moved from depicting young dreamers to older, more resistant holdouts to the past.

9   Walter Benn Michaels has understood the racial politics of Cather's valorization of supposedly "vanished" Indians as part of a rhetorically complex Progressive-era notion of "culture"—a notion, he argues, born of early-twentieth-century white Americans' anxieties in the face of massive immigration, and one that continues to shape our contemporary discussions of race. Michaels claims that this "culture," a name for the ideology of authentic American identity, continues to be defined by its ineffability—someone is always claiming to "have" it, though it is never clear how to get it; it is just given to you. This is a nasty bind, and it looks a lot like racism. Michaels is interested in it because of the logical contradiction it implies between what he calls "social" and "biological" ideas of identity.

> [Culture] is racist in that, refusing to identify "our" culture (whoever "we" are) with whatever it is we do and believe, it imagines instead that our culture is the culture of our ancestors, so that we can be understood, for example, to participate more fully in our culture when we find out about and imitate the social or religious practices of our great-grandparents. Their genetic makeup is (at least partially) ours through biology; their culture is ours only through the biologization of that culture. But culture involves also the critique of biology, for if culture were simply biological, we could never fail fully to participate in it. . . .
>
> Hence the extraordinary power of culture as a concept. (238)

The contradiction feels staged, however, because Michaels uses the word *culture* both critically, to describe the ideology he is studying, and thoughtlessly, as part of an ideology he participates in, an ideology of ideology as semantics. "Culture," in this second sense, does not involve a critique of racism—a political problem—but rather "the critique of biology," where "biology" is a private neologism of Michaels's, meaning only "sexual reproduction" ("Their genetic makeup is . . . ours through biology"). Michaels's mistaking of this false dilemma for an ideological problem is further symptomatized in his repeated use of the words *we* and *ours,* a gesture by which he means merely to communicate, between quotation marks, the contemporary urgency of the problem of the rhetorical essence of race, but which inevitably, through his sustained mimicry of the voice of those who think of the problem in this way, becomes his own voice as well, fascinated as he is by the idea's "extraordinary power." I discuss Michaels's argument at greater length in an earlier version of this chapter (Nealon).

10 One exciting development in queer Cather studies is the forthcoming publication of Jonathan Goldberg's book *Willa Cather and Others,* which takes great critical care to flesh out some of the cultural scenes in and through which Cather produced her novels, especially *One of Ours* and *The Professor's House.* By establishing Cather's personal and identificatory links to other women artists, in particular, Goldberg manages to demonstrate that wanting to "be like" another artist, regardless of her gender, is complexly haunted by genders not reducible to the bodies of the players involved. If I have been trying to demonstrate in these pages that Cather struggles with her sense of gender inversion through loving, punishing cross-gendered identifications with her characters, that is, Goldberg demonstrates that an enriched contextual and historical understanding of Cather can by itself complicate a simply "inverted" understanding of gender and sexuality—a very different, and more persuasive, approach to Cather than the discipline has thus far entertained.

3. The Secret Public of Physique Culture

1 In his introduction to *Homosexual Desire,* Jeffrey Weeks takes Hocquenghem to task for reproducing a "hydraulic" theory of libido when Hocquenghem declares that the repression of homosexuality, not homosexuality itself, produces paranoia. That is, Weeks accuses Hocquenghem of formulating a closed-system theory, one that fails to take into account the Lacanian sense of sexuality as signification, as open-ended. But Hocquenghem is not merely accusing the paranoia theorists of being paranoid: he is suggesting that the social bond (not, admittedly, a phrase he uses), rather than the interior of the individual person, is the medium of paranoia as well as the medium of homosexuality, which "only exists in groups." This claim entails, then, not merely a hot-potato game of queer theorists and patriarchal authority figures each calling the other paranoid but a consideration of how affect obtains in homosexual "situations" (since

affect is the best term psychoanalysis and its orbital vocabularies have for the idea of a "bond"): an analysis, a demonstration, bumping into someone on the street; even, no doubt, driving on the highway. This is why it is so important, in these theories, to "go out of your way to be extra friendly," a bathetic phrase that nonetheless encodes some of what I think has been lost in the post–Queer Nation era of U.S. lesbian and gay organizing—the need to imagine confrontation on "the street" as a scene not just of civility but of seduction.

2 In D'Emilio's landmark study, *Sexual Politics,* see especially chapter 5, which focuses on the conservatism the early homophile publications felt forced into, and chapter 8, which details the attention of various mass media outlets to the subcultures of U.S. homosexuals in the early 1960s.

3 For an overview of *ONE*'s struggle in the courts, see *Homophile Studies* 1 (1958): 60–64.

4 Lee Edelman suggests a theoretical model that takes into account, among other things, the limitations of sexological inquiries into homosexuality—a linguistic model indebted to Jacques Derrida and Jacques Lacan, by which he argues that male homosexuality impels the question of identifiability by its very nature: it has "the power to signify the instability of the signifying function *per se,* the arbitrary and tenuous nature of the relationship between any signifier and signified" (*Homographesis* 6). Edelman proposes that in patriarchy, male homosexuality exposes the "tenuous" nature of language because it threatens the idea of sexual difference between men and women from within masculinity—it upsets, in other words, the symbolic arrangement by which the definition of maleness becomes "sameness unto itself," and all difference is set down to femaleness. Male homosexuality hints that this arrangement is constitutively unstable because it suggests there may be different ways to be a man (11–12).

Elsewhere, in an essay called "Tearooms and Sympathy; or, The Epistemology of the Water Closet," Edelman brilliantly analyzes the 1964 scandal over Walter Jenkins, President Lyndon Johnson's chief of staff, who was arrested in a Capitol Hill men's room for "indecent gestures" with another man. Through a combination of historical evidence gathered from *Time, Life,* and the *New York Times,* Edelman makes clear that mid-century uncertainty about how to identify gay men allowed male homosexuality to become a condensation point for anxieties about the fate of the United States at the dawn of the nuclear age. Specifically, he argues that the notion of male homosexuality as a weakness of spirit, as a failure to carry on a masculine tradition of clenched bodily integrity, dovetailed with fears that nuclear war might bring all tradition, all transmission of culture to an abrupt end, unless all enemies were identified while still outside the nation's body.

5 Michael Warner writes about the market and media dynamics of fashioning

individuality out of brand names and image effluvia, long a Marxist preoccupation. Warner's particular contribution is to point out the ways in which bodily coherence itself is purchased through identifications with commodities and images ("Mass Subject").

6   In an essay on early-twentieth-century physical culture, Greg Mullins writes insightfully about the role of white male desires for black bodies and the need of white men to distance themselves from those desires. He describes the sexual dynamic by which white readers of Bernarr Macfadden's *Physical Culture* made themselves feel comfortable consuming images of naked African men:

> Representations of sexy African men . . . remain locked in a racist discourse which rigidifies the difference between reading, desiring subject, and pictorial, desirable object. . . .
>
> To admit that the African body is beautiful [however] immediately positions one on the slippery ground of desire, wherein "desire to be like" and "desire for" blend treacherously together. (44–45)

Mullins's understanding of the role of desire in cross-racial image consumption and in modeling our racial selves gives him a wider reach than Morgan's; the limitation in his essay is that the concepts he wishes to historicize, desire and identification, are designed by psychoanalysis to collapse into each other — and so, brought into a more "historical" register in order to explain a specific cultural dynamic, those terms suggest that the motion of history itself is the confusion of identification and desire. The psychoanalytic language, that is, takes over the context of a historical analysis too thoroughly and leaves out the sense in which not only are desires historicizable but historicity itself is an object of desire: we want, at every turn, our desires to give us some tale, nostalgic or otherwise, that locates us in relation to pastness or futurity. Instead of an interrogation of muscle culture as an instance of the way historical dynamics (racism, colonialism, the birth of homoerotic print culture) impel desire and identification to call up certain resources toward their inevitable collapse, Mullins is forced by the abstract nature of his grounding terms to settle for describing physical culture as an example of a psychoanalytic truth: desire and identification bleed together. Mullins's additional insight, that this bleeding confounds racist separations of white and black into subject and object, remains useful to remember.

7   For a brief discussion of Morgan's unpublished work on Glenn Carrington, see Waugh 35.

8   The *Grecian Guild* is notable for the variety of reader relationships it encouraged. There were letters columns in which, obliquely, sexual orientation began to appear as a topic; the "Grecian of the month" feature; a pen pal system that

prefigured contemporary gay male personal ads (as did ads in Macfadden's magazines, as Waugh points out); and the monthly "Thoughts on Our Creed" column, written by a guild member and devoted, usually, to more amusing analogies between physical culture and American history at large ("General Robert Edward Lee [1807–1870] of Virginia is a shining example for all Grecians because of his sterling character" [May 1957]).

9 I suggest of Quaintance that, if the politics of his historical fantasy life are a mess, they nonetheless contain a utopian understanding of history as offering manifold possibilities for hope that has its own corollaries in more rigorously theoretical writing. The particular writer I quote here is Raymond Williams, writing his autobiography in the first chapter of *The Country and the City*. Compare his account of his life's trajectory to Quaintance's.

> I was born in a village, and I still live in a village. But where I was born was under the Black mountains, on the Welsh border, where the meadows are bright green against the red earth of the ploughland, and the first trees, beyond the window, are oak and holly. Where I live now is in the flat country, on a headland of boulder clay, towards the edge of the dikes and sluices, the black earth of the fens, under the high East Anglian skies. . . .
>
> My own network, from where I sit writing at the window, is to Cambridge and London, and beyond them to the postmark places, the unfamiliar stamps and the distant cities: Rome, Moscow, New York. . . . I have stood in many cities and felt this pulse: in the physical differences of Stockholm and Florence, Paris and Milan: this identifiable and moving quality: the centre, the activity, the light. . . .
>
> I have known this feeling, looking up at the great buildings that are the centres of power, but I find I do not say, "There is your city, your great bourgeois monument, your towering structure of this still precarious civilisation" or I do not only say that; I say also, "This is what men have built, so often magnificently, and is not everything then possible?" (3–6)

I include this passage as evidence for the persistence and the continuity of the dream, in widely separate terrains, of history as the tracings of the future. Quaintance thinks this future can be achieved through solitary pursuit of a dream, whereas Williams sees possibility in collective effort. But the genre and style coincidences that link the Marxist theorist and the physique artist in their respective autobiographies—the turn to landscape description, the repetition of the first-person pronoun as a staving-off against the potentially overwhelming vastness of the History being confronted—are worth attention, as is the homosocial tremor in Williams's description of what "men" have wrought. What is most pressing to me in making this comparison, though, is to import from

Williams's exemplary book some of the dignity that lurks in Quaintance's self-portrayal, if we are willing to see it. The gay child struggling to manufacture a narrative of history into which his desire might fit, and the working-class boy who grows up to make his way into the metropolitan "centres"—both make recourse to the notion of history-as-possibility for a good reason. They share, differently inflected, a subaltern and specifically ambivalent response to History (a specifically modern history, one whose primary feature is its weight). Both men reject a heritage—for Quaintance, it is called "heredity"; for Williams it is the sheer material heft of European culture—while also identifying with its products, either by imagining himself "mixed up" with History or by recognizing the manly "magnificence" of that heritage.

10   Thom Fitzgerald's film *Beefcake* fictionalizes the story of a young man who gets caught up in the world of the Athletic Model Guild in Los Angeles and who discovers, much to his surprise, that the sweet, innocent gentleman who has been photographing him shirtless (Bob Mizer) is actually a homosexual. The film also contains documentary-style interviews with models and photographers from the period, none of whom, interestingly, ever identifies himself or the culture of physique photography as gay. The closet, it seems, still has a contemporary hold on male homosexuality, at least when that homosexuality is phrased as a form of incipient male sociability. My point here is to suggest that the closet can be seen as a perpetually re-occurring moment in the becoming-historical of male homosexuality: it cannot be overcome because it is continually sketching the set of conditions (a homosexual-everywhere) out of which we imagine other, more "self-identified" forms of homosexuality, as well as other, more progressive ideas about increased homosexual participation in history.

4. The Ambivalence of Lesbian Pulp Fiction

1   For a brief but entertaining discussion of the genesis of the many pulp subgenres in the 1950s, see Server. Lee Server specifically interviews Marijane Meaker, who as Vin Packer wrote *Spring Fire*. Meaker remarks on the astonishment of discovering a lesbian audience for her novel, which was imagined by her editor as aimed at men (Server 55).

2   Allan Bérubé has since amply documented exactly the "daily struggle" of mid-century gay men and lesbians to survive in the military.

3   Michèle Aina Barale, in a discussion of the first chapter of *Beebo Brinker,* suggests that Jack's masculine appearance, paired with Beebo's innocence in the city—it is, after all, Bannon's only novel in which Beebo is an ingenue—suggests that this configuration *seems* but is not heterosexual and is therefore subversive: it deceives uninitiated, straight readers while establishing space for a gay text

(613). As the books unfold, this initial "subversive" shock is lost, and Jack becomes one more in a variety of Bannon's examples of how to deal with feeling that your desires are wrong: in his case, a good-natured irony, alcoholism, and marriage to Laura.

4   The only mention of Bannon I have found by a woman of color writing about the 1950s in New York is Audre Lorde, who describes the way that pulp novels, Bannon's among them, focused primarily on pain and never "even mentioned the joys" (213). Lorde does not mention the pulps as a specifically all-white genre, reserving her discussion of mid-century white lesbian racism to passages concerning lesbian bars in Greenwich Village.

5   Ruby Rich makes this point in a roundtable discussion about Teresa deLauretis's essay "Film and the Visible" (Bad Object-Choices 274–75).

6   Biddy Martin, in her essay "Lesbian Identity and Autobiographical Difference[s]," argues that woman-identified, feminist writing in the 1970s obscured the possibility of differences among lesbians, not least those of race and class, in order to produce master-narratives that joined coming out as lesbians with an arrival in the welcoming arms of feminism. This narrative, Martin suggests, disavows the entire lesbian culture of butch-femme roles and practices that preceded it. Against this disavowal she cites Cherríe Moraga's "call for a 'theory' in the flesh,'" which she thinks is available in "the use of the language of the body's physical pains and pleasures and of the materiality of psychic and social life" (Martin 285). This is exactly the "materiality" I think Beebo embodies, in particularly butch form.

.... *references*

Acocella, Joan. "Cather and the Academy." *New Yorker* 27 Nov. 1995: 56–72.

Adam, Barry D. *The Rise of a Gay and Lesbian Movement.* Boston: G. K. Hall, 1987.

Adam, Barry D., Jan Willem Duyvendak, and André Krouwel. *The Global Emergence of Gay and Lesbian Politics: National Imprints of a Worldwide Movement.* Philadelphia: Temple UP, 1999.

Ahmad, Aijaz. *In Theory: Nations, Classes, Literatures.* New York: Verso, 1992.

Altman, Dennis. *The Homosexualization of America, the Americanization of the Homosexual.* New York: St. Martin's, 1982.

Anderson, Benedict. *Imagined Communities: Reflections on the Origin and Spread of Nationalism.* London: Verso, 1983.

Appadurai, Arjun. *Modernity at Large: Cultural Dimensions of Globalization.* Minneapolis: U of Minnesota P, 1996.

Bad Object-Choices, ed. *How Do I Look? Queer Film and Video.* Seattle: Bay, 1991.

Baldwin, James. *Go Tell It on the Mountain*. 1952. New York: Laurel, 1985.

Balibar, Etienne, and Immanuel Wallerstein. *Race, Nation, Class: Ambiguous Identities*. London: Verso, 1991.

Bannon, Ann. *Beebo Brinker*. 1962. Tallahassee, Fla.: Naiad, 1986.

———. *I Am a Woman*. 1959. Tallahassee, Fla.: Naiad, 1986.

———. *Journey to a Woman*. 1960. Tallahassee, Fla.: Naiad, 1986.

———. *Odd Girl Out*. 1957. Tallahassee, Fla.: Naiad, 1986.

———. *Women in the Shadows*. 1959. Tallahassee, Fla.: Naiad, 1986.

Barale, Michèle Aina. "When Jack Blinks: Si(gh)ting Gay Desire in Ann Bannon's *Beebo Brinker*." *The Lesbian and Gay Studies Reader*. Ed. Henry Abelove, Michèle Aina Barale, and David M. Halperin. New York: Routledge, 1993. 604–15.

Barnes, Djuna. *Nightwood*. 1936. New York: Random, 2000.

Batten, Guinn. *The Orphaned Imagination: Melancholy and Commodity Culture in English Romanticism*. Durham: Duke UP, 1998.

Bederman, Gail. *Manliness and Civilization: A Cultural History of Gender and Race in the United States, 1880–1917*. Chicago: U of Chicago P, 1995.

Berlant, Lauren, and Elizabeth Freeman. "Queer Nationality." *Fear of a Queer Planet*. Ed. Michael Warner. Minneapolis: U of Minnesota P, 1993. 193–229.

Bersani, Leo. *Homos*. Cambridge, Mass.: Harvard UP, 1995.

Berthoff, Warner. *Hart Crane: A Re-Introduction*. Minneapolis: U of Minnesota P, 1989.

Bérubé, Allan. *Coming Out under Fire: The History of Lesbians and Gay Men in World War Two*. New York: Plume, 1990.

Bhabha, Homi K. "DissemiNation." *Nation and Narration*. Ed. Homi K. Bhabha. London: Routledge, 1990. 291–322.

Birmingham, Stephen. "Far Out beyond Fitness." *Sports Illustrated* 27 July 1959: 58–64.

———. "For Love of Muscle." *Sports Illustrated* 3 Aug. 1959: 61–64.

Bogan, Louise. "American-Classic." *Willa Cather and Her Critics*. Ed. James Schroeter. Ithaca: Cornell UP, 1967. 126–33.

———. *The Blue Estuaries: Poems 1923–1968*. New York: Ecco, 1988.

Bravmann, Scott. *Queer Fictions of the Past: History, Culture, and Difference*. Cambridge: Cambridge UP, 1997.

Butler, Judith. *Bodies That Matter: On the Discursive Limits of "Sex."* New York: Routledge, 1993.

———. *Gender Trouble: Feminism and the Subversion of Identity*. New York: Routledge, 1990.

Carlin, Deborah. *Cather, Canon, and the Politics of Reading*. Amherst: U of Massachusetts P, 1992.

Carnes, Mark C. *Secret Ritual and Manhood in Victorian America*. New Haven: Yale UP, 1989.

Cather, Willa. *Five Stories*. New York: Vintage, 1956.

———. *Later Novels*. [Includes *Sapphira and the Slave Girl* (1940)]. New York: Library of America, 1990.

———. *My Ántonia*. 1918. Boston: Houghton, 1988.

———. *Not Under Forty*. New York: Knopf, 1936.

———. *One of Ours*. 1922. New York: Vintage, 1991.

———. *O Pioneers!* 1913. Boston: Houghton, 1988.

———. *The Professor's House*. 1925. New York: Vintage, 1990.

———. *The Song of the Lark*. 1915. Boston: Houghton, 1988.

Chandler, James. *England in 1819: The Politics of Literary Culture and the Case of Romantic Historicism*. Chicago: U of Chicago P, 1998.

Chauncey, George. *Gay New York: Gender, Urban Culture, and the Making of the Gay Male World, 1890–1940*. New York: HarperCollins, 1994.

Clark, David R. "For the Marriage of Faustus and Helen." *Critical Essays on Hart Crane*. Ed. David R. Clark. Boston: G. K. Hall, 1982. 56–67.

Cory, Daniel Webster [Edward Sagarin]. *Homosexuality: A Cross-Cultural Approach*. New York: Julian, 1956.

Crane, Hart. *The Complete Poems and Selected Letters and Prose of Hart Crane*. Ed. Brom Weber. New York: Anchor, 1966.

———. *Complete Poems of Hart Crane*. Ed. Marc Simon. New York: Liveright, 1986.

———. *O My Land, My Friends: The Selected Letters of Hart Crane*. Ed. Langdon Hammer. New York: Four Walls, 1997.

Damon, Gene [Barbara Grier]. "The Lesbian Paperback." Parts 1 and 2. *Tangents* 1 (June 1966): 9–10.

Dean, Tim. "Hart Crane's Poetics of Privacy." *American Literary History* 8.1 (spring 1996): 83–109.

DeLauretis, Teresa. *The Practice of Love: Lesbian Sexuality and Perverse Desire*. Bloomington: Indiana UP, 1994.

Deleuze, Gilles, and Félix Guattari. *Anti-Oedipus*. 1972. Minneapolis: U of Minnesota P, 1983.

D'Emilio, John. "Capitalism and Gay Identity." *Powers of Desire: The Politics of Sexuality*. Ed. Ann Snitow, Christine Stansell, and Sharon Thompson. New York: Monthly Review, 1983. 100–113.

———. *Sexual Politics, Sexual Communities: The Making of a Homosexual Minority in the United States, 1940–1970*. Chicago: U of Chicago P, 1983.

D'Emilio, John, and Estelle Freedman. *Intimate Matters: A History of Sexuality in America*. 2d ed. Chicago: U of Chicago P, 1998.

Dollimore, Jonathan. *Sexual Dissidence: Augustine to Wilde, Freud to Foucault.* Oxford: Clarendon, 1991.

Dos Passos, John. *Three Soldiers.* New York: Random, 1921.

Douglas, Ann. *Terrible Honesty: Mongrel Manhattan in the 1920s.* New York: Farrar, 1995.

Duberman, Martin Bauml, Martha Vicinus, and George Chauncey Jr. *Hidden from History: Reclaiming the Gay and Lesbian Past.* New York: New American Library, 1989.

Due, Linnea. *Joining the Tribe: Growing Up Gay and Lesbian in the 90s.* New York: Anchor, 1995.

Duggan, Lisa. "The Discipline Problem: Queer Theory Meets Lesbian and Gay History." *GLQ: A Journal of Lesbian and Gay Studies* 2.3 (1995): 179–91.

Dyer, Richard. "Children of the Night: Vampirism as Homosexuality, Homosexuality as Vampirism." *Sweet Dreams: Sexuality, Gender, and Popular Culture.* Ed. Susannah Radstone. London: Lawrence, 1988. 47–72.

Edelman, Lee. *Homographesis.* New York: Routledge, 1994.

———. "Tearooms and Sympathy; or, The Epistemology of the Water Closet." *The Lesbian and Gay Studies Reader.* Ed. Henry Abelove, Michèle Aina Barale, and David M. Halperin. New York: Routledge, 1993. 533–74.

———. *Transmemberment of Song: Hart Crane's Anatomies of Rhetoric and Desire.* Stanford: Stanford UP, 1987.

Eliot, T. S. *Collected Poems, 1909–1962.* New York: Harcourt, 1971.

Ernst, Robert. *Weakness Is a Crime: The Life of Bernarr Macfadden.* Syracuse: Syracuse UP, 1991.

Escoffier, Jeffrey. *American Homo: Community and Perversity.* Berkeley: U of California P, 1998.

Faderman, Lillian. *Odd Girls and Twilight Lovers: A History of Lesbian Life in Twentieth-Century America.* New York: Columbia UP, 1991.

Fiedler, Leslie. *Love and Death in the American Novel.* 1960. New York: Dalkey Archive, 1997.

Fitzgerald, Thom. *Beefcake.* Strand Releasing, 1999.

Foucault, Michel. *The History of Sexuality: An Introduction.* Trans. Robert Hurley. New York: Vintage, 1990.

———. "The Life of Infamous Men." 1977. *Michel Foucault: Power, Truth, Strategy.* Ed. Meaghan Morris and Paul Patton. Trans. Paul Foss and Meaghan Morris. Sydney: Feral, 1979. 76–91.

Frank, Waldo. *Our America.* New York: Boni, 1919.

Freedman, Estelle B., and John D'Emilio. "Problems Encountered in Writing the History of Sexuality: Sources, Theory, and Interpretation." *Journal of Sex Research* 27.4 (Nov. 1990): 481–95.

Friedman, Leon, ed. *Obscenity: The Complete Oral Arguments before the Supreme Court in the Major Obscenity Cases.* New York: Chelsea, 1970.

Gallagher, Catherine, and Steven Greenblatt. "Counterhistory and the Anecdote." *Practicing the New Historicism.* Chicago: U of Chicago P, 2000.

Garber, Eric. "A Spectacle in Color: The Lesbian and Gay Subculture of Jazz Age Harlem." *Hidden from History: Reclaiming the Gay and Lesbian Past.* Ed. Martin Baum Duberman, Martha Vicinus, and George Chauncey Jr. New York: New American Library, 1989. 318–31.

Gardner, Jared. "'Our Native Clay': Racial and Sexual Identity and the Making of Americans in *The Bridge.*" *American Quarterly* 44.1 (1992): 24–50.

Giles, Paul. *The Contexts of* The Bridge. Cambridge: Cambridge UP, 1986.

Goldberg, Jonathan. *Willa Cather and Others.* Durham: Duke UP, 2001.

Grier, Barbara. *See* Damon, Gene.

Grossman, Allen. "Hart Crane and Poetry: A Consideration of Crane's Intense Poetics." *Hart Crane: Modern Critical Views.* Ed. Harold Bloom. New York: Chelsea, 1986. 221–54.

Guterl, Matthew Pratt. "'All Was Closed and Sealed Tight': Jean Toomer, Physical Culture, and Blackness." Annual meeting of the American Studies Association. Seattle. 19 Nov. 1998.

Harper, Phillip Brian. "Eloquence and Epitaph: Black Nationalism and the Homophobic Impulse in Responses to the Death of Max Robinson." *The Lesbian and Gay Studies Reader.* Ed. Henry Abelove, Michèle Aina Barale, and David M. Halperin. New York: Routledge, 1993. 159–75.

Harper, Phillip Brian, Anne McClintock, José Esteban Muñoz, and Trish Rosen, eds. *Queer Transexions of Race, Nation, and Gender: Social Text* 52–53 (fall/winter 1997).

Harris, Daniel. *The Rise and Fall of Gay Culture.* New York: Hyperion, 1997.

Henry, George W. *Society and the Sex Variant.* 3d ed. New York: Collier, 1955.

Hobsbawm, E. J. *Nations and Nationalism since 1780: Programme, Myth, Reality.* Cambridge: Cambridge UP, 1990.

Hobsbawm, Eric, and Terence Ranger, eds. *The Invention of Tradition.* Cambridge: Cambridge UP, 1983.

Hocquenghem, Guy. *Homosexual Desire.* 1972. Durham: Duke UP, 1993.

Hooven, F. Valentine III. *Beefcake: The Muscle Magazines of America, 1950–1970.* Cologne: Taschen, 1995.

Hughes, Holly. *Clit Notes: A Sapphic Sampler.* New York: Grove, 1996.

Hunt, William R. *Body Love: The Amazing Career of Bernarr Macfadden.* Bowling Green: Bowling Green State U Popular P, 1989.

Irigaray, Luce. *This Sex Which Is Not One.* 1977. Trans. Catherine Porter. Ithaca: Cornell UP, 1985.

Irving, Katrina. "Displacing Homosexuality: The Use of Ethnicity in Willa Cather's *My Ántonia*." *Modern Fiction Studies* 36 (spring 1990): 91–102.

Jameson, Fredric. "Figural Relativism; or, The Poetics of Historiography." *The Ideologies of Theory: Essays 1971–1986. Vol. 1: Situations of Theory*. Minneapolis: U of Minnesota P, 1988. 153–65.

———. *The Political Unconscious*. Ithaca: Cornell UP, 1981.

Katz, Jonathan. *Gay American History: Lesbians and Gay Men in the U.S.A.* New York: Crowell, 1976.

Kennedy, Elizabeth Lapovsky, and Madeline D. Davis. *Boots of Leather, Slippers of Gold: The History of a Lesbian Community*. New York: Penguin, 1993.

Kennedy, John F. "The Soft American." *Sports Illustrated* 26 Dec. 1960: 15–17.

Kinsey, Alfred C., Wardell B. Pomeroy, and Clyde E. Martin. *Sexual Behavior in the Human Male*. Philadelphia: Saunders, 1948.

Laqueur, Thomas. *Making Sex: Body and Gender from the Greeks to Freud*. Cambridge, Mass.: Harvard UP, 1990.

Lee, Hermione. *Willa Cather: A Life Saved Up*. London: Virago, 1989. Reprinted as *Willa Cather: Double Lives*. New York: Pantheon, 1989.

Lewis, Sinclair. "A Hamlet of the Plains." *Willa Cather and Her Critics*. Ed. James Schroeter. Ithaca: Cornell UP, 1967. 30–34.

Loewenstein, Andrea. "Sad Stories: A Reflection on the Fiction of Ann Bannon." *Gay Community News* 7.43 (24 May 1980): 8–12.

Lorde, Audre. *Zami: A New Spelling of My Name*. Trumansburg, N.Y.: Crossing, 1982.

Martin, Biddy. *Femininity Played Straight: The Significance of Being Lesbian*. New York: Routledge, 1996.

Mencken, H. L. "Four Reviews." *Willa Cather and Her Critics*. Ed. James Schroeter. Ithaca: Cornell UP, 1967. 7–12

Menuhin, Yehudi. *Unfinished Journey*. New York: Knopf, 1977.

Michaels, Walter Benn. "The Vanishing American." *American Literary History* 2 (summer 1990): 222–40.

Miller, Neil. *Out of the Past: Gay and Lesbian History from 1869 to the Present*. New York: Vintage, 1995.

Millet, Kate. *Sexual Politics*. 1970. Champaign: U of Illinois P, 2000.

Mondimore, Francis Mark. *A Natural History of Homosexuality*. Baltimore: Johns Hopkins UP, 1996.

Moon, Michael. *A Small Boy and Others: Imitation and Initiation in American Culture from Henry James to Andy Warhol*. Durham: Duke UP, 1998.

Morgan, Tracy. "Pages of Whiteness: Race, Physique Magazines, and the Emergence of Gay Public Culture, 1955–1960." *Found Objects* 4 (1994): 109–26.

Morrison, Toni. "Black Matters." *Playing in the Dark: Whiteness and the Literary Imagination.* New York: Vintage, 1992. 1–28.

Mullins, Greg. "Nudes, Prudes, and Pygmies: The Desirability of Disavowal in Physical Culture." *Discourse* 15.1 (fall 1992): 27–48.

Nealon, Christopher. "Affect-Genealogy: Feeling and Affiliation in Willa Cather." *American Literature* 69.1 (Mar. 1997): 5–37.

Nestle, Joan. *A Restricted Country.* Ithaca: Firebrand, 1987.

Norton, Rictor. *The Myth of the Modern Homosexual: Queer History and the Search for Cultural Unity.* London: Cassell, 1997.

O'Brien, Sharon. *Willa Cather: The Emerging Voice.* New York: Oxford UP, 1987.

Paul, James C. N., and Murray L. Schwartz. *Federal Censorship: Obscenity in the Mail.* New York: Free Press, 1961.

Pazicky, Diana Loercher. *Cultural Orphans in America.* Jackson: UP of Mississippi, 1998.

Pease, Donald. "Blake, Crane, Whitman, and Modernism: A Poetics of Pure Possibility." *PMLA* 96 (1981): 64–85.

Peterson, Theodore. *Magazines in the Twentieth Century.* Urbana: U of Illinois P, 1964.

Polak, Clark. "The Story behind Physique Photography." *Drum* Oct. 1965: 8–15.

Quaintance, George. Interview. *Grecian Guild Pictorial* spring 1956: 14–17.

Riddel, Joseph. "Hart Crane's Poetics of Failure." *Hart Crane: Modern Critical Views.* Ed. Harold Bloom. New York: Chelsea, 1986. 91–110.

Rivière, Joan. "Womanliness as a Masquerade." *Formations of Fantasy.* Ed. Victor Burgin, James Donald, and Cora Kaplan. London: Routledge, 1986. 33–45.

Robinson, Paul. *The Modernization of Sex: Havelock Ellis, Alfred Kinsey, William Masters, and Virginia Johnson.* New York: Harper, 1976.

Robinson, Phyllis. *Willa: The Life of Willa Cather.* Garden City, N.Y.: Doubleday, 1983.

Roscoe, Will. "Was We'Wha a Homosexual?" *GLQ: A Journal of Lesbian and Gay Studies* 2.3 (1995): 193–235.

Rosowski, Susan J. *The Voyage Perilous: Willa Cather's Romanticism.* Lincoln: U of Nebraska P, 1984.

———. "Willa Cather's Subverted Endings and Gendered Time." *Cather Studies,* vol. 1. Ed. Susan J. Rosowski. Lincoln: U of Nebraska P, 1990. 68–88.

Rubin, Gayle S. "Thinking Sex: Notes for a Radical Theory of the Politics of Sexuality." 1984. *Lesbian and Gay Studies Reader.* Ed. Henry Abelove, Michèle Aina Barale, and David M. Halperin. New York: Routledge, 1993. 3–44.

Ryan, Maureen. "No Woman's Land: Gender in Willa Cather's *One of Ours.*" *Studies in American Fiction* 18 (spring 1990): 65–75.

Sedgwick, Eve Kosofsky. "Across Genders, Across Sexualities: Willa Cather and Others." *Tendencies.* Durham: Duke UP, 1993. 167–76.

———. *Epistemology of the Closet.* Berkeley: U of California P, 1990.

Server, Lee. *Over My Dead Body: The Sensational Age of the American Paperback, 1945–1955.* San Francisco: Chronicle, 1994.

Sollors, Werner. *Beyond Ethnicity: Consent and Descent in American Culture.* New York: Oxford UP, 1986.

Stein, Gertrude. "The Making of Americans." 1903. *Fernhurst, Q.E.D., and Other Early Writings.* New York: Liveright, 1971. 137–74.

Streitmatter, Rodger. *Unspeakable: The Rise of the Gay and Lesbian Press in America.* Boston: Faber, 1995.

Suárez, Juan A. *Bike Boys, Drag Queens, and Superstars: Avant-Garde, Mass Culture, and Gay Identities in the 1960s Underground Cinema.* Bloomington: Indiana UP, 1996.

Tashjian, Dickran. *Skyscraper Primitives: Dada and the American Avant-Garde, 1910–1925.* Middletown, Conn.: Wesleyan UP, 1975.

Tate, Allen. "Hart Crane." *Critical Essays on Hart Crane.* Ed. David R. Clark. Boston: G. K. Hall, 1982. 115–23.

Terry, Jennifer. "Lesbians under the Medical Gaze: Scientists Search for Remarkable Differences." *Journal of Sex Research* 27.3 (Aug. 1990): 317–39.

Trilling, Lionel. "Willa Cather." *Willa Cather: Modern Critical Views.* Ed. Harold Bloom. New York: Chelsea, 1985. 7–13.

Vaid, Urvashi. *Virtual Equality.* New York: Anchor, 1995.

Walters, Suzanna Danuta. "As Her Hand Crept Slowly Up Her Thigh: Ann Bannon and the Politics of Pulp." *Social Text* (fall/winter 1989): 83–101.

Warner, Michael. "Introduction." *Fear of a Queer Planet.* Ed. Michael Warner. Minneapolis: U of Minnesota P, 1993. vii–xxxi.

———. "The Mass Subject and the Mass Public." *The Phantom Public Sphere.* Ed. Bruce Robbins. Minneapolis: U of Minnesota P, 1993. 234–56.

Waugh, Thomas. *Hard to Imagine: Gay Male Eroticism in Photography and Film from Their Beginnings to Stonewall.* New York: Columbia UP, 1996.

Weinstein, Jeff. "In Praise of Pulp: Bannon's Lusty Lesbians." *Voice Literary Supplement* Oct. 1983. 8–9.

Weinstone, Ann. "Science Fiction as a Young Person's First Queer Theory." *Science Fiction Studies* 26.1 (Mar. 1999): 41–48.

Weissman, Aerlyn, and Lynne Fernie. *Forbidden Love: The Unashamed Stories of Lesbian Lives.* Women Make Movies/National Film Board of Canada, 1992.

Willhoite, Michael. *Members of the Tribe: Caricatures of Gay Men and Lesbians.* Boston: Alyson, 1993.

Williams, Raymond. *The Country and the City.* Oxford: Oxford UP, 1973.

Williams, William Carlos. *In the American Grain*. New York: New Directions, 1925.

Wilson, Edmund. "Two Novels of Willa Cather." *Willa Cather and Her Critics*. Ed. James Schroeter. Ithaca: Cornell UP, 1967. 25–29.

Winters, Yvor. "The Progress of Hart Crane." *Critical Essays on Hart Crane*. Ed. David R. Clark. Boston: G. K. Hall, 1982. 102–8.

Woodress, James. *Willa Cather: A Literary Life*. Lincoln: U of Nebraska P, 1987.

Yingling, Thomas E. *Hart Crane and the Homosexual Text*. Chicago: U of Chicago P, 1990.

Yusba, Roberta. "Twilight Tales: Lesbian Pulps 1950–1960." *On Our Backs* summer 1985: 30–31, 43.

Zabel, Morton D. "Willa Cather: The Tone of Time." *Willa Cather*. Ed. Harold Bloom. New York: Chelsea, 1985. 41–50.

Christopher Nealon is Associate Professor of English
at the University of California, Berkeley.

Library of Congress Cataloging-in-Publication Data
Nealon, Christopher S. (Christopher Shaun).
Foundlings : lesbian and gay historical emotion
before Stonewall / Christopher Nealon.
p. cm. — (Series Q)
Includes bibliographical references and index.
ISBN 0-8223-2688-4 (cloth : alk. paper)
ISBN 0-8223-2697-3 (pbk. : alk. paper)
1. Gays—United States.   2. Gays—United States—
Identity.   3. Homosexuality—United States.
I. Title   II. Series.
HQ76.3.U5 N43   2001
306.76'6'0973—dc21   2001023933